EXILE AND THEOLOGY OF CREATION:

*A Socio-Historical Study of the
Creation Motif in Isaiah 40-55*

EXILE AND THEOLOGY OF CREATION:
A Socio-Historical Study of the Creation Motif in Isaiah 40-55

P. Rajendra Babu

2011

Exile and Theology of Creation: A Socio-historical Study of the Creation Motif in Isaiah 40-55 — published by the Rev. Dr. Ashish Amos of the Indian Society for Promoting Christian Knowledge (ISPCK), Post Box 1585, Kashmere Gate, Delhi-110006.

© Author, 2011

All rights reserved. No part of this book may be reproduced or transmitted in any form or by any means, electronic, mechanical, photocopying, recording, or by any information storage and retrieval system, without the prior permission in writing from the publisher.

The views expressed in the book are those of the author and the publisher takes no responsibility for any of the statements.

ISBN: 978-81-8465-157-7

Laser typeset by

ISPCK, Post Box 1585, 1654, Madarsa Road, Kashmere Gate, Delhi-110006 • *Tel:* 23866323

e-mail: ashish@ispck.org.in • ella@ispck.org.in
website: www.ispck.org.in

Contents

Foreword ix
Preface xiii
Abbreviations xvii

Chapter One
Introduction

1.1.	Statement of the Problem	1
1.2.	Elaboration of the Problem	1
1.3.	Importance of the Problem	6
1.4.	Definitions	8
1.5.	Brief Survey of the History of Research	9
1.6.	Scope of the Study	19
1.7.	Methodology	20
	1.7.1. Why Socio-Historical Approach is Necessary?	22
	1.7.2. The Structural-Functional Model	26
	1.7.3. The Present Study	31

Chapter Two
Creation Motif in Ancient West Asia

2.1.	Introduction	33
2.2.	Creation Account in Mesopotamia	34
	2.2.1. The Sumerian	34
	2.2.1.1. Creation of Human Being	37
	2.2.1.2. Creation by Word	39
	2.2.1.3. Conclusion from the Sumerian Material	40

	2.2.2.	Babylonian Account	40
		2.2.2.1. Atrahasis	41
		2.2.2.2. Creation of Human Being in Atrahasis	42
		2.2.2.3. Enuma Elish	43
		2.2.2.4. Creation of Stars and Moon	46
		2.2.2.5. The Creation of Human Being	46
	2.2.3.	Minor Cosmogonies	48
	2.2.4.	Conclusion	49
2.3.	Creation in Egyptian Thought		49
	2.3.1.	Heliopolitan Tradition	50
	2.3.2.	Memphis Tradition	51
	2.3.3.	Hermopolitan Tradition	53
	2.3.4.	Conclusion	55
2.4.	Creation in Canaanite Texts		56
	2.4.1.	Ugaritic Texts	57
	2.4.2.	Phoenician	60
2.5.	Conclusion		61

Chapter Three
Creation Motif in the Hebrew Bible

3.1.	Introduction	64
3.2.	The Priestly Account of Creation	64
	3.2.1. Creatio ex nihilo	68
	3.2.2. P's Anthropology	70
	Conclusion	72
3.3.	The Yahwistic Account of Creation	73
	3.3.1. J's Classical Anthropology	75
	3.3.2. Purpose of Human Being	76
	3.3.3. Formation of Animals	77
	3.3.4. Creation of Woman	77
	Conclusion	78
3.4.	Creation in the Psalms	79

CONTENTS   vii

      3.4.1. Communal Lament   80
      3.4.2. Hymns   82
                Conclusion   88
3.5. Creation in Wisdom Literature   89
      3.5.1. Creation in the Book of Proverbs   91
            3.5.1.1. Proverbs 3:19-20   92
            3.5.1.2. Proverbs 8:22-31   94
      3.5.2. Creation in Job   96
            3.5.2.1. The First Speech of Yahweh:
                        38:1-40:2   97
            3.5.2.2. The second speech of Yahweh:
                        40:6-41:26   99
3.6. Conclusion   100

Chapter Four
The Period of Exile: A Socio-historical Survey

4.1.   Introduction   103
4.2.   Sources   105
4.3.   The Assyrian Rise to Power   107
4.4.   The End of Northern Kingdom   109
4.5.   Judah's Movement to the Exile   110
4.6.   The Rise of the Neo-Babylonian Empire   114
4.7.   The End of Judah   114
4.8.   Number and Dates of Deportations   116
4.9.   Number of Judeans deported to Babylon   118
4.10. Condition of Judah during Exile   120
4.11. Israel in Babylonian Exile   124
      4.11.1. Social Situation of the Babylonian Exile   125
      4.11.2. Sociological Development during the Exile   130
4.12.Conclusion   140

Chapter Five
Introduction to Isaiah 40-55

5.1.   Introduction   141

5.2.	The Unity of the Book of Isaiah	145
5.3.	Literary Questions of Isaiah 40-55	149
5.4.	Socio-Historical Setting of Isaiah 40-55	155
5.5.	Domicile of Deutero Isaiah	160
5.6.	The Community of Deutero-Isaiah.	164

Chapter Six
An Exegetical Study of Selected Passages with Creation Motif

6.1.	Exegetical Study of Selected Passages with Creation Motif		174
	6.1.1.	Hope on the Creator	174
	6.1.2.	Creator is the Protector	209
	6.1.3.	Creator's Commission	218
	6.1.4.	Creator of Israel	228
	6.1.5.	Creator leads the History	237
	6.1.6.	Good and Evil, Both from the Creator	250
	6.1.7.	Creator's Plan Cannot be Questioned by Creatures	256
	6.1.8.	Creation: A Purposeful Act of Yahweh	266
6.2.	Summary of the Exegetical Study		273

Chapter Seven
Concluding Remarks

7.1.	Conclusions	278
7.2.	The Decisive Reality of Exile behind DI's Creation Theology	281
7.3.	Structure of the Exilic Society and Creation Theology	283
7.4.	The Function of Creation Theology in DI	285
7.5.	Creation Theology and Other Motifs in DI	287
7.6.	Relevance of the Study	289

BIBLIOGRAPHY **291-302**

Foreword

Curious readers and researchers of the Bible have repeatedly said in the past that the Old Testament begins with the story of creation but not the theology of the Old Testament. A survey of the classical volumes of Old Testament theology would certainly testify to this interesting comment. The theology of creation was never a passionate theme for biblical theologians until the very last part of the twentieth century. For various reasons several of them treated it as a subsidiary theme in their theological deliberations. However, since the last decade of the twentieth century there is renewed interest among Old Testament theologians in reexamining the significance of the theme, particularly in the wake of ecological backlashes in various parts of the planet, and also in response to accusations holding the Hebrew Scriptures responsible for the same.

This renewed interest in the theology of creation is influenced by two factors.[1] First, all Old Testament scholars are come to a realization that the creation is an integral part of the faith of Israel. They can no longer accept the theological position that bypasses a theology of creation. As Leo G. Perdue has pointed out 'it is impossible intellectually to speak of history and redemption without setting forth the relationship of these fundamental themes to the theology of creation'[2] Second factor is the rediscovery of

---

[1] Water Brueggemann, "The Loss and Recovery of Creation in Old Testament Theology," *Theology Today* 53/2 (1996) 177-190.

[2] Leo G. Perdue, *The Collapse of History: Reconstructing Old Testament Theology* (Minneapolis: Fortress Press, 1994), 115.

the importance of the wisdom literature for the theology of creation. All this began in the 1960's and 1970's when a shift in paradigm took place in Old Testament studies.

Dr. Rajendra Babu's book "Exile and the Theology of Creation: A Socio-Historical Study of Creation Motif in Isaiah 40-55" is an example of this renewed interest. In this book, he has shown a keen interest in perusing the theology of creation in Deutero-Isaiah. He has given particular attention to the development of the motif of creation in the exilic period and has clearly shown how the motif of creation enabled the people in exile experience life in the midst of threats of life.

One of the strengths of this book is the integrated approach the author uses in terms of the methodologies he employs in his work. Although he discusses the limitations of the historical critical method, he does make use of the historical critical method, along with the socio-historical method, which he employs widely in his study. This is indeed a healthy trend in Biblical Hermeneutics. It is an attempt to advocate the uniqueness of each method with its own strength and limitations. It is also a depiction of the richness of knowledge that would emerge when the methodologies are used in an integrated manner.

The second and third chapters of this book elaborately deal with the creation motif in the Ancient West Asia and in the Bible traditions. These chapters provide a vast amount of information, which reflect the author's comprehensive knowledge of the subject and his analytical skill as well. Chapter four is a socio-historical survey of the period of exile in which the writer delineates the social situation in Babylonian exile and also throws light on the sociological development during the period. Chapter five provides an extensive introduction to the book of Isaiah and a survey of the scholarly debate on various issues associated with the Deutero-Isianic corpus. In chapter six the writer deals with key texts of Deutero-Isaiah that deal with the creation motif. The translation of selected texts, explanation of text critical notes and the exegetical steps, on the whole, give evidence to the writer's knowledge and experience as a theological teacher.

The findings of the study are significant and very interesting too. The observation that the prophet Deutero-Isaiah was not an individual but a small community with a distinct world view; the use of creation theology to persuade the exiles to acknowledge Cyrus as Yahweh's agent of redemption; the function of creation theology as a theology of integration bringing together different exilic groups; the role of creation theology granting support to the suffering and the displaced communities etc., are significant truths which are very relevant to our times. The overall conclusion of the writer that the "Creation is not an event that took place once for all in the distant past. It emphasizes Yahweh's continuous sustaining of the world order" is indeed valid and makes the study academically brilliant and practically tenable and challenging.

Rev. Dr. J. R. John Samuel Raj
Principal
United Theological College, Bangalore

Preface

Exile is a poignant reality for millions of human being. Every day, thousands of people are forced to leave their home country or place of residence due to several reasons such as invasion of super powers, terrorist attack, connivance of real estate mafia, government policies like Special Economic Zone (SEZ) etc. How these people relate themselves to the place where they reside as refugees, or how these uprooted people find meaning of their existence in the new circumstances and the quest for their identity are important concerns of the modern world. Curious readers could observe that the creation theology in Deutero-Isaiah was developed as a result of an active interaction with various kinds of existential concerns of the people of Israel during their Babylonian exile, and their attempt to find meaning and purpose in life in the midst of numerous threats present in their daily life.

An active interrogation of these claims demands an integrated methodological approach. So, the use of historical critical method along with the socio-historical method held the most promising in this study. This approach helped me greatly not only examine the literature and social setting of ancient Israel, but also the social forces underlying the production of that literature.

While writing this dissertation, I have incurred many debts, impossible to repay yet gratefully acknowledged. Right from the time of formulation of the title to the completion of the dissertation, my Guide Rev. Dr. K. V. Mathew has been with me to sharpen and expand the horizons of my critical thoughts and engagement with the research work with his scholarly comments, appropriate guidance and the meticulous correction of the text. So, I am particularly grateful to him for his valuable contributions in this pursuit. Also I am greatly indebted to Rev. Dr. Geevarghese Mathew for his insightful comments and valid suggestions which were very helpful in the process of this research work.

I am thankful to the Fr. Dr. John Mathews, Registrar FFRRC, Rev. Dr. M. C. Thomas, MT Seminary, and Prof. Dr. D. Jones Muthunayagom, UTC, Bangalore for their valuable comments which helped me to gain much clarity with regard to my methodological perspective. My sincere thanks also go to Rev. Dr. Samson Prabhakar the Director, SATHRI for his continued moral support throughout my doctoral study programme.

Writing this book would not have been possible without the financial support from the CRISP, LC-MS. I am greatly indebted to Rev. Dr. Herbert Hoefer, the theological consultant, India, and Mr. Kenneth L. Reiner, the manager of CRISP, and for their endeavor in getting the CRISP scholarship and also for their efforts to provide with me an exposure programme to the Concordia Seminary, St. Louis, USA. This exposure programme gave me a great opportunity to interact with a number of scholars at Concordia Seminary, St. Louis and to make use of its excellent Library. I also wish to express my sincere gratitude to Rev. Dr. A. R. Victor Raj, Concordia Seminary, St. Louis, Mr. James Kell & family, West Bend, Wisconsin and Mr. Philip Stout & family, Casper, Wyoming for their generous hospitality extended to me during my exposure programme at Concordia Seminary, St. Louis. My special word of thanks also goes to the Board members of Wyoming Women Missionary League, USA and especially the President Ms. Chris Fiechtl for their generous support and prayers during my study programme.

I express my sincere thanks to the FFRRC office staff, especially Ms. Darly for her prompt assistance with regard to various administrative tasks involved in relation to my study programme. My sincere thanks also go to the Librarians of M.T. Seminary,

Kottayam, Orthodox Seminary, Kottayam, KUT Seminary, Thiruvanathapuram and the UTC, Bangalore.

I also would like to thank the administration of the Concordia Theological Seminary, Nagercoil for granting me sufficient leave to undertake my doctoral study programme and all my fellow faculty members at CTS for their moral support to complete this study.

I am especially grateful to Rev. Dr. John Samuel Raj, Principal, United Theological College, Bangalore for writing a 'Foreword,' and to Dr. Dan Mattson, LC-MS who took the initiative to pay the authors share of expenses towards the publication of this book, and to the ISPCK for publishing this book.

Finally, I would like to express my warmest appreciation and gratitude to my wife Mohana and to my children, Shana and Shine for standing with me with good will, understanding and prayers, each in their own way, and to my son-in-law Rev. Sam Thompson who was a great help to me in collecting the needed materials and especially my granddaughter Sasha, who eased my stress and always kept me cheerful and positive.

I am especially grateful to my Gracious God for His call and diverse opportunities and space he has provided me to grow spiritually and academically to continue to serve His people and especially for enabling me and sustaining me to undertake this research work and strengthening me to bring it to its completion.

P. Rajendra Babu

Abbreviations

AB	The Anchor Bible
ABD	The Anchor Bible Dictionary. Edited by D. N. Freedman. 6 vols. New York, 1992.
ANET	Ancient Near Eastern Texts Relating to the Old Testament. Ed. by J. B. Pritchard. Princeton, 1955
Aqu.	Aquila
AV	Authorized Version
BA	Biblical Archaeologist
BDB	F. Brown, S. R. Driver & C. A. Briggs, *A Hebrew and English Lexicon of the Old Testament*. Oxford: Chavendon Press, 1907
BHS	*Biblia Hebraica Stuttgartensia*
BK	*Bibel und Kirche*
BWANT	Beiträge zur Wissenschaft vom Alten und Neuen Testament
BZAW	Beihefte zur Zeitschrift für die alttestamentliche Wissenschaft
CBC	The Cambridge Bible Commentary
CBQ	*Catholic Biblical Quarterly*
1 Chro	1 Chronicles
2 Chro	2 Chronicles

COT	*Creation in the Old Testament*. Ed. by Bernhard W. Anderson, Philadelphia: Fortress Press, 1984
Dan	Daniel
Deut	Deuteronomy
DI	Deutero-Isaiah
Exod	Exodus
ExpTim	*Expository Times*
Ezk	Ezekiel
Gen	Genesis
HAR	*Hebrew Annual Review*
Hos	Hosea
HTR	*Harvard Theological Review*
IB	Interpreters Bible
IDB	*Interpreters Dictionary of the Bible.* Ed G. A. Buttrick, et al. 4 vols. Nashville, 1962.
Int	*Interpretation*
Isa	Isaiah
J	Yahwist source
JBL	*Journal of Biblical Literature*
Jer	Jeremiah
JJS	*Journal of Jewish Studies*
JNES	*Journal of Near Eastern Studies*
Josh	Joshua
JSOT	*Journal for the Study of the Old Testament*
JSOTSup	*Journal for the Study of the Old Testament Supplement Series*
JSS	*Journal of Semitic Studies*
JTS	*Journal of Theological Studies*
Judg	Judges

ABBREVIATIONS

1 Kgs	1 Kings
2 Kgs	2 Kings
Lam	Lamentation
Lev	Leviticus
LXX	Septuagint
Matt	Mathew
MS	Manuscript (s)
MT	Masoretic Text
Nah	Nahum
Neh	Nehemiah
NERT	*Near Eastern Religious Text Relating to the Old Testament.* ed. By Walter New Jersey: Princeton University Press, 1950.
NIB	The New Interpreters Bible
NICOT	The New International Commentary on the Old Testament
NIV	New International Version
NRSV	New Revised Standard Version
Num	Numbers
OT	Old Testament
OTL	Old Testament Library
P	Priestly source
PCB	Peake's Commentary on the Bible. Ed. Matthew Black & H. H. Rowley Philadelphia: Fortress Press, 1984.
Prov	Proverbs
Ps	Psalms
Rom	Roman
RSV	Revised Standard Version
1 Sam	1 Samuel

2 Sam	2 Samuel
SBT	Studies in Biblical Theology
SJOT	*Scandinavian Journal of Old Testament*
SJT	*Scottish Journal of Theology*
SOTSMS	Society for Old Testament Study Monograph Studies
Symm.	Symmachus
Syr.	Syriac version
Tg.	Targum
TDOT	*Theological Dictionary of the Old Testament*, Ed. By G. Botterweck and H. Ringgren, Tr. D. E. Green, et al. Grand Rapids: Eerdmans, 1974.
Theod.	Theodotion
TLOT	*Theological Lexicon of the Old Testamen.* Ed. E. Jenni and C. Westermann.
VT	*Vetus Testamentum*
VTSup	Supplement to Vetus Testamentum
Vg.	Vulgate
WBC	World Biblical Commentary
ZAW	*Zeitschrift für die alttestamentliche*
Zech	Zechariah

CHAPTER ONE
Introduction

1.1. Statement of the Problem

According to the most accepted critical view, a greater and an emphatic discussion on the Old Testament concepts of the Creator and creation took place during the period of exile, and Deutero Isaiah was the first writer, who considered it extensively and drew theological conclusions from the belief in Yahweh as the Creator. This does not mean that the belief in Yahweh as the Creator did not exist in Israel before the period of exile. But it was only in the period of exile that Israel made it meaningful to the whole context of her faith. This shows a possibility of influence of the history and the social context of the exile behind the formation of the creation theology. So, any attempt to understand the theological significance of 'creation' without considering the socio-historical context of exile will be inadequate. Therefore the basic question of this inquiry is: How does the socio-historical context of exile contribute to Deutero Isaiah (or the Community of Deutero Isaiah) for the development of a theology of creation and its significance to the community of faith today.

1.2. Elaboration of the Problem

The Old Testament scholarship is nearly unanimous in regarding the creation faith in ancient Israel as chronologically late and theologically secondary. This is, on the one hand, due to the fact that the extended statement about Yahweh's creation of the world appeared in the later texts, viz. Deutero Isaiah (hereafter DI), Priestly writings and the late Psalms.[1] And on the other hand, it was due to the over emphasis given to the historical character of God's revelation.[2] For example, Gerhard von Rad begins his famous essay on creation as follows: "The Yahwistic faith of the Old Testament is a faith based on the notion of election and therefore primarily concerned with redemption".[3]

In this essay, he advocated the hypothesis that the creation faith in the Old Testament is subordinate to the salvation faith. Further, he added that it has no 'independent status as an article of faith in itself.' In order to substantiate this hypothesis he quotes from Deutero Isaiah and stresses that in DI, creation faith "performs only an ancillary function. It seems as a magnificent *foil* (italics mine) for the message of salvation".[4] He also argues that the creation faith within Israel was comparatively a late development.

Von Rad's view of 'creation' as late and subordinate to the salvation history has been followed by a large number of scholars. Bernhard W. Anderson writes: "The earliest cultic summaries of Israel's faith did not refer to Yahweh as creator, but concentrated, rather, on his mighty deeds on history by which he made himself known and constituted Israel as his people."[5] Creation motif is absent in most of the prophets too.[6] Boman also presumes the non-

---

[1] Although J source is considered as the first layer of editing the biblical text which dated to *ca.* 900-850 B.C.E., "P" of the sixth century B.C.E. or a bit later, is regarded as the final redactor of J.

[2] See Rolf P. Knierim, *The Task of Old Testament Theology: Substance, Method, and Cases* (Michigan, Grand Rapid: William B. Eerdmans Publishing Co, 1995), 178-181.

[3] Gerhard von Rad, "The Theological Problem of the Old Testament Doctrine of Creation" in *The Problem of Hexateuch and Other Essays* (London: Oliver & Boyd, 1965), 131.

[4] Gerhard von Rad, "The Theological Problem...," 134.

[5] B.W.Anderson, "Creation" *IDB*, vol. 1, 726.

[6] The creation doxologies in Amos 4:13; 5:8-9; 9:5-6, according to von Rad, are "theological accretions, arising from the reflections of a later writer" (See G. von Rad, op. cit., 135).

INTRODUCTION

existence of creation faith before DI.[7] In this connection Brevard S. Childs writes: "Israel's faith developed historically from its initial encounter with God as redeemer from Egypt, and only secondarily from this center was a theology of creation incorporated into its faith"[8]

Does this necessarily argue that the creation faith was unknown to early Israel? The *argumentum e silentio* of the relevant Old Testament evidence is an insufficient basis for the conclusion that belief in Yahweh as Creator of the world was not found in pre-exilic Israel.[9] Also the absence of creation terms like קנה, ברא, יצר, עשׂה and בנה need not necessarily mean that the idea of the 'world being created' was not taken for granted, nor does it disprove that it was explicitly acknowledged. W. F. Albright, Freedman, F.M. Cross and others proposed that the divine name "Yahweh" originally was a causative verb from the meaning "he causes to be" and that the formula in Exodus 3:14 means he "causes to be what came into existence."[10] However, in the past decades scholars have carried on a lively debate on the question whether Yahweh was originally a creator deity.[11]

According to Westermann, 'The Old Testament never speaks of belief in the Creator: there never occurs a sentence such as 'I believe the world was created by God'. Because, he argues, 'for the man of the Old Testament it was not possible that the world could have originated in any other way'.[12]

---

[7] T. Boman, "The Biblical Doctrine of Creation," *CQR*, 165 (1964), 140-151.
[8] Brevard S. Childs, *Biblical Theology of the Old and New Testaments* (Minneapolis: Fortress Press, 1992),110.
[9] Stefan Paas, *Creation and Judgement: Creation Text in Some Eight Century Prophets* (Leiden-Boston: Brill, 2003), 18.
[10] F.M. Cross, *Canaanite Myth and Hebrew Epic: Essays in the History of the Religion of Israel*, (Cambridge: Harvard University Press, 1973), 64ff.
[11] J. P. Hyatt, "Was Yahweh Originally a Creator Deity?," *JBL*.86 (1976) 369-77. In this article Hyatt rejected the view of W.E Albright and others that Yahweh was originally a creator deity.
[12] C. Westermann, *Creation*, trans. J. J. Scullion (London: SPCK, 1974), 5.

The belief in divine creation is of course very old, attested literarily as early as the *Sumerians* of the third millennium B.C.[13] Moreover as Schmid points out 'there were no cultures in ancient West Asia that did not speak rather extensively of creation in literary forms and contexts'.[14] As George M. Landes points out, "there is no high god- that is, no deity of cosmic and widespread significance- who could qualify as such without possessing as a crucial attribute the power to create."[15] There is no doubt that the Psalmists were familiar with the creation faith of Israel (e.g., Ps.8, 19, 104 etc.) Further, a number of scholars have recognized a close relation between creation and Israel's cultic institutions.

Moreover, when Israel recalled her story of Exodus, the wilderness wandering, and the giving of the land, Yahweh's delivering actions were not depicted as involving only historical and political events, but also the use of forces and elements of nature. It was probably presumed that only the Creator-God, the One who made the sea, the animals, the heavenly bodies, and all of nature, could employ these elements in His redemptive work. 'But out of all her experience in liberating events, Israel did not only at some distant later date infer that the Liberator-God must be the creator-God, but rather, because she already knew Yahweh as Creator of heaven and earth, she understood how it was that wind and sea, birds and insects, sun and moon could be used as instrument supporting the divine liberating activity'.[16] So it must be admitted that the belief in creation existed from the beginning as an integral element of God in Israel.

Therefore the real question is not whether the early Israel possessed the notion of divine creation, but rather why were they reluctant to confess her God as Creator in her early writings? As

---

[13] See, S. N. Kramer, *The Sumerian: Their History, Culture, and Character* (Chicago: Univ. of Chicago Press, 1963), 112-113.
[14] See H. H. Schmid, "Creation, Righteousness, and Salvation", in *Creation in the Old Testament* edited by B. W. Anderson (Philadelphia: Fortress Press, 1984), 103.
[15] George M. Landes, "Creation and Liberation" in *COT*, 136.
[16] George M. Landes, "Creation and Liberation," 137.

Gerhard von Rad has pointed out, when a serious attack, which the faith of Israel had to meet with regard to the conception of nature, came from the Canaanite Baal religion, she did not oppose the nature religion on the ground of the doctrine of creation; on the contrary, she objected to it in terms of Israel's redemptive history.[17] If she already knew her God as the Creator of heaven and the earth, why she did not challenge the nature religion of Baal on the ground of the doctrine of creation?

It is a striking fact that it was in the period of the exile that Israel first reckons seriously with the doctrine of creation. In fact, the creation faith receives its fullest articulation in Deutero Isaiah during exile. This raises many questions. What made Israel to revive this tradition suddenly during the exile? Did the theology of creation develop essentially as a result of historical exile? It is conceivable that the exile provided the impetus for the formation of creation theology. If so, what was the socio- historical context of the exile, and how did it contribute to DI's development of the theology of creation? And how does the theology of creation help them to cope with the socio-historical problems of the exile? And what are its implications to other motifs in DI, such as monotheism, universalism, mission etc?

Another question is about the community behind the formation of the creation theology. Did Deutero Isaiah develop it as an individual theologian or was this a formation of the faith community? And if it was developed by the community, what was its implication to the socio-political and economic life of the community?

And finally, what is the significance of Deutero Isaiah's creation theology for the modern faith community? And how is the theology of creation relevant to the present exilic context of modern faith community? The study endeavors to find answers to these questions.

---

[17] See G. von Rad, "The Theological Problem ...", 132.

1.3. Importance of the Problem

Both 'creation' and 'exile'[18] have become prominent themes of today's theological discussion. This renewed interest in creation has resulted in part from the existential crisis of our age such as the nuclear holocaust, the pollution of our planet, ozone depletion, climatic change etc. Another reason is the recognition that it is impossible intellectually to speak of history and redemption without setting forth the relationship of these fundamental themes to the theology of creation.[19] In some important sense, the understanding of human nature, history, and redemption are defined by the theology of creation.

The reason for the renewed interest in the exile is based on the fact that the Old Testament itself, in its canonical form, has arisen from the crisis of exile as a response to that crisis. When discussing OT history and literature, things are measured on a chronological scale of them being 'pre-exilic' or 'post-exilic.' The concept of 'sin-exile-restoration' has made a major impact on theological thinking, both in the Old Testament itself and in subsequent theological discussion. As Daniel Smith has suggested, 'exilic theology' promises to be the most provocative, creative, and helpful set of ideas that modern Christian can derive from the ancient Hebrew religious reflections on their experiences.[20]

Moreover, the exile as a symbol has been found to be increasingly a powerful source for the illumination of our circumstance. Transcultural experience is an increasingly important feature of the modern world. According to Brueggemann the exile symbolizes social, moral, and cultural displacement and the

---

[18] Some prefer the term "deportation" to "exile" noting that the latter term is more of a theological construct than a historical reality (Davies, Grabbe). However, all agree that significant social and cultural changes occurred in this tumultuous period.

[19] See Leo G. Perdue, *The Collapse of History: Reconstructing Old Testament Theology* (Minneapolis: Fortress Press, 1994), 115.

[20] Daniel L. Smith Christopher, *A Biblical Theology of Exile* (Minneapolis: Fortress Press, 2002), 6.

INTRODUCTION 7

dominance of false values.[21] The metaphor, then, reveals the danger inherent for 'aliens' in exchanging their true identity conferred by God for that promoted by the dominant culture. Exile was thus the test and temptation of Israel and to this context DI developed his theology of creation. Thus, the theology of creation developed during the exile has significance even for the present faith community.

Creation in Deutero Isaiah then was not a philosophical inquiry about the origin of the universe etc. It developed when Israel was threatened by its surroundings. It was developed from its existential crisis. Creation theology rightly can be called a 'crisis theology.' So, in a world where existential problems are very severe, an in-depth study of theology of creation is particularly appropriate as it provides a perspective from which a comprehensive understanding and resolution of the problems could be envisaged.

Moreover, the biblical basis of mission also begins with the concept of 'creation'. (see Acts.17:24-31: St. Paul lays the OT creation as a platform for his message of Jesus Christ) 'Creation' provides the basic biblical worldview of reality: God, the earth, and humanity in reciprocal relation to each other. It also sets before us the basic human obligations: love and obedience towards God; care and keeping the earth; and mutual love and care for one another. As Schmid has rightly pointed out, the creation faith did not deal only with the origin of the world. Rather it is concerned above all with the present world and the natural environment of humanity now.[22]

Besides, India's pluralistic context also demands a wider perspective about God and his plan for the world, which can be fully elucidated through a proper understanding of creation

---

[21] See Brueggemann, "Second Isaiah: An Evangelical Reading of Communal Experience", in *Reading and Preaching the Book of Isaiah*, edited by Christopher R. Seitz (Philadelphia: Fortress Press, 1988), 74-75.

[22] H. H. Schmid, "Creation Righteousness...," 103.

theology. This study will be an attempt towards evolving such a wider perspective.

No serious attempts have been made so far to explore the significance of the exile for the formation of a theology of creation and the significance of creation theology for the modern faith community. So, this study intends to open a path in that direction.

1.4. Definitions

In this study, the term "exile" is used both as a historical datum and as a paradigm of the condition of the modern faith community. As a historical datum, it refers to the historical exile in Babylon in the sixth century.[23] As a 'paradigm of the condition,' it refers to the danger inherent within the faith community in exchanging its true identity conferred by God for those of the dominant cultures that exist today. And also, as pointed out earlier, it symbolizes the social, moral, and cultural displacement, and the dominance of false values that impact the faith community.[24] (See 1Peter 1:1. Here its author employs it as a useful metaphor to designate the faith community). Moreover, as Smith-Christopher points out, the 'exile' is the daily reality for millions of human beings in this century.[25]

Also it is necessary to elucidate what is meant by 'creation motif.' The Old Testament does contain a rich vocabulary that implies creation. So, it is essential to observe from the outset that the theme of 'creation' in the Old Testament is not necessarily restricted to generally recognized creation terminology such as יצר and ברא, but it is also found in motifs more closely related to the product of these activities. So, when this study uses the term

---

[23] In this paper 'exile' refers to the so-called Babylonian exile. However, the fact of Egyptian *golah*, and other exiles will also be considered for our purpose.

[24] W. Brueggemann, *Hopeful Imagination: Prophetic Voice in Exile* (Philadelphia: Fortress Press, 1986).

[25] Daniel L. Smith-Christopher, *A Biblical Theology of Exile*, 28.

INTRODUCTION 9

'creation motif,' it refers to the ideas and concepts that support the belief in Yahweh as Creator, both in the sense of *actions* of God that leads to an ordered universe as well as the *universe itself*, which results from those actions and continues to stand in a relationship of dependence upon the Creator, without stating it explicitly.

1.5. Brief Survey of the History of Research

For a long time, judgements about the significance of the theme of creation for Old Testament theology were governed by the predominant role, assigned to the theme of history in the Old Testament.[26] This idea of subordination of the theology of creation to the theology of history influenced most of the scholars of the last generation.

Predominance of History: In his famous *Theology of Old Testament* (1975), W. Eichrodt wrote: 'The creation is thus from the very first integrated into a spiritual process in which each individual event acquires its value from the overall meaning of the whole; that is to say, into history...both the Yahwist and Priestly writers *make the creation the starting point of a history.*'[27] This emphasis on historical matters was fed by the development of the idea of history as the arena of revelation. In turn, Barthian theology[28] with its disdain for natural religion and natural revelation further submerged any real concern for creation per se. A classical example of this approach to the creation can be found in von Rad's work becoming a dominant consensus among scholars.

> The Old Testament is a history book; it tells of God's history with Israel, with the nations, and with the world, from the creation of the world down to the last things, that is to say, down to the time when dominion over the world is given to the Son of Man (Dan. vii.13f.). This history can be described as saving history because,

---

[26] H. G. Reventlow, *The Problem of Old Testament Theology in the Twentieth Century* (Philadelphia: Fortress Press, 1985), 138.

[27] W. Eichdrot, *Theology of the Old Testament*, vol. 2, trans. J. A. Baker (Philadelphia: Westminster Press, 1975), 100-101.

[28] For Karl Barth's view on creation, see his "Doctrine of Creation" in *Church Dogmatics* III/1.

as it is presented, creation itself is understood as a saving act of God....[29]

On the basis of the study of 'creation' in Psalms and in Deutero Isaiah, von Rad came to the conclusion that creation was an ancillary doctrine in relation to Israel's primary faith in a historical salvation. He wrote: "the doctrine of creation was never be able to attain to independent existence in its own right."[30] Further, in his writings, he continually emphasizes the subordinate, serving role of creation. For him, creation serves to underpin salvation history. Von Rad also believed that the creation element had entered into Israel from the side of wisdom. In his early essays he even argued that wisdom entered as a foreign element and therefore it is peripheral to Israel's historical faith.

However, in his later treatment, he corrected this misapprehension of wisdom and did much to show the independence and positive contribution of Wisdom's theology of creation. In his renowned book *Wisdom in Israel*,[31] he moved well beyond his earlier view. In this book, he sees wisdom theology as a reflection upon creation, its order, its gifts, its requirements and its limits. Furthermore, he presents an excellent exposition of Proverb 8, Job 28, and Ben Sirach 24, which is clearly a theology of creation. Here we see his gradually growing perception of the occurrence of creation in that particular field of Israel's literature with which salvation history has little to do, viz. Wisdom. There, creation has a far independent role. What is more, creation obtains the status of the mediator of revelation alongside of salvation history.

Von Rad's pupil R. Rendtorff followed his teacher in assigning the subordinate role of creation faith in DI further, and came to the conclusion that in this prophet the notion of creation and

---

[29] Gerhard von Rad, *Old Testament Theology*, vol. II, trans. D. M. G. Stalker (New York: Harper & Row, 1965), 357.
[30] Gerhard von Rad, "Theological Problem...", 142.
[31] Gerhard von Rad, *Wisdom in Israel* (Nashville: Abingdon Press, 1972), 144-157.

election are closely related concepts.³² Stuhlmeuller's work also points in the same direction. He wrote: "The major theme of redemption surfaces so forcefully and so continuously through the Book of Consolation, that the idea of creation must be accepted as a secondary motif."³³

Preeminence in Mythical Language: Frank Moore Cross's influential book *Canaanite Myth and Hebrew Epic* was articulated as a challenge to this view. In his book, Cross has argued that the Israelites mythologized historical events, such as the victory at the Red Sea. (Exodus15). He even recognized a historical kernel in such a myth.³⁴ According to Cross, the mythic language was borrowed from Canaan and elsewhere to enable Israel to speak of divine transcendence. Thus, Cross disagrees with von Rad and other members of the German school for their view of late dating of creation theology. According to Cross, the name Yahweh was an abbreviated form of the longer cultic formulation, "He is the one who creates the heavenly armies," and he argued that very early Yahweh was understood both as a creator deity and as a divine warrior who fought on Israel's behalf. Nevertheless, though he could establish his argument through extra biblical sources, it suffers under the limitation of the etymology of the Tetragrammaton. Moreover, the context of the passage Exodus 3:14-15 does not deal with the cosmic issue at all, rather the emphasis there is on liberation.³⁵

Precedence in Synthesis: Among the American scholars who have contributed significantly to the understanding of creation as a theme in Israelite religion and Old Testament theology is Bernhard W. Anderson. His studies of creation synthesized the theological work of scholars like von Rad and F. M. Cross. Among Anderson's writings, *Creation in the Old Testament* is an important collection of classic articles that deal with Old Testament creation,

---

³² See. H. G. Reventlow. *The Problem of Old Testament Theology*, 139.
³³ Carroll Stuhlmueller, *Creative Redemption in Deutero Isaiah* (Rome: Biblical Institute Press, 1970), 1.
³⁴ F. M. Cross, *Canaanite Myth...*, 64ff.
³⁵ See, George M. Landes, "Creation and Liberation", 137.

12 EXILE AND THEOLOGY OF CREATION

introduced by his own insightful programmatic essay.[36] Here, he gives a summary of the development of creation theology in different traditions of early Israel.

Anderson argues that there are two different traditions of creation in the Old Testament: the older Exodus-Covenant formulation in which Yahweh is a warrior and the creator of a people, and the later David- Zion tradition. The former is represented by the Song of the Sea in Exodus 15, which contains the mythical patterns of defeat in chaos, enthronement on the sacred mountain (temple), and proclamation of kingship over the cosmos. Anderson contends that this mythic hymn traces the origin of Israel to a historical event, not to primeval times. By contrast, the second tradition, the election of David and Zion is grounded in the order of creation.

In his treatment of creation in DI, Anderson sees a complete synthesis of these different traditions. The God who creates the cosmos and who maintains order in the face of threats of chaos now re-creates a people out of the chaos of bondage and prophetically anticipates a new creation.[37] Thus in DI, Anderson elucidates the theology of creation under the category of "Creation and New Creation" where history, soteriology, and creation are combined into an eschatological vision.

Preference of a presupposition: Differing from the above views, P.B. Harner has observed a prominent role of the creation faith in DI.[38] According to Harner, 'creation faith is an integral part of his total proclamation.' "He (DI) does not merely presuppose it as a

---

[36] Bernhard W. Anderson, ed., *Creation in the Old Testament*, Issues in Religion and Theology 6; (Philadelphia: Fortress Press, 1984). See also his *Creation versus Chaos: The Reinterpretation of Mythical Symbolism in the Bible* (New York: Association Press, 1967); and *From Creation To New Creation* (Minneapolis: Fortress Press, 1994).
[37] B. W. Anderson, *Creation in the Old Testament*, 21.
[38] P. B. Harner, "Creation Faith in Deutero Isaiah," *VT* 17 (1967), 298-306.

basis for his good news of imminent restoration. He joyously proclaims it as a part of the whole message that he wishes to bring to a people languishing in exile. Israel on her part needs to realize that Yahweh is Creator of all the ends of the earth...."[39] Though his observation of creation theology as an integral part of DI's message is appreciable, he did not elucidate the decisive reality of exile, specially the socio-historical circumstance, which made it an integral part of DI's message.

Predilection for Order: Another important development in creation theology came as a result of the renewal of wisdom studies. The work of Hans Heinrich Schmid is important in this regard. Although he has not written a full length OT theology, his proposal on creation is highly noteworthy. Contrary to the tendency of earlier OT theology, which emphasized Israel's history as the medium of God's revelation and reduced creation to a sort of appendix subsequently attached, Schmid emphasized the theme of creation.[40] He wants to give a far more central theological significance to creation. Moreover, the theme of creation was not only, and not primarily, an account of the *beginning* of the world: it was more an account of an *order* under which the world existed and was governed. The order of creation, moreover, was linked to the order of law. He tries to demonstrate that in ancient West Asia, the notion of 'righteousness' (צדקה) was an overall concept for world order. Israel shared this ancient West Asian way of thinking about world order. This order, founded by creation and therefore guaranteed by the creator, did not only comprise the cosmic order but was oriented in a much wider sense, including politics and law. Schmid argued that creation forms the horizon of biblical theology, for ordering of creation is the will of Yahweh as structured into a fabric of creation.

However, it was Walter Zimmerli who enunciated the dictum, "Wisdom thinks resolutely within the framework of a theology of

---

[39] P. B. Harner, "Creation Faith...," 302.
[40] H. H. Schmid, "Creation, Righteousness, and Salvation...," 102-117.

creation"[41] In this essay he also stated that wisdom theology is creation theology.

Predisposition for Synthesis: The most significant work in creation theology has been done by Claus Westermann.[42] Notably, in his inquiry into the biblical account of origins (*Genesis 1-11*), he has given a significant impetus to a deeper understanding of what Israel meant when it spoke of Yahweh's creative work. It is generally regarded as the landmark for its broad coverage and sober judgement. In method, Westermann is predominantly a form critic; from that perspective he has published extensively on the Psalms, Job, and Isaiah 40-66. As Walter Brueggemann has correctly observed, Westermann brings together two major theological poles in the Old Testament that are fundamental to its depiction of God: soteriology (history) and blessing (creation). In discussing the first Westermann almost agrees with von Rad's position. Here Yahweh is the redeemer who acts through history for the sake of the chosen people. However, Westermann believes that the key to understanding the stories about the origins is to be found in the ancient correlation between myth and ritual.[43] In ancient times, stories about the beginning of the world were not written down out of interest for the origins of existence, but out of concern for the continuance of the present.

In the second, Westermann focuses on creation texts, psalms and the wisdom literature in addressing the theme blessing, the divine power that enhances and sustains life. Blessing is the divine power that preserves the ongoing order of life and creation. Breaking with von Rad, who saw creation merely as the first of

---

[41] Walter Zimmerli, "The Place and Limit of the Wisdom in the Framework of the Old Testament Theology," *Scottish Journal of Theology* 17 (1964), 148. For further elaboration of this thesis, see H-J. Hermisson, "Observations on the Creation Theology in Wisdom," in *COT*, 118-34.

[42] Claus Westermann, *Creation* (London: SPCK, 1974); *Genesis I-11* (Minneapolis: Augsburg, 1984); *Blessing in the Bible and the Life of the Church* (Philadelphia: Westminster, 1978); and *Elements of Old Testament Theology*, 1982).

[43] C. Westermann, *Creation*, 13f.

God's historical acts, thus as a continuum from the beginning into history, Westermann argued that creation is beyond history. According to Westermann creation was the presupposition of faith, not the object of faith. However in his classical commentary on Deutero Isaiah, Westermann shares the view of von Rad.

Brevard Childs also seriously questioned subordinating the theme of creation and urged that the two themes not be approached as if one were subordinate to the other, but see them as interactive and corrective.[44]

Programmatic Rationality: Another important scholar addressing the issue is Rolf Knierim. Knierim has not written a comprehensive theology of creation. However, his several programmatic essays are highly significant.[45] Recognizing the plurality of Old Testament theologies, Knierim seeks a monotheistic structure that relates and systematizes these features into a consistent whole.[46] According to Knierim, the Old Testament does not speak about God alone but about God in relationship to a reality that consists of cosmos and nature, history and society, and the individual. The task of Old Testament theologians is to relate these three spheres to the sovereignty of God. "Justice" and "righteousness," which include the fundamental concept of order, is the key in describing and understanding this relationship.

In contrast to many, Knierim subordinates history to creation. For Knierim, the most universal domain of God's sovereignty is creation, not history. God's sovereignty is not dependent on history but precedes, transcends, and will follow history. While humans are dependent on the cosmos for life, they were not originally a part of its order. Indeed, the continuation of the cosmos does not require human beings, although it is often threatened by their

---

[44] Brevard Childs, *Old Testament Theology in a Canonical Context* (Philadelphia: Fortress, 1985), 32 f.
[45] See. Rolf Knierim, "Cosmos and History in Israel's Theology" in *Task of Old Testament Theology: Substance, Method, and Cases* (Cambridge: William B. Eerdmans Publishing Co. 1995), 171-224.
[46] See. Leo G. Perdue, *The Collapse of History...*, 126.

presence. History, thus, is subordinate to cosmos. Moreover, Knierim argues that human history as well as Israel's history receives its meaning only when it witnesses to and acts out God's universal dominion.[47]

Priestly Redaction for Cosmogony: Perhaps the most vigorous criticism on von Rad's theology of creation came from Richard J. Clifford in his essay, "The Hebrew Scripture and the Theology of Creation."[48] Clifford's main point is that there are deep differences in defining creation between modern and ancient views that von Rad did not sufficiently take into consideration.

Also, Clifford questions von Rad's distinction between creation and soteriology. Creation theology is soteriological in that it purports to show organized life emerging from disorganized chaos. What is more, none of the Communal Laments (Psalms 77, 74, 89, 44, 78, 135, 136, and 104) distinguishes between the creation of the world and the creation of Israel or between the redemption of the one and of the other. In DI, the situation is comparable as regards the recreation/ redemption of Israel. Here, however, "the perspective differs from Genesis, where the creation of the world took place once and for all.[49]

Clifford next turns to the classic reports on creation at the beginning of the book of Genesis. The first creation narrative in Genesis 1:1-2:4 is P's preface to the whole.[50] Now "the Priestly redaction intends Genesis 2:4-11:26 ...to be a single cosmogony," so that here again, creation and history are not distinguished. Genesis 1-11 points in the direction of the call of Abraham and the election of Israel against the background of the care of God for the whole world.

---

[47] Rolf Knierim, *Task of Old Testament Theology*..., 194.
[48] Richard J. Clifford, "The Hebrew Scripture and the Theology of Creation," *Theological Studies* 46 (1985), 507-23. See also his *Creation Accounts in the Ancient Near East and in the Bible*, The Catholic Biblical Quarterly Monograph (Washington: The Catholic Biblical Association, 1994).
[49] R. J. Clifford, "The Hebrew Scripture...," 519.
[50] R. J. Clifford, "The Hebrew Scripture...," 521.

INTRODUCTION

Prioritizing the vulnerability: One of the best and the more recent treatments of creation come from Jon Levenson, a student of F. M. Cross, who carries his teacher's interest in Canaanite myth and the Divine Warrior. His book, *Creation and Persistence of Evil*, grows out of his concern to address the difficult questions posed by the Jewish Holocaust.[51] In this book he tries to reconcile the doctrine of divine sovereignty with equally important affirmation of the life-sustaining justice of God. To answer the fundamental question of post-Holocaust thought, Levenson explains that the notion of *creatio ex nihilo* is an inadequate characterization of creation in the Hebrew Bible. This has led in turn to ascribing "a false finality or definitiveness" to creation that ignores the vulnerability and fragility of the cosmos. Also he works out the relationship between cosmos and history, not only in understanding God as both the Creator and Lord of history, but also in appreciating the dialectic of human submission to divine suzerainty and God's dependence on humanity.

Levenson argues that it is within Israel's historical experience that chaos seemed to gain the upper hand. Thus, the assertion of Yahweh's sovereignty is often opposed. Levenson believes that liturgy, by activating divine power, mediates the two contradictory affirmations of God as Lord of creation and history, on the one hand, and as the one who contested and even appears at times to be defeated, on the other hand. Levenson's work is provocative and compelling. He provides a systematic presentation of the various materials in the Hebrew Bible without negating the plurality of voices.

Levenson's study, with its accent on Yahweh's struggle for creation against chaos, provides an introduction to Terence E. Fretheim's daring article, "The Plagues as Ecological Signs of Historical Disaster".[52] In this article, Fretheim makes an amazing

---

[51] Jon Levenson, *Creation and the Persistence of Evil: The Jews Drama of Divine Omnipotence* (San Francisco: Harper & Row, 1988).

[52] Terence E. Fretheim, "The Plague as Ecological Signs of Historical Disaster", *JBL*, 110 (1991), 385-396.

statement: "Pharaoh's oppressive measures against Israel (in the Book of Exodus) are viewed as fundamentally anti-life and anti-creation."[53] Fretheim then undertakes a detailed analysis of the plague cycle in the book of Exodus, and suggests that the plagues are disruptions of creation caused by the anti-life, anti-creation policies and practice of slavery. As a response to Pharaoh's destructiveness, Yahweh acts in the Exodus not simply to save Israel but to restore creation. "Generally for Exodus, God's liberation of Israel is the primary but not the ultimate focus of the divine reality. The deliverance of Israel is ultimately for the sake of the entire creation."[54] Moreover, Fretheim reclaims the canonical ordering of creation. He suggests that Exodus is to be understood in the light of Genesis, and redemption and law in the light of creation.[55]

In short, from the above survey of the research, it is obvious that the Old Testament scholarship has moved along several clearly demarcated line and development in its study on creation. However, in spite of these diverse attempts on the theme 'creation,' many of them are only a general study on the theme. Only a few have paid particular attention to the creation motif in DI. But even those studies have not made any serious attempt to explore the decisive reality of exile behind the formulation of the creation theology in DI. Moreover, they failed to take note of the socio-historical circumstances of the exile in which Deutero Isaiah (or the community of DI) developed their theology of creation. Exegetically, those studies failed to take account of the fact that all ideas, concepts and knowledge are socially determined. Also they failed to relate the reality of exile and the theology of creation in a meaningful way, so that the present 'exilic community' could make use of it to today's 'exilic' challenges. Therefore, the present study of the creation motif in Isaiah 40-55 will hopefully elucidate the contribution of socio-historical circumstances of exile in

---

[53] Terence E. Fretheim, "The Plague as Ecological Signs...," 385.
[54] Terence E. Fretheim, "The Plague as Ecological Signs...," 392.
[55] Terence E. Fretheim, "The Reclamation of Creation," *Interpretation* 95 (1991) 354-365.

formulating a theology of creation and its relevance to the present faith community.

1.6. Scope of the Study

Since our main concern is to bring forth DI's theology of creation in its socio-historical context, only passages relevant to our theme are chosen for an exegetical analysis and our historical survey is limited to the Babylonian Exile and its social setting. Even though, our study is confined to the theology of creation in DI, this study will make use of the creation texts that are found in other exilic literature such as Jeremiah, Ezekiel, and the exilic Psalms in order to understand the influence of the socio-historical context of the exile on the formation of the theology of creation.

The reason why an inquiry into creation in the Old Testament often begins with DI is obvious, since the dating of the Psalms and even of the stories of the 'beginning' find much less agreement among scholars. In this respect, we have with Deutero-Isaiah a rather reliable point of departure. Because this prophet can be related to Israel's exile.[56] From this point it becomes easier to classify other texts as well.

There are other reasons why this study of creation is focused on Isaiah 40-55. They are among the most important, and have been among the most influential chapters in the entire Bible. They have already exerted their theological influence within the Old Testament period, as the later Old Testament writings show.[57] They played a crucial role in the development of some of the great themes such as 'universalism', 'mission of Israel' etc., which are very closely related to the theme of 'creation'.

Moreover, there is a form-critical reason why this study is focused on Deutero-Isaiah. Westermann's disciple Rainer Albertz

---

[56] There are scholars who do not accept DI's exilic background. For a classical example of this view: see, Barstead Hans, *The Babylonian Captivity of the Book of Isaiah* (Oslo: Novus forlag, 1997).

[57] R. N. Whybray, *The Second Isaiah* (Sheffield: Sheffield Academic Press, 1995), x.

distinguishes in Deutero- Isaiah two contexts in which creation is mentioned. The first is the *Bestreitung*, the second the *Heilsorakel*.[58] In the *Bestreitung* (Disputation), which is not a well-defined genre, statements about creation are unambiguously used to support the prophet's argumentation.[59] With regard to their form, they are characterized by participles. In substance they are about the creation of heaven and earth. The conclusion is obvious then: in these contending, reasoning texts, Deutero- Isaiah has used hymnic utterances to endorse his assertions.[60] With the *Heilsorakel* (Oracle of Salvation), things are different. There, the utterances about creation are the foundation of Yahweh's promise of salvation. Because the *Heilsorakel* corresponds with the lament, we should also look here for the origin of the utterance about creation.

1.7. Methodology

In order to explore the fuller meaning of the creation motif in DI, all the available models of Historical criticism, such as text critical, form critical, literary critical and tradition-historical critical factors are taken into account. However, the historical-critical method has exposed its limits to answer adequately the social milieu in which the exilic people lived and the social struggle, which they experienced and the social environment, which made them to formulate the theology of creation. This requires a sociological interpretation of the text in the historical context or a sociologically oriented historical criticism in order to explore how far the socio-historical context of the exile contributes to develop a theology of creation. As Bizzell has pointed out: "it would be impossible to understand the meaning of the social programme of a Jewish prophet without taking into account the conditions that produce it"[61] This means that the biblical sociologist is necessarily

---

[58] See Stefan Pass, *Creation and Judgment*..., 16.
[59] Stefan Pass, *Creation and Judgment*..., 16
[60] Stefan Pass, *Creation and Judgment*..., 16
[61] W. B. Bizzell, *The Social Teachings of the Jewish Prophets: A Study in the Biblical Sociology* (Boston: Sherman, French & Co., 1916), 1, cited by J. David Pleins, *The Social Visions of the Hebrew Bible* (Louisville: Westminster John Knox Press, 2001), 11.

dependent on good historical work. Thus a careful sociological and historical work is the prerequisite for a sociological study that seeks to interact with the prophetic social vision as a *material production*.[62] It compliments and improves the prevailing method of biblical interpretation through more rigorous attention given to the sociological dimension of the exegetical task.[63]

The question of the social world of the Bible has been one of the major goals of biblical scholarship since the early nineteenth century. This can be traced back to the pioneering work of W. Robertson Smith.[64] Early practitioners included Louis Wallis, Max Weber and the so-called "Chicago School," Johannes Pedersen, Roland de Vaux, and Antonin Causse.[65] Robertson Smith and Julius Wellhausen believed that the study of pre-Islamic Arabic sources, as well as careful observation of contemporary West Asian life and culture could give clues about many of the customs and beliefs of the Old Testament material.[66] Nevertheless, none of these scholars developed a social- historical method as such in biblical interpretation. The historical and literary questions about ancient Israel that have traditionally preoccupied biblical scholars have often overlooked the social realities of life experienced by the vast majority of the population of ancient Israel.

---

[62] W. B. Bizzell, *The Social Teachings of the Jewish Prophets...*, 11.

[63] John H. Elliott, *A Home for the Homeless: A Sociological Exegesis of I Peter, Its Situation and Strategy*, (Philadelphia: Fortress Press, 1981), 1.

[64] Scottish theologian and biblical scholar Robertson Smith is generally considered the founder of social anthropology. See Mary Douglas, *Purity and Danger: An Analysis of the Concept of Pollution and Taboo*, London: Routledge and Kegan Paul, 1966, 13. However, many of Robertson Smith's ideas have been subsequently abandoned or even disproved by anthropologists or biblical scholars, yet his approach to the social data and the questions he brought to the biblical texts from the social perspective have had a lasting impact.

[65] See, Ronald A. Simkins and Stephen L. Cook eds., *The Social World of Hebrew Bible: Twenty- Five Years of The Social Science in the Academy*, Semeia 87, (Atlanta: SBL, 1999), 2.

[66] See J. W. Rogerson, *Anthropology and the Old Testament* (Atlanta: John Knox Press, 1978), 27.

The credit for the first serious attention paid to social-scientific research may be attributed to George Mendenhall. In his seminal essay "The Hebrew Conquest of Palestine" (1962) Mendenhall consciously constructed a new model for explaining the historical process of the Israelite establishment in Palestine within an economic, sociological and political framework.[67] In this essay he challenged the traditional assumptions and gave expression to a rising dissatisfaction within the limits of historical-critical method and stimulated new method of social-scientific inquiry in the biblical field.

However, it was with Gottwald that the sociological approach to the Old Testament obtained a prominent role in biblical criticism.[68] Gottwald understood the sociological method, as providing tools for reconstructing the whole social system of ancient Israel, including functions, roles, institutions, customs, norms, judicial and religious organization, military and political structures, and material aspect of culture. He saw this as complimenting traditional historical studies in order to reconstruct ancient Israel as a lived totality.[69] Gottwald's monumental *Tribes of Yahweh* (1979) and his *Hebrew Bible: A Socioliterary Introduction* (1985) are marked by a conscious attempt to account for the complexities and nuances of biblical traditions and Israelite social structures, and their approach to the biblical society both from a structural-functional and cultural materialist perspective.

1.7.1. Why Socio-Historical Approach is necessary?

The reasons for this can be begun with considering the text as it is. The text always has a social dimension. The prophets' ministry, message, and action are rooted in a social matrix and cultural

---

[67] George E. Mendenhall, "The Hebrew Conquest of Palestine," *Biblical Archaeologist* 25 (1962), 66-87.

[68] Nevertheless some scholars have made a strong critique on Gottwald, and Mendenhall on account of their lack of strong footing in social theory.

[69] N. K. Gottwald, "Sociological Method in the Study of Ancient Israel," in *Encounter with the Text: Form and History in the Hebrew Bible*, edited by M. J. Buss (Philadelphia: Fortress Press, 1979), 70.

forces. These texts evolved out the social milieu in which the prophets grew up and contextualized their utterance in that milieu. That means the prophets and the people lived in and were molded by a social system and a culture, and their actions are intelligible only in reference to them. So, without addressing their social contexts one may miss the significance of the texts even if their literary and historical contexts are considered.

Practitioners of the historical-critical method have generally shown an interest in the social features of the ancient world. Historical critics have also shown interest in social history, in developments and changes over time in the social organization of the biblical communities, their varying relations to the larger society, and in the developments of a larger society itself of which the biblical communities were a small and generally vulnerable minority.[70]

In the twentieth century, the development of the methods of source criticism, form criticism, and tradition criticism, in particular, promoted an intense interest in the social setting or *Sitz im Leben* of traditions and their tradents and the manner in which traditions undergo modification under changing social conditions.[71] Form criticism, which was launched by Hermann Gunkel has had a powerful influence on biblical studies during the twentieth century. It provided importance to the sociological investigation in so far as this method attempts to identify the social setting (*Sitz im Leben*) out of which the various genres of tradition have come and to which they are inseparably related. However, later form critics, lacking Gunkel's breadth of understanding and out of touch with the social science, came to restrict the life settings largely to cultic situations. Redaction critics also have shown an interest in the social circumstances influencing authors and their compositional strategies. But here too, it did not advance beyond hunches to a comprehensive analysis of the interrelation of text

---

[70] John H. Elliott, *What is Social- Scientific Criticism*? (Minneapolis: Fortress Press, 1993), 11.
[71] John H. Elliott, *What is Social- Scientific Criticism*, 12.

and social context. In both instances these sub disciplines of the historical- critical method failed to fulfill their own promises.[72]

Moreover, historical- criticism, as a result of its preoccupation with historical questions, did not show much interest how the ancient society was organized and operated. Or how attitudes, expectations, values, and beliefs were shaped by the natural and social environment? Nor, how did they share social and cultural knowledge and provide the basis for shared meanings and effective communication? How and why did conceptualizations of God and community vary over time according to changing circumstances? How did religious beliefs and symbolizations develop? How were they employed to advocate and justify deliberate responses to specific and changing social situations?[73]

In response to the questions above and also to attempt at resolving these issues, biblical scholars now agree that a more sophisticated method is required for examining and understanding the biblical writings as products of and response to their social and cultural environment. Out of this realization biblical scholars have turned to the social science with the intention of expanding and improving the historical critical method. And in this sense, the social-scientific criticism compliments the conventional historical critical analysis by enabling historical criticism to do what it is intended to do. As Elisabeth Schussler Florenza insists, modern historical research has always had a social interest: "I don't think there is a historical method without a social or sociological awareness and conceptualization."[74] Socio-historical criticism recognizes that the biblical texts have a social context in addition to a historical context- that the biblical authors and contemporary readers are social beings, subject to social forces, and that the

---

[72] John H. Elliott, *What is Social- Scientific Criticism*, 12.
[73] Cf. John H. Elliott, *What is Social- Scientific Criticism*, 13.
[74] Cited by Dale B. Martin, "Social-Scientific Criticism," in *To Each Its Own Meaning: An Introduction to Biblical Criticism and Their Application*, edited by Steven L. McKenzie and Stephen R. Haynes (Louisville, Kentucky: Westminster John Knox Press, 1999), 125.

biblical texts embed a social system.⁷⁵ If we wish to reconstruct ancient Israel as a lived totality, historical method and sociological method are the requisite complimentary disciplines. While the history is concerned with the sequential articulation of Israelite experience, the sociological approach is concerned with the structure and function of patterns of relationship both at a given moment and in their trajectories of change in history.⁷⁶

Thus a combination of historical and sociological approach holds the most promise for advances in the study of the Hebrew Bible. This approach examines not only the literature and social setting of ancient Israel, but also the social forces underlying the production of that literature. As Davis pointed out, there is a "society behind the text" and there is a "society within the text."⁷⁷ Therefore, the sociological study of Israel is necessary in order to place it within its appropriate historical context. Sociological study asks not only what a text said "then and there," but also how and why that text was designed to function, and what its impact upon life and activity of its recipients and formulators was indeed to be.⁷⁸ However, outlining a strict social world methodology is nearly impossible. As James Flanagan states:

> Social world studies do not offer a single method or theory in the usual sense of the terms. Their dependence on standard biblical methodologies, archaeology, and comparative sociology make them derivative and eclectic in ways that defy methodological purity....⁷⁹

Therefore, the principal method to be employed in the present study will be a socio-historical method. It combines the task and methods of the historian with those of the social and cultural

---

⁷⁵ Ronald A. Simkins et al., *The Social World of Hebrew Bible...*, 4.

⁷⁶ Gottwald, "Sociological Method in the Study...," 69.

⁷⁷ See Philip R. Davis, "The Society of Biblical Israel," in *Second Temple Studies 2: Temple and Community in the Persian Period*, edited by Tamara C. Eskenazi and Kent H. Richards (Sheffield: Sheffield Academic Press, 1994), 23.

⁷⁸ John H. Elliott, *A Home for the Homeless...*, 8.

⁷⁹ J. Flanagan, *David's Social Drama: A Hologram of Israel's Early Iron Age*, The Social World of Biblical Antiquities Series, 7 (Sheffield: Almond Press, 1988), 53.

anthropologist. While other methods of study are important, it is fundamental to recognize that the biblical texts convey meaning derived from a specific culture and social context. It is rooted in interacting groups of people organized in social structures that controlled the chief aspects of public life such as family, economy, government, law, war, and religious belief. This model studies the texts as both a reflection of and a response to, the social and cultural setting in which the text was produced.

There are however many ways of approaching the study of social structure and human behavior. The ideas of Marx, Weber, Durkheim, and others have given rise to dozens of theories about how our lives are shaped by social structure. In the sociological approach there are three dominant perspectives: the *Structural-Functional model*, the *Conflict Model* and the *Symbolic Interaction Model*.[80] This study focuses mainly on the Structural-functional model to explain the society during the Exile.

1.7.2. The Structural-Functional Model

Emile Durkheim is considered the founder of the structural-functional approach.[81] Structural- functional model addresses the question of social organization and how it is maintained. This theoretical perspective has its roots in natural science and the

---

[80] See also Bruce J. Malina; there are three main types of social-science models that one might use to understand social interaction. These three are called the structural-functionalist model, the conflict model and the symbolic interaction model. The structural- functionalist theory addresses the question of social organization and how it maintained. See. *The Bible and Liberation*, edited by Norman. K. Gottwald (Maryknoll, New York: Orbis Books, 1983), 16.

[81] However the Structural-functional model in the present study does not depend on any particular scholar. Structural-functional model had been proposed by many classical as well as modern sociologists like Auguste Comte, Herbert Spencer, Emile Durkheim, Talcott Parsons et al. And there is no consensus among these sociologists in their definition on structural-functional model. Therefore, this study is considering a general framework of the structural-functional theory. But at the same time this study realizes the difficulty in laying down a general framework of the structural-functional model due to the fact that the sociologists whom we refer is often in disagreement.

analogy between society and an organism.⁸² In the analysis of a living organism, the researcher's task is to identify the various parts (structures) and determine how they work (function).⁸³ In the study of the society, a researcher with this perspective tries to identify the structures of society and how they function. It focuses primarily on the structure and function of social groups, institutions, and ideologies within societies.⁸⁴

Assumptions Underlying Structural Functionalism: In the sense that any study of society must begin with an identification of the parts of society and how they work, structural functionalism is basic to all perspectives.⁸⁵ Scholars who use this perspective are distinguished from other social analysts by their reliance on three major assumptions.

1. *Stability*: The chief evaluative criterion for any social pattern is whether it contributes to the maintenance of society.

2. *Harmony*: As parts of an organism work together for the good of the whole, so the parts of the society are also characterized by harmony.

3. *Evaluation*: Change occurs through evaluation- the adaptation of social structures to new needs and demands and the elimination of unnecessary or outmoded structure.⁸⁶

The structural-functional approach identifies and analyzes the basic structures of a given society and examines their interrelationship; it is further interested in how the component parts of a society (its institutions, family, structures, beliefs, and so on) function within the wider society.⁸⁷ Thus, to understand

---

[82] David B. Brinkerhoff & Lynn K. White, *Sociology*, 3ʳᵈ ed. (New York: West Publishing Co., 1991), 13.

[83] David B. Brinkerhoff and Lynn K. White, *Sociology*, 13

[84] Charles E. Carter, "Social Scientific Approach," in *The Blackwell Companion to the Hebrew Bible*, edited by Leo G. Perdu (Oxford: Blackwell Publishers, 2001), 38.

[85] David B. Brinkerhoff and Lynn K. White, *Sociology*, 13.

[86] David B. Brinkerhoff and Lynn K. White, *Sociology*, 13.

[87] David B. Brinkerhoff and Lynn K. White, *Sociology*, 24.

any aspect of a society, each specific part must be seen in relation to the society as a whole.[88]

Talcott Parsons asserts that the structure of a system is that a set of properties of its component parts and their relations or combinations which, for a particular set of analytical purposes, can both logically and empirically be treated as contrasting within definable limits.[89] Having established the existence of a social structure, functional analysis turns to a consideration of how that structure operates in practice. Thus, a structural-functionalist assumes that a certain degree of order and stability are essential for the survival of a social system.

Thus, the structural-functional model seems more productive to delineate the structure and functions of the exilic community. It also helps us to understand how the structure motivated them to articulate a theology of creation. Moreover, this model helps us to understand the existence of different groups among the exiles and their interrelationship and its impact on the exilic society as a whole. Finally, it helps us to understand the social system and how this system and the theology of creation contributed positively to maintain the equilibrium of the exilic society.

However, limiting this study only to the structural-functional model will be inadequate. The success of applying the structural functional model on prophetic oracle depends on the relevant source materials which the text contains. Unfortunately, this source material is scanty and difficult to use. Thus all sociological information has to be extracted laboriously by a process of *analytical* and *comparative* conclusions.[90] And several oracles in DI do not

---

[88] M. Haralambos and R. M. Heald, *Sociology: Theme and Perspective*, (Slough: University Tutorial Press, 1980), 9.

[89] Talcott Parsons, "Functional Theory of Change," in *Social Change: Source, Patterns and Consequence*. edited by Eva Etzioni- Halevy and Amitai Etzioni (New York: Basic Books, 1968), 72-73.

[90] *Analytical conclusions* are drawn from texts which provide indirect sociological information such as conflict between groups or symbolic mode of expression (e.g. 'great deep' Isa. 51:10). *Comparative conclusions* are drawn from case studies of similar deportation found in the contemporary world.

yield to such a process. Moreover, several passages in DI show those other models – conflict model and symbolic interaction model- are relevant in order to get a full understanding of the exilic society and the decisive reality of exile behind the formation of creation theology. Therefore this study will consider those models also in the process of expounding the texts.

Objections are often made to the legitimacy of a sociological study of the biblical texts.[91] It is objected, for example, that sociology covers only general patterns, and leave the individuals out of account. Certainly it is true that sociology of the exilic community is confined to its more general, structural aspects. It is well aware of its limitations and does not claim to do justice to every aspect of the subject. However, this method will help us to delineate more clearly the general background of the exile, which was a decisive factor behind the DI community in its theological articulations.

With regard to the structural-functionalist theory, it is often criticized for failing to adequately deal with change, or the process of social change. It is felt, that it is far more likely to deal with the static structure than with the change of process. At this point too, we cannot completely disregard the criticism. But at the same time this method helps us to understand DI's theology of creation with a different perspective. Generally, scholars connected the theology of creation in DI with the coming of Cyrus and liberation and the new hope for the return from the exile. But the structural-functional model helps us to see other functions of creation theology such as integration of the community.

Here, the question is about the social structure of the exilic community and its consequences. So this study focuses on the social structure of the exilic community, especially during the period of Deutero-Isaiah.

---

[91] M. Robert Mulholland, Jr., 'Sociological Criticism,' in *New Testament Criticism and Interpretation: Essays on Methods and Issues*, edited by David Alan Black and David S. Dockery (Grand Rapids, Michigan: Zondervan Publishing House, 1991), 304-6.

Much, if not most, of the recent explicitly sociological study of the Old Testament and ancient Israel adopt the structural-functional model. Robert R. Wilson has made a significant contribution to this approach with reference to the study of prophets.[92] He addresses the sociological and anthropological dimensions of the prophetical text, seeking to locate the prophets in their 'social matrix'. Wilson's impressive book, *Prophecy and Society in Ancient Israel*, attempts to illustrate these at work. Moreover, in his article "The Community of Second Isaiah," Wilson had shed some light on the features of the exilic community.[93] However, he did not make any serious attempt to provide a socio-historical analysis of the society out of which DI and his community speak. But, even though he did not pay any attention to the formation of the creation theology, his observation concerning the features of the exilic community is highly significant to understand the setting of the creation theology.

The vast majority of exilic studies grapple with the political history or the development of religious institutions, practice, and ideas. But this study will undertake a comprehensive sociological analysis of the Babylonian Exile. In the process of reconstruction of the history of exile, this study will make use of social data and comparative materials towards the reconstruction of the political economy and social history of exile.

All social sciences are at their heart comparative in nature. This comparison of societies and cultures allows social scientists to make observations in one culture that may apply to another culture, though distant in time and perhaps place. The use of models might involve examining the role and functions of other Diaspora societies. A comparative analysis of the characteristic features of exile will be utilized to get a comprehensive understanding of exile, especially during the period of DI.

---

[92] See Robert R. Wilson, *Prophecy and Society in Ancient Israel* (Philadelphia: Fortress Press, 1980).

[93] Robert R. Wilson, "The Community of Second Isaiah," in *Reading and Preaching the Book of Isaiah*, edited by Christopher R. Seitz (Philadelphia: Fortress Press), 1988. 53-70.

Daniel Smith has proposed a series of social models for analyzing the social context of the Babylonian exile. He argues that the exilic community can be examined in the light of other societies that have undergone similar levels of upheaval and identifies four major social coping strategies: structural adaptation, competition for leadership, developing new boundaries and rituals, and production of literature of resistance.[94]

Therefore, this study will examine the well documented case of modern communities that have been subjected to forced migration and minority status in order to see what comparative light they throw on the plausibility of various hypotheses about the Jewish exiles. This socio-historical study will enable us to gain a fuller and more accurate understanding of the social environment of the exiles, in which they developed the theology of creation and to relate it more meaningfully to the present world.

1.7.3. The Present Study

The present study begins with an introduction, which provides a review of recent research, and the problem to be investigated. The first chapter explains the methodology. Its primary thrust is methodological because it explores the relationship of the creation theology in DI to its social context of the Babylonian exile. The principal method to be employed in this study is a "socio-historical analysis. A definition of important terminology will be provided and the different models on which the present study is based will be explained.

The second and third chapters concentrate on the creation motif in the Ancient West Asia and in the Bible respectively. The stories of creation in the literatures of Mesopotamia, Egypt and Canaan will be discussed briefly. The biblical traditions on creation such as Priestly, Yahwist and Wisdom traditions also will be discussed briefly. Moreover, as certain Psalms explicitly deal with 'creation,' they are also included in this study. Even though many

---

[94] Daniel L. Smith, *Religion of the Landless: The Social Context of the Babylonian Exile* (Bloomington: Meyer Stone Books, 1989), 74ff.

of these psalms reflect the idea of creation expressed elsewhere, we will consider it separately, to help us to trace the root of creation theology in Israel's liturgical traditions. This is not a socio-historical study. The purpose of these chapters is to equip ourselves to see the creation motif in DI in its West Asian background and to discern the uniqueness of creation in DI.

This will be followed by a comprehensive sociological analysis of the Babylonian Exile and its social setting. In the process of reconstruction of the history of exile, this study will make use of the social data and comparative materials towards a reconstruction of the political economy and the social history of exile. The analysis of the characteristic features of the exile will be utilized to get a comprehensive understanding of the exile, especially during the period of Deutero-Isaiah. This will help us to understand the social location of DI as well as the precious context in which the theology of creation developed. This chapter will give due attention to the problem of the historicity of the exile as some scholars have expressed their doubts about it.

The fifth chapter is set aside for a brief introductory study of Isaiah 40-55. There is a heated discussion among scholars about the unity of Isaiah, its authorship etc. Therefore, a discussion on the authorship of Deutero-Isaiah, domicile of DI, the community of DI, the social setting of Deutero-Isaianic community etc., is included in this chapter.

The sixth chapter is devoted to a comprehensive exegetical study of the relevant texts using the socio-historical approach as the principal method.

In the concluding chapter, the findings of the research will be summarized, and a brief attempt will be made to see how far the present study is relevant to the modern faith community.

CHAPTER TWO

Creation Motif in the Ancient West Asia

2.1. Introduction

One cannot hope to give a true-to-life picture of Israel's religion without indicating its proper place within the world in which and out of which it arose.[1] Geographically Israel was part of the ancient West Asia. History and archaeological evidences show that their political and cultural relationships with its neighbors were manifold and varied. Israel was molded in the ancient West Asian social and cultural matrix. Scholars assume that perhaps the entire ancient West Asia shared a common culture and basic religious concepts. Therefore a brief survey of the creation motif in the ancient West Asia is not out of place. However, the survey is not based on socio-historical approach. The purpose of this chapter is to introduce the milieu in which the community of DI developed their theology of creation.

S.G.S Brandon wrote the first comprehensive work on ancient West Asian creation.[2] Brandon's book, *Creation Legends of the Ancient Near East*, opens with a brief chapter on the origin of the concepts of creativity and beginning in time. This is followed by

---

[1] Th. C. Vriezen, *The Religion of Ancient Israel* (London: Lutterworth Press, 1967), 22.
[2] S. G. S. Brandon, *Creation Legends of the Ancient Near East* (London: Hodder and Stoughton, 1963).

the creation myth in Egypt, Mesopotamia, Israel, and Greece. The data available for Mesopotamia during his time was hardly sufficient for a comprehensive treatment. Since the mid 1960s much Akkadian material has come to light; *Atrahasis* was properly published only in 1969, *Enuma Elish* is much better understood today, and many 'minor' cosmogonies have come to light and much more work has been done over the past four decades in this area.

2.2. Creation Account in Mesopotamia

There are two groups of people in particular which have left their mark on the cultural development of Mesopotamia: the Sumerians and the Babylonians.

2.2.1. *The Sumerian*

Sumer is a land that came to be known in classical time as Babylon, situated in the southern half of modern Iraq. Its people, the Sumerians, developed probably the first highly sophisticated civilization in the history of humankind.[3] Sumerians settled there towards the end of 4th millennium B.C.E. Their origin is unknown. Ringgren assumes that they came from the east or northeast.[4] However that may be, there is a general agreement that the foundation of Mesopotamian culture was laid by the Sumerians.[5]

Among the vast quantities of clay tablets excavated in Mesopotamia are a number of cosmogonies written in the Sumerian and Akkadian languages. The texts range in date from the middle of the third to the end of the first millennium B.C.E. Also it differs in genre and purpose, making classification very difficult. When we survey the variety of legends dealing with the origin of things it would seem that there was no common pattern in the Sumerian thought on this subject. However, there is a reason

---

[3] Cf. S. N. Kramer, "Sumer," *IDB*, vol.4, 454.
[4] Cf. Ringgren, *Religions of the Ancient Near East* (London: SPCK, 1973), 1.
[5] S. G. F. Brandon, *Creation Legends....*, 67.

to think that they regarded water as the primordial substance out of which the world emerged.

Texts from Nippur traditions draw our special attention. An important feature of Nippur creation scenario is the pre-creation period:

An (being) Bel (an en- né), made heaven resplend [ent],

earth was in darkness, the lower world was [invi]sible;

the waters did not flow through the opening (in the earth),

nothing was produced, on the vast earth the furrow had not been made.

The high priest of Enlil did not exist, the rites of

purification were not carried out,

the h[ierodul]e(?) or heaven was not adorned, she did not

proclaim [the praises?].

[Heaven (and Ea]rth were joined to each other (forming) a unity,

they were not [married].

The moon did not sh[ine,] darkness spread;

Heaven showed its shining face in Dagan [=heavenly dwelling],

as it coursed, it could not reach the fields.

The rule of Enlil over the land had not yet come about,

the p[ure Lad]y? of E'anna had not yet [receiv]ed [offerings]?

The gr[eat gods], the Anunna, were not yet active,

the gods of heaven, the gods of ea[rth] were not yet there.[6]

The text depicts the period before creation. Heaven and earth were undifferentiated; they had not yet separated so that they could come back together in marriage. Only heaven enjoyed light; the underworld waters did not yet flow up to the earth through an opening to fertilize the fields through rivers and canals.

---

[6] R. J. Clifford, *Creation Account in the Ancient Near East and in the Bible*, The Catholic Biblical Quarterly Monograph Series 27 (Washington, DC: The Catholic Association, 1994), 28.

According to the Eridu tradition, Enki the spring water fertilizes earth by means of rivers and canals, causing life (including human life and cities) to rise along their banks. Included in this is the distinct tradition of Enki's creating individual human beings out of clay.[7] In the Eridu tradition, the principle of life is not cosmic but chthonic; water from under the earth makes the earth fertile.[8] Water plays a large role in Enki's myths and cult. Everything that lives in water arises from water; in other words, it owes its existence to the god of water.

Five myths describe Enki as the creator:[9] *Enki and the World Order, Enki and Ninhursag, Bird and Fish, Enki and Ninmah*, and the *Sumerian Flood Story*. In *Enki and the World Order*, Enki creates in several stages- by bringing water up to the world and designating the gods of culture. *Enki and Ninhursag* open with a picture of the society not yet created by Enki before going to the act of creation. *Bird and Fish* attribute the existence of towns on the banks of canals to Enki. The satirical *Enki and Ninmah* describe Enki's forming man from clay. The fifth, Sumerian Flood Story divides the establishment of human race into two stages.

Enki and the World Order is known from Old Babylonian copies, and dated by Wilcke in the Isin Period (1953-1730 B.C.E.)[10] It consists of a hymnic section and two narrative sections. In the first narrative section, Enki travels to several places- Nippur, Ur, Meluhha, Dilmun- and blesses them. He then imparts fertility to the fields by inseminating the Tigris and Euphrates with water from beneath the earth; the rivers will bring that water to the fields. Creation is through providing water, as found essential for life.

In the second narrative section of *Enki and the World Order*, Enki assigns the gods' responsibility for the culture of Sumer. Three gods are made responsible for the supply of water to Sumer, another god for fishing in fresh water and still another for fishing

---

[7] R. J. Clifford, *Creation Account*..., 32.
[8] R. J. Clifford, *Creation Account*..., 32.
[9] See R. J. Clifford, *Creation Account*..., 33.
[10] R. J. Clifford, *Creation Account*..., 34.

in salt water; there is a goddess for grain, two gods for architecture, one each for wild and domestic animals, one for judicial administration, and a goddess for spinning and weaving. This list is not complete but it shows that Enki's creation includes organizing the world of human society.[11]

The second myth opens with a picture of Sumer and Dilmun before creation.

At Dilmun, no crow cries "ka'gu,"
no francolin [type of partridge] goes "dander,"
no lion kills,
no wolf takes a lamb.
Unknown the dog herding the goats,
unknown is the pig, eater the grain.
The widow does not spread malt on the roof,
no bird in the sky forages for it
................................[12]

Like other cosmologies, this text describes the pre-creation state concretely in terms of the absence of particular elements of society rather than abstractly as unspecified nothingness.[13]

2.2.1.1. Creation of Human Being
The fourth myth, *Enki and Ninmah*, deserve special attention. It specifically narrates the creation of human being from clay moistened with water. Its first section tells how the god at the command of the mother goddess Nammu, and with her and Ninmah's help, created human beings as substitute workers for the minor gods who were unhappy at work. Human beings as

---

[11] R. J. Clifford, *Creation Account...*, 34.
[12] R. J. Clifford, *Creation Account...*, 36.
[13] One can find the same expression in Genesis 2:5: "when no plant of the field was yet in the earth and no herb of the field had yet sprung up," used to describe the condition before creation.

substitute workers for the gods are also the theme of the Akkadian epic *Atrahasis*.[14] At Nammu's request Enki molds the form of the human being.

O my son, rise from thy bed, from they.....work what is wise,

Fashion *servants* of the gods, may they produce their.....

Enki accedes to his mother's request, and gives directions for the making of the new creature:

O my mother, the creature whose name thou hast uttered, it exists,

Bind upon it the ......of the gods

Mi the heart if the clay that is over the abyss

The good and princely fashioners will thicken the clay

Thou, do thou bring the limbs into existence;

Ninmah (the earth mother goddess) will work above thee,

...(goddesses of birth) will stand by thee at thy fashioning,

O my mother, decree thou its (the new born's) fate,

Ninmah will bind upon it the ...of the gods

...as man [sic]...[15]

Enki creates human beings, with the help of the mother goddesses, as surrogate laborers for the unwilling gods. The next scene depicts a banquet, presumably a celebration of the creation of human being. The poem goes on to describe how Ninmah creates certain deformed and inferior types of human being, who also have 'their destiny decreed', that is, they receive a function and their livelihood.

---

[14] The motif occurs in the standard version of *Gilgamesh* I, where Enkidu is created by the gods as a response to the problem of Gilgamesh, who is terrorizing Uruk.

[15] S. G. F. Brandon, *Creation Legends...*, 77; NERT, 77.

The idea that the clay is the basic substance of which humankind is fashioned is significant, perhaps this may have arisen from the conviction that human being is essentially a product of the earth – which he/she was made of it, he/she is nourished by it, and eventually he/she returns to it.[16] Moreover, according to this poem, the human being is created for one purpose only: to serve god by supplying them with food, drink, and shelter, so that they might have full leisure for their divine activities.[17]

However, another version said that after Enlil separated heaven and earth, he created the pickaxe, and with it made a hole in the ground, so that the human being grew out of it.[18] The remarkable thing in this narrative is that the creation of the human being is not a separate tradition from the creation of the world. It tells of the origin of humankind as toilers within the world.

2.2.1.2. Creation by Word

According to Kramer, the Sumerians believed in creation by the 'word' of the deity. 'All that the creating deity had to do according to this doctrine was to lay his plans, utter the word and pronounce the name'.[19] The evidence is found in one of the hymns to the moon god:

> Thou! When thy word settle down on the
> Earth green vegetation is produced,
> Thou! Thy word makes fat the sheepfold
> And the stall; it makes living creatures widespread.[20]

Here, in fact the Sumerians are witnessing to the power of the word of their king. Therefore, it is no wonder if they apply the same to the words of their deities.

---

[16] S. G. F. Brandon, *Creation Legends...*, 77.
[17] See S. N. Kremer, 'Sumer,' 461.
[18] Ringgren, *Religion of the Ancient...*, 21.
[19] S. N. Kramer, *The Sumerian Mythology* (Philadelphia: 1944), 115.
[20] *ANET*, 386.

2.2.1.3. Conclusion from the Sumerian Material

When we survey the variety of legends dealing with the origin of things, it would seem that there was no common pattern in the Sumerian thought on this subject. However, there is reason to think that they regarded water as the primordial substance out of which the world emerged or was created. They believed that the sea and water surrounded the universe on all sides, and therefore, concluded that the primeval sea had existed from the beginning and was a kind of 'first cause' and the 'prime mover'. From this primeval sea, personified as *Nammu*, was brought forth heaven and earth.

Another remarkable factor in Sumerian cosmology is the god's assigning to each person or thing a "destiny" or a plan of the universe. For the Sumerians, the 'origin' was the defining moment. Therefore, cosmogonies were a serious matter to them. Its intention was not to convey historical and scientific information (in a modern sense) about creation, but rather to ground or explain a contemporary reality or system.

2.2.2. Babylonian Account

It is generally accepted that the Babylonians inherited the cultural legacy of the Sumerians.[21] According to Speiser, 'the religion of historic Mesopotamia was in its essentials an original Sumerian contribution'.[22]

So, one can find several Sumerian genres and themes in the Babylonian materials. As in the Sumerian texts, the intent is not to convey historical and scientific information of creation but rather to ground or explain a contemporary reality or system.

There are several accounts of cosmogonies. Sometimes the scholars arrange them according to their status- minor or function-bound, and according to their form-anthological or exploratory.

---

[21] Cf. Alexander Heidal, *The Babylonian Genesis*, 2nd ed., (Chicago & London: The University of Chicago Press, 1951), 12f.

[22] E. A. Speiser, ed., *The World History of Jewish People*, vol. 1 (London: W. H. Allen, 1964), 234.

The minor cosmogonies presuppose the originating moment to be decisive for the present. They are bound by a single operation, giving the essential information for its performance, e.g., how to cure an ailment, dedicate a temple properly, provide the context for an entertaining debate, show that heavenly bodies are divine signs determining the times for rituals.[23] Anthological cosmogonies, on the other hand, occur within a story. The story explores broad questions such as divine governance and the purpose of human society in addition to cultural themes such as knowledge, social boundaries, and morality.[24] *Atrahasis* and *Enuma Elish* are the two main anthological cosmogonies which deal with creation extensively.

2.2.2.1. Atrahasis

It now appears as the classical Babylonian text about the creation and the flood, though it is closely related to the Sumerian text of flood. This myth developed from the Sumerian myth of *Enki and Ninmah*. The myth begins in the period when only gods existed, and the lesser gods, the Igigu, did the tiresome labor for the senior Anunnaki gods. After laboring for many years the Igigu refused to serve. The crisis was resolved by Enki and the mother goddess by creating human beings from the mix of clay and the flesh and blood of an Igigu as substitute workers. However, as the humankind increases, its tumult becomes intolerable to the gods, and especially to their lord Enlil. So Enlil with other gods took steps to destroy the human race by a series of plagues culminating in a world-wide flood. Only Atrahasis, the pious king of humankind (his name means all-wise) and his family survived, building at Enki's suggestion a boat to ride out of the flood. The gods, deprived of their human servants, realized how dependent on their human workers they had become. Therefore they relented and allowed repopulation, while adding safeguards against overpopulation- mortality and limits of reproduction.[25]

---

[23] R. J. Clifford, *Creation Accounts...*, 74.
[24] R. J. Clifford, *Creation Accounts...*, 74.
[25] According to A. D. Kilmer, the main issue in this myth was overpopulation. See his article "The Mesopotamian Concept of

2.2.2.2. Creation of Human Being in Atrahasis

The most remarkable aspect of creation in Atrahasis is the creation of human beings. It continues the Sumerian tradition of *formatio* from moistened clay, adding to the material the blood and "ghost" of a god. The epic is "the most important single witness to Babylonian speculation on the origins and nature of man [sic]."[26]

The lines on the creation of human being (192-284) constitute a unit: a separate scene precedes (the gods deciding to create) and follows it (the birth goddess creating); the key words from lines 192-193 reappear in lines 246-248 to form an *inclusio*.[27]

The broad context is the rebellion of the Igigu gods, which requires a new creature to labor in their stead. The gods command Nintu (a birth goddess) to create *lullû*-man to bear the yoke assigned by Enlil. She agrees on condition that Enlil provide the purified clay.

"On the first, seventh, and fifteenth of the month

I shall make a purification by washing.

Then one god should be slaughtered.

And the gods can be purified by immersion.

Nintu shall mix the clay

With his flesh and his blood.

Then a god and a man

Will be mixed together in clay.

Let us hear the drumbeat forever after,

Let a ghost come into existence from the god's flesh,

Let her proclaim it as his living sign,

And let the ghost exist so as not to forget (the slain god)."

Overpopulation and Its Solution as Reflected in Mythology," *Orientalia* 41 (1972), 160-77.

[26] R. J. Clifford, *Creation Accounts*.... 79.
[27] R. J. Clifford, *Creation Accounts*..., 79.

They answered "Yes!" in the assembly,
The great Anunnaki who assign the fates.[28]

Here, Enki commands Ninto to mix the slaughtered god's flesh and blood with the clay he will supply. In this connection Clifford writes: 'The Akkadian phrase "forever" usually occurs in contexts where something is to be commemorated; the drum (heart beat, pulse?) will commemorate, it seems, the dead god for all time. The next stanza describes how the ghost (*eṭemmu*) of the dead god, instead of wandering about, will remain in the god's flesh, which now becomes the *meteria ex qua* of man [sic]. There seems to be a play on *eṭemmu* ("ghost") and *ṭçmu* ("intelligence") of the dead god; the intelligence (and heartbeat?) of man comes from the god. The clever Enki determines the "formula" for man [sic]; clay from the terrestrial world and intelligence from the gods.'[29]

The origin of the human being is particularly striking in this epic. Mesopotamian cosmogonies repeatedly portrayed human beings simply as slaves of the gods, cogs in the machinery for divine care and feeding. But here human beings are important. The myth also explores the nature of the human being: mortality and limited procreation are the conditions for living peaceably with the gods in the post-diluvian age. Without such limits, the human race will expand beyond the capacity of the land to support it.[30] Here also the immediate issue is overpopulation.

2.2.2.3. Enuma Elish

Enuma Elish is the main source of our knowledge of Babylonian cosmogony. It is sometimes called the standard Mesopotamian creation text.[31] It gives us an account of the origin and the order of universe as a whole. It consists of almost 900 lines on the seven tablets. Its name, *Enuma Elish* (when on high) is given according

---

[28] S. Dalley, *Myths from Mesopotamia: Creation, the Flood, Gilgamesh and Others* (New York: Oxford University, 1989), 15.
[29] R. J. Clifford, *Creation Accounts...*, 80.
[30] R. J. Clifford, *Creation Accounts...*, 80.
[31] E. A. Speiser entitles it "The Creation Epic" in *ANET*, 60-72.

to the ancient West Asian custom for its opening words. It was recited regularly in the New Year Festival in Esangila, the temple of Marduk.

With new advances in dating and identifying its sources, it is possible to interpret *Enuma Elish* and its cosmogonies with more precision than before. The Old Babylonian date[32] once generally assigned to *Enuma Elish* is now recognized to be too early; most scholars today prefer either a late Kassite (fourteenth to twelfth century B.C.E.) or Isin II (Nebuchadnezzar I, 1125-1104 B.C.E.) date.[33] Scholars point out that the supremacy of Marduk over all the gods attested as such in *Enuma Elish* is not attested in Old Babylonian times; in the late eighteenth century B.C.E. In the Code of Hammurabi, Marduk is supreme over the earth but not over the gods. It was only during the time of Nebuchadnezzar I of Babylon (1125-1104 B.C.E.) did the old triad of Anu, Enlil, and Ea yield completely to Marduk.[34] Nebuchadnezzar replaced the triad of Anu, Enlil, and Ea rather than joining it, since the Semites (unlike Sumerians) preferred to worship very few high gods.[35]

The epic begins with a brief reference to the time when nothing except divine parents, Apsu and Tiamat, and their son Mummu existed.

> ¹When skies above were not yet named
> Nor earth below pronounced by name,
> Apsu, the first one, their begetter
> And maker Tiamat, who bore them all,
> ⁵Had mixed their waters together,
> But had not formed pastures, nor discovered reed-beds;

---

[32] See Heidel, *The Babylonian Genesis*, 13-14.
[33] See R. J. Clifford, *Creation Accounts...*, 83.
[34] Lambert, "The Reign of Nebuchadnezzar I: A Turning Point in the History of Ancient Mesopotamian History," in *The Seed of Wisdom: Essays in Honor of T. J Meek*, edited by W. S. McCollough (Toronto: University of Toronto), 1964), 3-13.
[35] R. J. Clifford, *Creation Accounts...*, 84.

CREATION MOTIF IN ANCIENT WEST ASIA

When yet no gods were manifest,
Nor names pronounced, nor destinies decreed,
Then gods were born within them.
¹⁰Lahmu and Lahamu emerged, their names pronounced
.....................................³⁶

The gods "were born" (*banû*, line 9); Lahmu and Lahamu "emerged" (*ŝûpû*), "their names pronounced" (line 10). All these verbs are used for creation elsewhere. The expression "to name" in line 1-2 are idioms meaning "to create."

According to this poem the primary form of the universe was water. Apsu was the primeval sweet-water ocean, and Tiamat the salt-water ocean, while Mummu probably represented the mist rising from the two bodies of water. It first reports the creation of gods by the primal couple Apsu and Tiamat, and the creation of further generation of gods. The uproar of the younger gods robs the aged Apsu of his repose. So Apsu decided to destroy them. But Tiamat opposes this with motherly concern. Despite this, the battle takes place in which Apsu is killed by *Ea*, one among the younger gods. Now of course, Tiamat seeks to take vengeance for her consort, and no god dares to go against her, except for Ea's son Marduk, but on one condition that he will be made the lord over the gods. Tiamat brings forth eleven enormous monsters, and sets god Kingu at the head of their ranks and fights a battle. In short, in this fearful battle, Marduk killed Tiamat and her helpers. Then he divided her body into two parts and with half of her body he fashioned heaven and with the other half earth. Tiamat's body becomes the basis for the formation of the earth:

V.⁵³He placed her head, heaped up [ ]
Opened up springs: water gushed out.
He opened the Euphrates and the Tigris from her eyes,
Closed her nostrils, [ ]

---

³⁶ S. Dalley, *Myths from Mesopotamia* ..., 233.

He piled up clear-cut mountains from her udder,
Bored waterholes to drain off the catchwater.[37]

Her natural outlets become vents for the fertilizing streams to flow through into the rivers, and her body becomes the foundation of the mountains.

2.2.2.4. Creation of Stars and Moon

After determining the proportions of the universe, Marduk then turns to ordering the astral bodies, the movements of which the Mesopotamians believed were the 'writing of the heaven's ordering the fates of nations and human beings.[38]

He constructed stations for the great gods,
Fixing their astral likeness as constellations.
He determined the year by designating the zones:
He set up three constellations for each of the twelve months,
....
In her (Tiamat's) belly he established the zenith
The moon he caused to shine, the night (to him) entrusting.[39]

2.2.2.5. The Creation of Human Being

When he had completed his work of creating and ordering the cosmos Marduk then turns to the creation of humankind. (VI. 1-34)

VI.5Let me put together, and make bones too.
Let me set up primeval man (*lullû*): Man shall be his name.
Let me create a primeval man.

The work of the gods shall be imposed (on him), and so they shall be at leisure.

---

[37] S. Dalley, *Myths from Mesopotamia...*, 257.
[38] S.G.F. Brandon, *Creation Legends..*, 103.
[39] *ANET*, 67-68.

The rebel god Kingu is summoned, and from his blood Ea creates man.

VI. 31They bound him (Kingu) holding him before Ea,
They imposed on him his guilt and severed his blood (vessels)
Out of his blood they fashioned mankind.
He imposed the service and let free the gods
After Ea, the wise, had created mankind,
Has imposed upon it the service of the gods
That work was beyond comprehension;
As artfully planned by Marduk, did Nudimmud create it. [40]

According to Brandon, these lines contain a number of problems that have severely caused much speculation among scholars and inspired some ingenious theories concerning the Babylonian conception of human nature and destiny.[41] Here, humankind is presented as formed from the blood of a rebellious god. Logically this derivation shows that human beings are essentially evil since they were created from the blood of a rebellious deity. Another aspect of creation of human being deals with the purpose of human life. The human being is made to do the work of which the gods grow weary, that is, the human being's toil lets the gods be free.

However there are stories, which give us a different picture. According to one legend, Bel (Marduk) created humankind by sacrificing himself.[42] Yet another account shows that humankind was regarded as being divine at least to some degree.[43]

After the creation of humankind, Marduk assigns to the gods their various stations in the universe, and they, in gratitude undertake the construction of his sanctuary at Babylon. The rest

---

[40] *ANET*, 67-68.
[41] S.G.F. Brandon, *Creation Legends...*, 106.
[42] A. Heidal, *The Babylonian Genesis*, 78.
[43] A. Heidal, *The Babylonian Genesis*, 68.

of *Enuma Elish* is not primarily a creation story. Its prime object is to offer cosmological reasons for Marduk's advancement from the position as chief god of Babylon to that of the head of the entire Babylonian pantheon. To do this, it traces his kingship back to the origin of the world, before any god existed. A fundamental contrast (always a rhetorically effective device in the Semitic world) underscores the antiquity and legitimacy of his kingship rather than Tiamat's.

There is another intention behind this text. This text claims Babylon's supremacy over all the cities of the land. Babylon's claim to supremacy was justified by the fact that it was the god of Babylon who had conquered Tiamat and had created and organized the universe. Thus this text also has a political motive behind this legend.

2.2.3. *Minor Cosmogonies*

Akkadian cosmogonies are also found in some short ritual texts. For example, several prologues to incantations show how cosmogonies functioned in rituals.

In an incantation against a toothache, the sufferer goes to a magician, who prays to the god Ea to call the worm back to the function he had assigned it in the order of creation.

> After Anu had created the heaven
> Heaven had created (*banû*) the earth
> ....
> The canals had created the marsh,
> (And) the marsh had created the worm
> The worm came weeping before Shamash
> His tears flowing before Ea:
> "What wilt thou give me for my food?
> What wilt thou give me for my drink?
> "I will give thee the ripe fig
> (And) the apricot."

CREATION MOTIF IN ANCIENT WEST ASIA   49

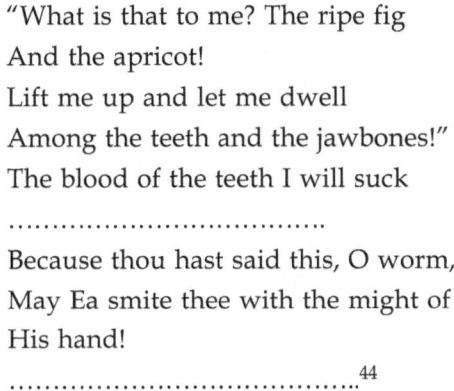

"What is that to me? The ripe fig
And the apricot!
Lift me up and let me dwell
Among the teeth and the jawbones!"
The blood of the teeth I will suck
....
Because thou hast said this, O worm,
May Ea smite thee with the might of
His hand!
...................................[44]

Here the magician recalls that, when the world was created the worm was destined to eat overripe fruit. The incantation illustrates how deeply rooted was the belief that the destiny of things were fixed on the day of creation. Deviation from this original order is the reason for the suffering. Consequently, the context of disease or suffering became the *Sitz im Leben* for the recitation of the creation myths.

2.2.4. Conclusion

Akkadian cosmogonies can be arranged as minor or function-bound cosmogony and anthological or explanatory cosmogony. The minor cosmogonies presuppose the originating moment to be decisive for the present. The original moment shows the right and intended use of elements within the universe. Cosmogonies in *Atrahasis* and *Enuma Elish* also show no interest in creation as a historical event in the modern sense but only as validating or exploring the present reality.

2.3. Creation in Egyptian Thought

Egypt was the major West Asian power geographically closest to Israel; on the Bible's own witness, it played a major role in Israel's formation. Egyptian thinkers avoided the subject-object distinction

---

[44] See A. Heidel, *The Babylonian Genesis*, 72-73.

of Western thought and preferred concrete imagery over abstract concepts in elaborating their thought.[45] As in Mesopotamia, cosmogonies played a major role in their prayers and rituals.

Egyptian cosmogonic thought has been influenced profoundly in every respect by the character of the land. The burning sun in its monotonous circuit and the annual flood of the Nile with its life-giving mud were the realities, which played a decisive role in the formation of their creation legends.

Egypt has a long recorded history. The religious concept of the land was never the same during this long span of time. Their cultic centers or the political centers shifted from place to place such as Heliopolis, Hermopolis, Memphis, and Thebes. The creation myth of Egypt, therefore, took their origin from these different religious centers, and its concept of creation, therefore, was most diverse. Heliopolis, Hermopolis, and Memphis are the three prominent traditions. Other traditions such as Crocodilopolis, Thebes, and Edfu also deal with creation.

2.3.1. Heliopolitan Tradition

Heliopolis (Greek for "Sun city," biblical On) south of modern Cairo, was the cult center of the sun god Re. As early as the Old Kingdom, Re was widely known as the creator. He was the creator of heaven and earth by virtue of being the sun god, who by his light and warmth daily awakened human beings, animals, and plants. Hence he was the god of seasons and his birthday fell on the New Year's Day. However, Re was not the major deity in the Heliopolitan cosmology.

The earliest expression of Egyptian cosmogonic thought was contained in a collection of hieroglyphic texts inscribed on the pyramids, commonly known as *Pyramid Texts*.[46] According to this text, the creation did not come out of nothing, but out of the

---

[45] R. J. Clifford, *Creation Account...*, 99.
[46] Cf. S.G.F. Brandon, *Creation Legends...*, 15.

primeval sea, the *Nun*. *Nun* in Egyptian thought was the primeval waste of waters. One Pyramid Text contemplates a primeval wastewater called *Nun*, existent before heaven and earth existed. According to Brandon, the underlying conception here is that these two fundamental constituents of the universe were already existent in *Nun* before they took their forms of heaven and earth.[47]

The major roles in the Heliopolis cosmogony were played by Atum and the Ennead (=nine gods). Atum generated from himself, either by masturbation or spitting, the first divine couple, Shu (atmosphere) and Tefnur, who gave birth to Geb (earth) and Nut (sky), who were then separated from each other by Shu. Subsequently there were born Osiris and Isis, Nephthys and Seth, to complete the Great Ennead. However, only the first five gods were regarded as cosmic. The famous shrine at Heliopolis known as Phoenix House was a place of Atum worship.

The Heliopolitan cosmology takes the form of a genealogical system comprising nine gods, the so-called *Ennead*. They include *Atum*, (the creator); *Shu* (the air); *Geb* (the earth); *Nut* (the sky) etc. The idea of a biological generation is operative here, and in that the origin of the world is accounted for in terms of the successive appearance of the divine personifications of its major parts, i.e., *Shu* = air; *Geb* = earth; *Nut* = sky.[48]

The Heliopolis cosmology asserts that the world developed from the monad.[49] The monad is the simple source from which all existence is derived; it is personified in the god Atum.

2.3.2. Memphis Tradition

Memphis, the capital during the Old and Middle Kingdoms, was the most important urban center in Egypt. *Ptah* was the god of this capital city. In all probability he was first considered a creator by

---

[47] S.G.F. Brandon, *Creation Legends*..., 15.
[48] S.G.F. Brandon, *Creation Legends*..., 18.
[49] "monad"= a hypothetical primitive living organism / god / or unit of organic life.

virtue of being the divine craftsman; only later was creation through word or sex ascribed to him.[50] Creation at Memphis was conceived on the model of artistic activity rather than on natural processes.

The text found on a stone dated to the reign of King Shabaka of the 25th Egyptian Dynasty (*ca.*710 B.C.E.), claims in its introduction that it was a copy of the much earlier papyrus document which had been found partially destroyed; and because of its importance, Shabaka ordered that it be restored and inscribed on stone.[51] His aim was no doubt to promote the unity of the kingdom, the restoration of Memphis as capital, and hence his own legitimization. This copy itself has suffered badly over the centuries with almost one-third of the text being destroyed as a result of the stone's having been used for milling.

The text has four main sections: the title of the King Shabaka, followed by a statement of the condition in which the original was found; the first part of the original document, which recounts *Geb*, the earth god's resolution of the conflict between *Horus* and Seth over the division of authority and territory after the death of *Osiris*; a long section which relates *Ptah's* creation of the cosmos, the gods, plants, crafts, towns, and all good things and the final section, which contains a brief description of the rescue of *Osiris'* body by his sisters, *Isis* and *Nephthys*. According to this text, *Ptah* is described as the creator:

> Through the heart and through the tongue something developed into *Atum's* image
> And great and important is *Ptah*,
> who gave life to all gods and their *kas* as well
> through this heart and this tongue
> through which *Horus* and *Thoth* became *Ptah*.[52]

---

[50] See R. J. Clifford, *Creation Account...*, 110.
[51] *NERT*, 4.
[52] James Allen, *Genesis in Egypt: The Philosophy of Ancient Egyptian Creation Account*, Yale Egyptological Studies 2 (New Haven, CT: Yale University, 1988), 43.

The creation activities of Ptah are described as taking place through the agency of his "heart" and "tongue"; the former being the seat of thought, while the latter represents the verbalization of the heart's thoughts. These lines also show that the intellectual creative principle is essentially embodied in *Ptah*, though components of it can be found in the gods *Horus* (command) and *Thoth* (perception).[53]

When the first dynasty established its capital at *Memphis*, it was necessary to justify the sudden emergence of this town and its central importance. For this, they exalted the local god of *Memphis*, *Ptah*, as the creator, and the city of Memphis as the central place.[54]

In this, a significant passage contains a list of deities who are stated to be manifestations or forms of *Ptah*.[55]

Even Nun and his consort of the Heliopolitan tradition is identified here as forms of *Ptah*. This claim in turn makes *Ptah* logically the creator of all gods of Egypt.

So were all the gods born
Atum and his Ennead as well,
for it is through what the heart plans and the tongue
commands that every divine speech has developed.[56]

The remarkable character of *Memphis* cosmology, especially for a student of OT, is the idea of creation by word of *Ptah*.[57] However, the idea of creation by word need not be regarded as a unique concept, because the Sumerians too shared a similar concept.

2.3.3. Hermopolitan Tradition

Hermopolis in the middle Egypt was so named by the Greeks,

---

[53] R. J. Clifford, *Creation Accounts*..., 111.
[54] R. J. Clifford, *Creation Accounts*..., 111.
[55] Cf. *ANET*, 5
[56] James Allen, *Genesis in Egypt*..., 44.
[57] Cf. *NERT*, 5.

who identified the city's chief god, Thoth, with their Hermes. Thoth was not, however, part of the local creation tradition. The Egyptian name of the city, *Ḥmnw* ("city of eight [primeval gods]"), underlines the Ogdoad's major role in the local cosmogony.

The Ogdoad consisted four pairs of gods: Nun and his female partner Naunet (primeval waters), Huh and Hauhet (flood), Kuk and Kauket (darkness), and Amun and Amaunet (concealed dynamism). The males are pictured as frog-headed and the females, as snake headed. The goddess however has no independent existence apart from the gods. The Ogdoad represented the conditions before creation.

This tradition describes a 'cosmic egg,' from which the maker of the world or some other primeval being emerged. Here the cosmic egg was produced by eight mysterious beings. This egg contained Re, the sun god, who was to be the creator of the world. These eight mysterious beings, Ogdoad, which produced the egg is therefore regarded as the elements or forces necessary antecedent of the beginning of creation. They constitute what might naturally be imagined to have the chief features of the primeval chaos that preceded the creation of the world.[58]

The significance of the egg is revealed in an inscription of a certain Petosiris of Hermopolis:

> I reserved a zone around the egg in the Great Pool to prevent it from being contaminated by the common people, for it is the place where Re was born in the First Time, when the land was still immersed in Nun, for it is the place of birth of all the gods who began to exist at the beginning, for it is in this spot that every being was born, for half the egg was buried in this spot, and there also are all the beings that issued from the egg.[59]

According to the New Kingdom texts from Hermopolis, Amun figures as the primordial god, being the creative principle and ruler over what exists. His name is derived from the verb 'imn (= to conceal or to be hidden), suggesting transcendence. Elsewhere

---

[58] S.G.F. Brandon, *Creation Legends*..., 43.
[59] R.J. Clifford, *Creation Account*..., 113.

Amun is manifested in the sun, the primeval mount (Ta-tenen), and the pre-creation universe. Thus the tradition describes both his immanent and transcendent nature. One poem states clearly that all things are manifestations of a single transcendent deity:

> All the gods are three:
> Amun, the Sun, and Ptah, without their seconds.
> His identity is hidden in Amun,
> his is the Sun as face, his body is Ptah.[60]

These are three expressions of one underlying deity, since the singular pronoun "his" is used. The deity is transcendent (his identity is hidden in Amun), he is manifest through the greatest force in nature, and he extends his form or essence into the multiple "developments" of the created world (his body is Ptah).[61] Earlier hints at Amun's role come to a climatic conclusion here: he is the ultimate cause.

2.3.4. Conclusion

We have made a brief survey of the creation legends associated with the three great cult centers of ancient Egypt. Although each center presents its own version of creation, the gist is the same. All these cosmogonies deal with the emergence of the first land from the primeval waters. A notable feature in Egyptian cosmogonic thought is that we do not find any evidence of struggle motif in it, as in the case of the Babylonian tradition. Another notable feature of the Egyptian cosomogony is the material out of which the heaven and earth are fashioned is not taken out of the substance of *Nun* as Marduk made from the body of Tiamat. Instead, either the original creator emerges from it or Nun itself possesses the potentiality of producing creative emanations from itself.

Another notable feature is that the cosmogonies were developed at important cities to exalt the principal local deity –

---

[60] R.J. Clifford, *Creation Account*..., 113.
[61] R.J. Clifford, *Creation Account*..., 113.

Re, Atum, Ptah, or Amun – to the rank of universal and officially recognized god of state, undergirding the city's claims to importance.

May be the most important feature of Memphite Theology of creation is the process of creation: creation by word of a single deity. Many scholars believe that the process described in the Memphite Theology influenced Genesis 1 either directly or indirectly.[62] However, the important difference between Egyptian and biblical cosmogonies must be mentioned. In Egyptian cosmogonies everything is contained within the inert monad, even the creator god. The creation process is sometimes depicted as a self-development within Nun, while at other times the creator is independent of his creation; these depictions may represent two sides of the same coin. But in Genesis 1, the creator is unequivocally distinct from the *materia*, the distinction being underlined by repetition of the divine name and by a variety of the verbs of creative action. Further, the manner of creating activity in Genesis - speaking a word to darkness and waters - may have been at the inspiration of the Memphite Theology, but the assumptions behind each text are quite different.

However, no Egyptian text gives clear and unambiguous answers to the question why the world was created. In contrast, amid the variety of biblical accounts, Yahweh always creates for a purpose.

2.4. Creation in Canaanite Texts

At the beginning of the second millennium B.C.E., the West Semitic tribes appeared in the region of the Upper Euphrates and founded their kingdom around the city of Mari.[63] These people were called 'Amorites'. At about the same time, some related tribes invaded what is now Palestine. Bible usually makes a distinction between the Amorites in the hill country and the Canaanites in the coast (Gen 10:16; Exod 3:8). But recent archaeological studies show that

---

[62] Cf. Frank T. Miosi, "Memphite Theology," *ABD* Vol.4, 691.
[63] H. Ringgren, *Religion of the Ancient...*, 124.

they are not two different people, but only a special geographical development of Amorite culture in the coastal district, which acquired the name Canaan.⁶⁴ Canaan, according to Schmidt, was exposed to the cultural influence from the north and south, especially from Mesopotamia and Egypt.⁶⁵

However, on the northern part of this coast a distinct culture developed the so-called Phoenician culture. It is a disputed question, exactly where we should draw the boundary between the Canaanite culture in general and the Phoenician in particular, and it depends on whether the Ugaritic culture should be called early Phoenician or not.⁶⁶ Nonetheless, here we are concerned with the Phoenician concept of creation and that of the Ugaritic concept separately for the sake of clarity.

For a long time our primary source of Canaanite religion was the polemical texts from the Old Testament. Therefore our knowledge of Canaanite and Phoenician religions was extremely small. There are however, three main sources available now (outside the Bible) for understanding Canaanite cosmogonies: the Ugaritic texts of the Late Bronze Age (pre-1200 B.C.E.); the divine epithet "creator of heaven and earth," which occurs in Phoenician, Aramaic, and Punic inscriptions from the eight century B.C.E. to the second century C. E.; and a late first century C.E. compendium of mythology by Philo of Byblos.

2.4.1. Ugaritic Texts

The Canaanite religion, which we have come to know through the discoveries of texts at Ras Sharma, ancient Ugarit does not give us an actual creation account. But the supreme god El is sometimes described as the 'creator of the created'. Thus the act of creation is indicated through epithets. El, chief of the pantheon, is five times called *bny bnwt* (the creator of creation / creatures)⁶⁷ Like Akkadian

---

⁶⁴ H. Ringgren, *Religion of the Ancient...*, 124.
⁶⁵ Cf. H. Schmidt, *The Faith of the Old Testament: A History*, (Philadelphia: The Westminster Press, 1983), 136.
⁶⁶ See H. Ringgren, *Religion of the Ancient...*, 124.
⁶⁷ See R. J. Clifford, *Creation Accounts...*, 118.

banû, Ugaritic *banaya* has a wide range of meanings –from constructing building to begetting gods or humans (in the latter meaning sometimes *'b* as "father").⁶⁸ The epithet usually occurs in the context of divine or human appeals to El's mercy to emphasize the supplicants' claim on El, based on his fatherhood. El's wife Asherah has an analogous epithet *qnyt 'lm*, "creator of the gods."⁶⁹ From these epithets J. C. de Moor concludes: "To the Canaanites creation and procreation were aspects of one and the same concept."⁷⁰ El created the world, the gods, and human beings. Unfortunately the details of El's creative acts are not presented in the extant texts; we have only epithets.

An important Ugaritic evidence bearing on cosmogonies is the so-called Baal cycle, six tablets describing the storm god's battle with Yamm (sea) and with Mot, the god of death, in which finally Baal gains victory. However, some scholars are reluctant to consider it as a genuine creation text. For example, J. C. Greenfield states: "The Ugaritc texts record no creation or flood story, although fragments from Akkadian texts excavated at Ugarit deal with elements of these stories."⁷¹ However, others interpret Baal's battles and victories as cosmogonies. For example, Loren Fisher here discerns cosmogony in certain themes:

> In this conflict theme [between Baal and Sea or Death] related to kingship, temple building, or creation? I think this is an improper question....conflict, kingship, ordering of chaos, and temple building are all related to an overarching theme that I would call "creation."⁷²

---

⁶⁸ R. J. Clifford, *Creation Accounts*...,118 (But we should note that Hebrew *banâ* never means "to beget")

⁶⁹ R. J. Clifford, *Creation Accounts*..., 118.

⁷⁰ J. C. de Moor, "El the Creator," in *The Bible World: Essays in Honor of Cyrus H. Gordon*, edited by G. Rendsberg et al., (New York: Ktav, 1980), 187.

⁷¹ J. C. Greenfield, "The Hebrew Bible and Canaanite Literature," in *The Literary Guide to the Bible*, edited by R. Alter and F. Kermode; Cambridge, MA: Harvard University, 1987), 547.

⁷² L. Fisher, "Creation at Ugarit and in the Old Testament," *VT* 15 (1965), 316.

It is worth noting that the conflict account bears striking similarities to the Babylonian Creation story, Enuma Elish. Peter C. Craigie writes:

> The story, in outline form, is typical of one part of common Near Eastern creation myths. First in the cosmogonic process, there are the gods of the primeval, chaotic waters; second, there come those gods who represent the ordered aspects of the emerging world. Then there emerges the classical tension between the powers of chaos and the forces of order, and only when order has triumphed over chaos can creation be said to be fully established. In this story it is Yamm who represents the primeval forces in mythological terms, it is Baal's victory over Yamm that symbolizes the conquest of chaos by order. In this sense, the first part of the story has overtones of creation mythology; it is not a complete creation story, but it is typical of one classical portion of creation mythology.[73]

The center of gravity of these myths is different from the Babylonian myth of creation. However, the basic motif is identical. Just as Marduk's victory over Tiamat establishes the earth, so the Baal's triumph over Mot preserves fertility. Thus the focal point can be understood in terms of the chaos –order theme. It looks at reality from the point of view of human existence. It recognizes the element of chaos and order as an ever-present reality. Therefore, through the cultic activity of the myth they affirm not only the belief in the triumph of order over chaos, but also make an attempt to secure the continuity of that triumph.

In short, the question whether the Baal cycle is a true cosmogony is unanswerable. Some of the elements of cosmogonies are there – the building of a temple, the maintaining of fertility and of kingship (hence of social order); on the other hand, Baal does not make anything and, more importantly, is not ultimately powerful. He sits on the throne through El's decree, as both of Anat's and Asherah's intercession for him attests. As long as the relationship of El and Baal in the Ugaritic texts is not fully known, a satisfactory understanding of cosmogony in the Baal cycle is not possible.[74]

---

[73] P. C. Craigie, *Ugarit and the Old Testament* (Grand Rapids: Wm. B. Eerdmans, 1983), 63.
[74] See R. J Clifford, *Creation Accounts*..., 126.

2.4.2. Phoenician

Our main source of Phoenician cosmogony is the work of Philo of Byblos (*ca.* C.E. 50-150).

According to Philo two elements existed at the beginning, dark wind-shaped air and a dark miry chaos. From this substance, Wind (πνεμα) and Desire (ποθος) came out as a result of a sexual union. They brought forth a being Mot (μοτ). From this creature there then arose rest of the creation in the form of an egg, which 'shone forth' together with the sun, the moon, and the stars.[75] When the air became light and warm, there arose 'through the heat of the sea and of the land' clouds and rain, thunder and lightning, so that rational creatures were terrified and began to move as male and female on the land and in the sea.[76]

Damascius has two versions of the story of creation. According to one, at first there were three primary principles, namely Chronos (Χρονος = time), Pothos (ποθος = desire) and Omichle (ομιχλη = darkness). From the Pothos and Omichle there arose Aer (the air) and Aura. These then gave birth to Otos, which is the spiritual basic material.[77] However, this account is short and vague. We cannot, therefore, draw valid conclusions from it.

According to the other version, the first principles were Aither and Aer. The highest Intelligence, Ulômos (ουλομος) came out of it. By masturbation Ulômos brought forth the Chusor, and brought forth heaven and earth.[78]

Unfortunately for comparative purpose, the Canaanite religious evidence is far more random than that of Egypt and Mesopotamia and it has been too often made a foil for the alleged superiority of the Bible. The undoubted creator gods are El and his wife Asherah. One of the modes of creating is sexual generation,

---

[75] Ringgren, *The Religions of the Ancient...*, 144 ff.
[76] Ringgren, *The Religions of the Ancient...*, 144.
[77] Ringgren, *The Religions of the Ancient...*, 144.
[78] Ringgren, *The Religions of the Ancient...*, 145.

which is conveyed by the Ugaritic verbs *banaya* (to beget, to build) and *qanaya* (to beget, create). Baal's victory however, over Sea and Death and the political and the social order resulting from it (symbolized by his temple) cannot be called a cosmogony.

The remarkable thing is the concept of water as chaos or primeval sea and wind (cf. Gen. 1:2), which corresponds to the *rûah*, is a very familiar image both in Babylon and Israel. The point is that, the starting point for creation is similar in all these (Phoenician, Babylonian, Israelite) cosmogonies.

2.5. Conclusion

Finally as a way of conclusion, we must now move on and consider in brief the significance of creation as a concept in ancient West Asia.

First of all we have seen that there was no culture in Ancient West Asia that did not speak rather extensively of creation in various literary forms and contexts. One of the most pregnant forms of expression about creation was the myth. The modern human may not appreciate the myths of ancient West Asia. But the myth, to them, was an expression of human understanding of reality.[79] Therefore, for them, the myth about the primeval event was a determinative factor for their present life. This is the reason for the close connection of the creation myth with the cult.

We saw that the myth of creation has its setting in the New Year Festival. The concept of the act of creation has a wide range of significance here. The notion that the primeval act, which took place outside time, now breaks into history to become the present, as it overlays the idea that the created world can be maintained only by being constantly renewed.[80]

---

[79] Cf. Childs, *Myth and Reality in the Old Testament*, Studies in Biblical Theology No. 27, (London: SCM Press Ltd, 1960), 17.

[80] Benedict Otzen, Hans Gottlieb, and Kund Jeppesen, *Myth in the Old Testament* (London: SCM Press, 1980), 9.

Thus, according to the West Asian creation faith, it not only deals with the origin of the world, but also (as it is concerned above all) with the present world and the natural environment of humanity now.

Secondly (this is related to the first one), the order established through creation and its repetition every year has significance in the political realm. This is clearly seen in the motif of the battle against chaos (*chaoskampf*). In Mesopotamia and Ugarit, the *chaoskampf* appears not only in cosmological context but also just as frequently in political context also.[81] The repulsion and destruction of the enemy, and thereby maintenance of political order, always constitute one of the major dimension of the battle against chaos.[82]

Another notable feature is that the act of creation was often described in order to indicate the superiority of the deity. The primeval struggle takes places not on the question of creation, but on the question of authority and sovereignty. For example, in *Enuma Elish*, Marduk does not fight with Tiamat that he might create the heaven and earth, but, primarily, to establish his sovereignty.

The great liturgical rhetoric of creation was sponsored by the great royal regimes, which easily co-opted the evocative theological assertions of created order for their specific political accomplishments and interests. Thus creation faith was used for royal ideology and propaganda. There is no reason to imagine that the royal establishment in Jerusalem was immune to this temptation (cf. I Kgs 8:12-13; Ps 89:3-37). In Ps 89, the guarantees given to the house of David come along with the celebration of the goodness and reliability of Yahweh's created order.

Also, as Clifford points out, 'many ancient cosmogonies are narratives and depend on plot and character for their movement;

---

[81] Cf. C. H. Schmidt, "Creation, Righteousness, and Salvation" 104.
[82] C. H. Schmidt, "Creation, Righteousness, and Salvation" 104.

they must be read as drama rather than "objective" description.'[83] Because of this dramatic quality, ancient people apparently did not find it difficult to accept several versions of creation. We can however assume that each sociological context they lived in, prompted them to define a theology of creation appropriate to their context.

The idea of creation by word is another important feature, especially for the student of OT. Its traces can be found in Sumer and Egyptian cosmogonies. This idea is most probably a projection of the authoritative word of the king who brought order in the society.

---

[83] R. J. Clifford, *Creation Account...*, 199.

CHAPTER THREE
Creation Motif in the Hebrew Bible

3.1. Introduction

In the previous chapter, we reviewed briefly the creation motif in ancient West Asia. Here our task is to examine the same in the Hebrew Bible and thus prepare a ground for our investigation into the creation motif in the Book of Isaiah 40-55. Our main sources for this study are the Priestly and Yahwistic account of creation, which are given in Genesis 1-3, the Wisdom Literature, and Psalms. We may discuss the creation motif in each separately and briefly. No conscious attempt has been made to apply the sociological theory to delineate the idea of creation in these writings. As we noted above in chapter 2, here also our purpose is to perceive the theological background of DI's theology as we search the texts for the creation motif.

3.2. The Priestly Account of Creation

In this section, we deal mainly with the first chapter of the Bible (Gen 1:1-2:4a). This portion is assigned to P by nearly all critical scholars. P is often regarded as the final redactor of the entire Pentateuch, though some scholars postulate a distinct redactor (=R) who brought the J and P traditions together.[1] The function of the

---

[1] For the persuasive arguments that P was a redactor, and the writings are supplementary rather than an independent tradition in the analogy of J and E, see F. M Cross, *Canaanite Myth and Hebrew Epic* (Cambridge, Mass.: Harvard University Press, 1973), chapter II.

CREATION MOTIF IN THE HEBREW BIBLE   65

present text is reasonably clear. The creation account in Genesis 1 is P's preface to the J story for the exiles. However, we cannot limit the prefatory function of Genesis 1 to J only, rather it extends to the whole Pentateuch, which was written for an exiled community worried about losing its ancestral land and concerned about whether they would continue as a people. However, as von Rad pointed out, it was not "written" once upon a time; but rather, it is doctrine that has been carefully enriched over centuries by very slow growth.[2] A careful study of its form and content indicates that the present version is the result of traditions whose development extended over a considerable period of time.[3]

There is no doubt that P utilizes the older materials.[4] It reflects creation stories and cosmogonies of Mesopotamia and Egypt. The numerous points of contact between the P account of creation and the Babylonian creation epic, Enuma Elish and Atrahasis, have long been noted. There is not only a striking correspondence in various details, but also even the order of creation is very similar to the Babylonian account of creation.[5] However, the attempt to show that Genesis 1 is directly dependent on Enuma Elish is still left open.[6] Probably P must have made use of old data, which was more or less common to ancient West Asia.

Nevertheless, P does not accept those theologies. P's account of creation is something unique. 'The decisive difference between Genesis 1 and the Babylonian account of creation is that creation

---

[2] G. von Rad, *Genesis: A Commentary*, OTL (Philadelphia: The Westminster Press, 1972), 47.
[3] B. W. Anderson, 'Creation' in *IDB*, vol. I, 726.
[4] See. H. Gunkel, "The Influence of Babylonian Mythology upon the Biblical Creation Story" in *COT*, 25ff.
[5] See E. A. Speiser, *Genesis*, AB, (New York: Doubleday & Co., 1964), 9.
[6] Speiser, who translated Enuma Elish for *AENT* and also wrote a commentary on Genesis, simply adopted A. Heidel's chart of the sequence of act in Enuma Elish and Genesis 1, assuming that it proved borrowing. However, Heidel was more cautious than Speiser. To the question of 'borrowing', he wrote as conclusion; "I believe that *the whole question must still be left open*." (*The Babylonian Genesis*, 2nd ed.; Chicago: University of Chicago, 1951), 139.

in Genesis 1 is not the result of a struggle; the dramatic element is missing' in P.[7] Also among many creation myths of the ancient West Asia, a creation account opening without a theogony is another unique feature of P's creation theology.

According to P, the creation, in essence, is not a myth or a saga. It is addressed to the exiles. The text is a liturgical narrative, which tells the tale of creation in a stylistic way. It is a liturgical assertion against the temptations of the Babylonian gods in exile and thus in concert with Isaiah of the exile. It is therefore intimately related to the experience of the despairing Israel. Its themes answer pressing exilic questions about national existence and possession of the land.

P begins with the declaration, "In the beginning God created the heavens and the earth." The relation between the first two or three verses is controversial and not yet a settled problem.[8] On the ground of linguistic analysis and in the light of literary parallel found in Eluma Elish we should regard v.1 as a dependent clause.[9] This way of understanding the grammar of the verse suggests that God is said to be at work on the already present reality (chaos), which God orders by speech and enlivens by the spirit. Probably P must have made a literary synthesis of elements from Babylon, Egypt and Canaan.[10] However, we need not question the originality of the creation faith in Israel and it is clear, by this, that P urges the readers to know and experience God as Creator. P felt that it was important that his exilic audience first know God's identity as Creator. So Brueggemann describes it:

---

[7] Claus Westermann, *Genesis 1-11: A Commentary*, translated by J. J. Scullion (Minneapolis: Augsburg Publishing House, 1984), 81.

[8] There are two views about the first verse of the Bible. (i) Verse 1 as an independent clause, e.g., von Rad, *Genesis*, 48; Eichrodt, 'In the Beginning' in *Israel's Prophetic Heritage*, edited by B. W. Anderson, 1ff: (ii) Verse 1 as a dependent clause, i.e., 'when God set out to create heaven and earth..' Budde, W.F.Albright, Eissfeldt, Speiser, Brueggemann et al. hold this view.

[9] E. A. Speiser, *Genesis*, 12.

[10] W. F. Albright, *Yahweh and the God of Canaan* (Garden City, NY: Doubleday, 1968), 80.

The mood of this rhetoric is to evidence that God is serenely and supremely in charge. There is no struggle here, no anxiety, and no risk. If it is correct, as critical consensus holds, that this is an exilic text, then the intent and the effect of this liturgical narrative is to enact by its very utterance a well-ordered, fully reliable, generative world for Israelites who are exiles in Babylon. The world given in these liturgical utterances is a "contrast- world", compared to the world of exile that holds threat, anxiety, and insecurity. On this reading, the chaos already extant in v.2 represents the reality of exile- life at risk and disorder. The effect of the liturgy is to create an alternative world or ordered life, made possible by Yahweh's powerful word and will. Exilic Israel can live in this world and, if they choose, withdraw (emotionally, liturgically, politically, geographically) from the disordered world of Babylon, which in this recital is powerfully delegitimated.[11]

The arrangement in the P account of creation is difficult to understand. The eight work of creation are prompted by ten divine commands and executed on six different days. The following are the eight works:

1. Genesis 1: 3-5 : Creation of light
2. " 6-8 : " firmament
3. " 9-10 : " sea and land
4. " 11-13 : " plants
5. " 14-19 : " heavenly bodies
6. " 20-23 : " living bodies in air and water
7. " 24-25 : " land animals
8. " 26-31 : " human being[12]

P's presentation of creation through Word takes a particular form. He distributes each work into the component part of creation command:

Introduction of the command : God said
The command : let there be
Completion : it was so

---

[11] W. Brueggemann, *Theology of the Old Testament: Testimony, Dispute, Advocacy* (Minneapolis: Fortress Press, 1997), 153.
[12] Cf. C. Westermann, *Genesis*, 110 ff.

Judgement	:	God saw that it was good
Time sequence	:	it was evening ...one day.[13]

God's creation by means of 'word' is majestically presented here. Nevertheless, as Westermann has suggested, it is not necessary to divide them as 'word versions' or 'act versions.' It is important to note that God's speech does not stand isolated from divine deeds (see, 1:6-7; Isa 48:3; Ezk 37:4-6)

This literary style forestalled any misunderstanding of the creation account as mere information.[14] The whole of the Priestly work is permeated with the conviction that all events have their origin in God's commanding word.[15]

This 'theology of the word' is exceedingly influential in subsequent theological reflection. This is a most exalted way of speaking about Yahweh's generative sovereignty.

3.2.1. *Creatio ex nihilo*

In the light of verses 1-2 it is hardly possible to affirm that P has a *creatio ex nihilo*. Nowhere in the seven-day creation scheme of P's creation narrative does God create the waters; they are almost likely primordial. However, on theological grounds von Rad and Eichrodt argue for a creation out of nothing.[16] The Priestly writer, in the light of the text, has no scientific or philosophical motif so that he should begin with *creatio ex nihilo*. Westermann is right in his judgement that the question, "Is it *creatio ex nihilo* or not?" is not relevant to the text.[17] It has long been suggested that the God we encounter in the first creation narrative is more a God who brings order to things than one who actually creates. He separates

---

[13] C. Westermann, *Creation*, trans. J. J. Scullion (Philadelphia: Fortress Press, 1974), 49.
[14] C. Westermann, *Creation*, 49.
[15] C. Westermann, *Creation*, 49.
[16] Cf. Gerhard von Rad, *Genesis*, 49; Walther Eichrodt, *Theology of the Old Testament*, vol. II,101ff.
[17] Cf. C Westermann, *Genesis*, 109.

things from each other that things do not belong together and transfer them to their correct positions.[18] The verb ברא is certainly significant. It signifies the effortlessness of creation.[19] But there is another verb בדל which occurs frequently throughout the chapter, and which is characteristic both of Priestly linguistic tone and the Priestly view of creation. This verb can be translated as 'to make division', 'to part', or 'to separate from each other'. Thus the light and darkness are separated from each other (Gen. 1:14); the firmament of heaven separated the water above from the waters below (vv.6ff) etc. בדל is a truly Priestly word. Therefore, according to P, the creation is ordering of the material world from disorder.

When creation began, the condition of earth was חשך, תהו ובהו and תהום. Here the translation 'formlessness' or 'shapelessness' (O.Procksch, G. von Rad) are not quite accurate.[20] Westermann following Ridderbos and Delitzsch says, 'these notions are much more ominous for Israelite than for us, 'there is something fearful about this pair of words.'[21] Thus, here we get a picture of confusion and chaos, which was very common in the ancient West Asian myth. Through creation, God subdued the chaotic condition and brought order into this world.

The רוח introduced in v.2 belongs to God. It should be understood as the creative spirit of God in contrast to chaos.[22] It is thus the life-giving agent and stands for the invisible reality of the transcendent God.

The first thing that God created was light. Here P is not indebted to any traditions. This should be understood in the context of P's overall view as seen in the framework of six-day scheme with the conclusion of the seventh.[23] Therefore, it is not

---

[18] B. Otzen, H. Gottlieb, & K. Jeppesen, *Myths in the Old Testament* (London: SCM, 1980), 27.
[19] Cf. G. von Rad, *Genesis*, 49.
[20] Cf. Westermann, *Genesis*, 103.
[21] Westermann, *Genesis*, 103.
[22] Westermann, *Genesis*, 107.
[23] Westermann, *Genesis*, 112.

the creation of light, but the separation of light and darkness that set in motion the march of rhythm of time.[24]

In the account of creation of the heavenly bodies, P uses the old traditions what has been handed down to him. However, here P deliberately rejects the divinity of heavenly bodies, which was a dominating factor in the astral cult of the surrounding world. According to P, the heavenly bodies are nothing but created things. And P makes it clear that these were created for certain functions, and by virtue of their functions they belong to the order of creation.

The creation of plants and animals must also be considered in this background. Sumerian myth gives some extra divine nature to the plants. But P states, plant-species are vegetation; they are the constitutive part of the world fitted into the whole process of the world-creation.[25] We can say, as Westermann pointed out, 'it is a step towards a scientific explanation of creation of the plants'.[26]

3.2.2. P's Anthropology

Another significant contribution is P's anthropology. God has created man and woman in his image (צלם) and likeness (דמות). Exactly what is meant by 'image' has long been discussed.[27] Here P's radical anthropology can only be fully appreciated when it is compared with that of Babylonian theology, and its view of creation and human being as presented in Enuma Elish. After Marduk had killed the rebel goddess Tiamat and consigned her helpless consort Kingu to the charge of the god of death, he cut Tiamat into two parts and formed sky from the upper part and earth from the lower part. Later Marduk as an answer to gods' complaints about their heavy work, created humankind from the blood of Kingu, the ringleader of revolt, and the heavy work, which was formerly done by gods was imposed on human beings. Accordingly, human beings have two major defects: (i) their

---

[24] Westermann, *Genesis*, 112.
[25] Westermann, *Creation*, 45.
[26] Westermann, *Creation*, 45.
[27] For divergent opinions of scholars regarding 'image,' see Westermann, *Genesis 1-11*, 148-58.

vocation is to do the dirty work of gods; (ii) human beings are essentially evil, since they are created from the blood of the rebellious deity.[28]

Viewed against this background the human beings in Priestly work take on sharper contours. Perhaps one can even detect a polemic directed against the Babylonian concept of human being. Here P affirms to his exilic audience that they are not merely prisoners of war or captives. Rather they really are the kings and queens of God's estate, his agents in charge of the world.[29] Therefore P affirms that even though now they are captive, they have been created in the image of God. Thus, as Walter Brueggemann has pointed, 'this text is not an abstract statement about the origin of universe, rather it is a theological and pastoral statement addressed to a real historical problem'.[30]

This kerygmatic intention of P is further explicated in the proclamation of the phrase, "be fruitful and multiply and fill the earth and subdue it; and have dominion," to a people who had lost the land and perhaps the courage to return to it.[31] This is a subversive and empowering text addressed to the exiles. It denies the Babylonian claims to sovereignty, and attempt at empowering the marginalized exiles by routing their future in the power and purpose of the Creator.

The Priestly views are most obviously present in its brilliant presentation of creation in six days, so that the entire scheme was crowned by the institution of Sabbath.[32] Thus P 'introduces his work, a work which moves from creation to the institution of cult, and thereby, given to the creation event an orientation.'[33]

---

[28] Ralph W. Klein, *Israel in Exile* (Philadelphia: Fortress Press, 1979), 128.
[29] Ralph W. Klein, *Israel in Exile*, 128.
[30] W. Brueggemann, *Genesis*, Interpretation Commentary (Atlanta: John Knox Press, 1982), 25.
[31] W. Brueggemann, "The Kerygma of the Priestly Writers," in *The Vitality of Old Testament Tradition*, edited by Walter Brueggemann & Hans Walter Wolff (Atlanta: John Knox Press, 1975), 101-113.
[32] B. Otzen, *Myths in the Old Testament*, 28.
[33] C. Westermann, *Creation*, 41.

The Sabbath is ordained into the very fabric and structure of created life, and thus, it was given a cosmic significance. Yet the observance of the day of rest remain concretely and precisely a Jewish enactment, whereby Jews in Babylonian exile (and in every other circumstances) visibly and publicly distinguish themselves from a world that is too much given to the power of restless anxiety and control.

The world is *good* in the sense that the basic necessities of life are all there. God never deserted his creation or set it run like a wound-up clock that would eventually stop or ruin itself but he continues to create and uphold it. Thus, he guards the continuing existence of his creation. The goodness and perfection of the created world do not stand alone but depend on God the Creator and his continuing act of sustenance.

Conclusion

The function of the creation story is reasonably clear. It was given as a preface to the J-story of creating and populating the world, and thus providing an interpretive lens of Israelite reading of the whole Pentateuch in the exilic situation. P's creation story challenges the exilic community to view their exilic situation from a different point of view. P's main intention of describing Yahweh as the Creator is to link its significance to the exilic community's practical living in the hostile world.

Secondly, Israel was not the only people in ancient West Asia with creation stories. Sumerian, Mesopotamian, and Egyptian accounts have been unearthed in the last two centuries, which shows striking similarities with the creation account in Genesis. It does not imply that Israel directly borrowed the idea of creation from their neighboring countries, rather, the comparison with those text shows that Israel lived in a culture with a lively interest in these questions. While some have claimed that Israel used one or more of these accounts directly, it is now more common to speak of a widespread fund of images and ideas upon which Israel drew for its own account. The important aspects of P account of creation can be summed up in the following words:

1. The absence of theogony and creation as a consequence of combat.
2. The lack of interest in primeval chaos.
3. The prevailing monotheism.
4. The basic divine concept behind the creation as God's power and authority revealed through His word.
5. The high value given to human beings and thus a room for hope, by making him/her in God's image.

3.3. The Yahwistic Account of Creation

The Yahwist is the earliest collector and compiler of the oral traditions of Israel. It is difficult to put forward a date without ambiguity. However, the dating most often proposed are either in the era of David and Solomon (Noth, Sellin, Weiser et al.), or in the ninth century (Hölscher)[34]

J uses various traditional materials in his creation account, without much modification or reworking. The mythological features in P have been forced so much into the background. But in the case of J, these are visible on the surface of the narrative.[35]

In contrast to P, one cannot speak here of a creation which includes the entire world system. The general perspective of P's narrative is cosmic. This contrast is apparent from the respective initial sentence. P's account starts with the creation of "heaven and earth" (Gen.1: 1), whereas J's narrative begins with the making of "earth and heaven" (Gen.2: 4b). This means 'the Yahwist was not concerned primarily with the creation of heaven and earth or man's [sic] relation to the cosmic scene, but rather man's [sic] earthly environment'.[36] As D. J. McCarthy has pointed out, 'in the J part of primeval history, there is no real concern for the origin

---

[34] See. G. Fohrer, *Introduction to the Old Testament*, trans. D. Green (London: SPCK, 1970), 151.
[35] Cf. Otzen, *Myths in the Old Testament*, 40.
[36] B. W. Anderson, *Understanding the Old Testament*, 2nd ed. (New Jersey: Prentice-Hall, Inc., 1966), 174.

of the world. All the interest is directed towards its good ordering'.³⁷ Here the subjects are primarily human relationship to God and human relationship with the world in which he/she lives. This relationship is evident in the word play אדמה - אדם (arable land). The human being seems to be related to the land in some way, and in fact is created from it. On the other hand, the אדמה is dependent on human (אדם) cultivation (cf. vv.5,15)

'Not only do the two narratives have different foci and intentions, it is clear that each has also its own particular cultural background.'³⁸ According to P, water represented as תהום, is associated with danger. Besides, the similarity between תהום and the Babylonian mythical being *Tiamat*, was noted by many scholars. (Westermann, G. von Rad, et al.). This shows that the foundation of the Priestly conception is Babylonian. But according to J, in contrast, 'drought is the major threat to human existence'.³⁹ Water is regarded as the 'assisting element of creation' and the most important necessity for the cultivation of land and human existence. These characteristics clearly betray the Syro-Palestinian background.

Even the description of 'chaos' in J is different. J does not say anything about a primeval cosmic situation with a threatening character, instead they lists various absent materials which are necessary for making the earth inhabitable to humankind: 'there were no plant of the field…no herb…no rain…no human being to till the ground, etc. (Gen.2: 5). Here J's worldview is remarkably narrow. His cosmos indicate a world which the human being creates through labor. It clearly betrays a Palestinian peasant's feelings of community with the earth he cultivates.⁴⁰

Despite the difference in approach, emphasis, and authorship, in the subject matter, it is ultimately the same in both versions.

---

[37] Dennis J. McCarthy, 'Creation Motif in Ancient Hebrew Poetry' in *COT*, 76.
[38] B. Otzen, *Myths in the Old Testament*, 40.
[39] B. Otzen, *Myths in the Old Testament*, 40.
[40] B. Otzen *Myths in the Old Testament*, 41.

We have noted some similarities between P and Mesopotamian traditions. The account of J also points in the same direction. Perhaps we may assume that both were sharing from a common source.[41] However, each develops its accounts in its own distinctive way.

3.3.1. J's Classical Anthropology

According to W. Brueggemann, an anthropology based on this text is not adequate, because its role is limited.[42] He has his own justification for this. Yet we cannot ignore J's unique contribution in this regards.

In v. 7 we read: "then the Lord God formed human being from the dust of the ground, and breathed into his nostrils the breath of life, and the human being became a living being"(NRSV). P does not say how the human being was created, nor does he say that human was created by word. But, J answers that question. J says, God *formed* human being from the ground. The idea of human being formed from the earth as it was so widespread. There was an Egyptian parallel where god *Khnun* fashions humankind on a potter's wheel. Therefore, this motif is not peculiar to J. Rather J is repeating a traditional story, which was current for thousands of years before him.[43] But 'what is new in J is that he speaks of God of Israel as the Creator of all people'.[44] And he uses it to say that 'man [sic] receives his existence from God, human existence is nothing else but a created existence'.[45]

The tradition, which J has passed on to us, is still valid. It reminds that the human being consists of elements that belong to this earth. It occurs again at the end, Gen. 3: 19: "you are dust and to dust you shall return". Thus, J points out two facts concerning human beings.

---

[41] Cf. A. Heidal, *The Babylonian Genesis*, 69ff.; *ANET*, 68.
[42] Cf. Brueggemann, *Genesis*, 41.
[43] Westermann, *Creation*, 77.
[44] Westermann, *Genesis*, 204.
[45] Westermann, *Creation*, 77.

(i) It 'refers to human frailty to the fact that he/she is bound to a course of life which leads from birth to death'.[46]

(ii) It asserts the 'bond of life between human being and earth given by creation'.[47]

According to J, a human being is not merely a product of clay; he/she also participates in the divine. This idea is expressed clearly in the statement that "...and breathed into his nostrils the breath of life, and human became a living being" (Gen. 2: 7b) (NRSV). In P, this special relationship of human being is implied by the concept of the 'image of God'. But in J this special relationship is depicted by the image of a human as the recipient of the breath of life. Human being thus became a *living being*. Thus, J asserts that the life of a human being is a gift from God, and that when he/she dies; Yahweh takes back the breath of life. (cf. Ps. 104: 29f; Job 34: 14f).

3.3.2. *Purpose of Human Being*

According to K. Budde 'man [*sic*] is in paradise for a blissful enjoyment, not to work and guard it'.[48] This shows how completely the meaning of this section is misunderstood. This misunderstanding crept in as a result of adaptation of the Persian loan word, which through the Greek translation παραδεισος, evokes a definite image in western language.[49] J states quite clearly that God put man in the garden 'to till and keep it'. This means that it is not a 'fairy land, no Utopia, no Paradise for blessed bliss, but that it is a land which needs tilling and care'.[50] The idea of a paradise as a place or a state of blessed enjoyment is completely foreign to the Old Testament. The notion, which puts a very low value on manual labor, is not an Old Testament concept, but it

---

[46] Westermann, *Creation*, 78.
[47] Cf. G. von Rad, *Genesis*, 77.
[48] K. Budde, *Die biblische Urgeschichte (Gen 1-12:5) untersucht* (1883), cited by Claus Westermann, *Genesis*, 220.
[49] Westermann, *Creation*, 80.
[50] Westermann, *Creation*, 81.

comes from some commentators who were influenced by mediaeval feudalistic notion of work. Work is regarded as an essential part of human state not only in the creation narrative of J but also in the whole of Old Testament.

3.3.3. Formation of Animals

This section opens with the recognition that man in himself is incomplete.[51] He is in need of a suitable helper or a partner, because God recognizes the fact that 'it is not good that man should be alone' (Gen.2: 18). This shows that the concern for human welfare stands at the beginning of Yahweh's activity.[52] Therefore, God formed the animals and brought them to the man and man gave them its name. Giving of name, according to the Old Testament, is an expression of man's power over the rest of creation. 'Dominion' in P and 'naming' in J expresses the same idea.

Here the context in which the animals are created is completely different from that of P. According to P, the animals are part of God's created world, and they were regarded as a species of living beings and thus the creation of animals is given in the context of the creation of the world. But J, on the other hand, regards animals from the point of view of their meaning for human being.[53]

3.3.4. Creation of Woman

'But for man there was not found a helper fit for him' (Gen.2: 20). Some scholars believe that the narrative of forming animals, as a series of unsuccessful experiments to find a partner for man.[54] But this could not be so. Probably, this was to point out man's sense of loneliness.

---

[51] Cf. R. Davidson, *Genesis 1-11*, CBC (Cambridge: Cambridge University Press, 1973), 36.
[52] W. Zimmerli, *Old Testament Theology in Outline* (Edinburgh: T&T Clark, 1978), 32.
[53] Cf. Westermann, *Creation*, 83.
[54] H. Gunkel, K. Budde, L. Kohler et al. think that it tells of a number of attempts to create humans which misfire. See C. Westermann, *Genesis*, 225.

Here the narrator uses old traditions. The woman's construction from the rib taken out of man's side was a myth known to ancient West Asia. Often this myth conveys the idea of woman's inferiority and subordination to man. But J takes it over and shows the positive aspect of the myth. J attempts to motivate 'the close relationship between man and woman, as well as to emphasize that woman's relation to man is in principle different from that of the animals.[55]

The recognition by God in v.18, 'it is not good that man should be alone' is significant. In order to meet *this lack* God makes a new decision, "I will make him a helper fit for him". Thus, J acknowledges the fact that the people do not find the true meaning of human life in the mere fact of existence.[56] 'The people find the meaning of life only in human community; it is only this that makes true humanity'.[57]

Conclusion

It is regularly noted in theological studies of the Hebrew Bible that the cosmic perspective in J is narrow than that in P.[58] For example, according to P, the Sabbath is fixed in the order of creation, but it is not in J. Secondly, Priestly account of creation depicts the construction of the entire universe, while the J creation focuses exclusively on the earth and the birth of plant and animal life. Another notable difference in the outlook is that the Priestly creation narrative begins: "In the beginning when God created *the heavens and the earth*" (Gen 1:1), while J begins: "In the day that the Lord God made *earth and heavens*" (2:4b). The reverse order, as it happens, is appropriate to the respective points of view.[59] P portrays a cosmic crisis in which the habitable world is threatened, while J version merely reports rain. In short, P portrays Yahweh in conceptually broader terms than those of the J's portrayal. The

---

[55] Cf. B. Otzen, *Myths in the Old Testament*, 45.

[56] Cf. Westermann, *Genesis*, 226.

[57] Westermann, *Genesis*, 226.

[58] See G. von Rad, *Old Testament Theology*, vol.1, 148f; E. A. Speiser, *Genesis*, XXV ff.

[59] See Speiser , *Genesis*, 18f.

exilic influence on P might have made them to be more cosmic in their portrayal of the deity.

It is important to note that J's creation account begins with creation and ends with historical narrative. J, with its creation narrative, unites a sense of historical cause and effect with a traditional respect for the privileged moment of creation. The important thoughts of J's creation account can be summed up in the following words:

1. In J, there is no real concern for the origin of the world. His main concern is relationship of human beings with God and with the world in which he lives.

2. The creation, according to J, is an act of transforming the waste into habitable land. Therefore, water is regarded, in contrast to P, as the most important necessity for human existence.

3. Human being receives his/her existence from God and human existence is nothing but a created existence. Human being is given a place above other living beings.

4. J asserts human frailty. Since he/she was created from dust, he/she remains limited and conditioned by the fact that he/she is made of dust and returns to dust.

5. According to J, work is regarded as an essential part of human existence.

6. Creation of woman points out the fact that the people do not find the true meaning of human life in the mere fact of existence. But they find the meaning of life only in human community.

3.4. Creation in the Psalms

The significance of the creation theology in the psalms has captured the interest of many scholars only in recent years.[60] In this study,

---

[60] See R. Albertz, *Weltschöpfung und Menschenschöpfung: Untersucht bei Deutero-jesaja, Hiob und in den Psalmen,* (Calwer Theologische Monographien 3; Stuttgart: Calwer, 1974), 176. In his survey he has noted the lack of

we look at creation mainly on the basis of two genres of Psalter, namely the communal lament and the hymn. The focus on these two genres is deliberate. The study of ancient West Asian literature shows that the creation accounts function differently according to the genre in which they occur. Creation motif in an incantation, for example, functions differently from a creation motif in an astrological text. So the creation psalms also need to be treated based on its *Gattung*.

Richard Clifford, following R. Albertz, describes about two distinct creation traditions: creation of the world (*Weltschöpfung*) and creation of human beings (*Menschenschöpfung*). The former tradition is found in the genre of hymn, where it serves to emphasize Yahweh's majesty. The latter occurs in the genre of lament, where it forms the basic appeals to Yahweh's mercy.[61] One can find an incorporation of these two genres in Deutero-Isaiah. Also in many hymns and historical psalms in the Psalter, the deeds of Yahweh in history and creation are recited in close connection with each other. Psalm 136 is a good example for this, where creation is depicted as the work of Yahweh in history.

3.4.1. Communal Lament

A regular feature of communal lament is a recital of the glorious past (e.g., Ps. 44:2-9; 74:12-17; 77:12-21; 80:9-12; 83:10-13; 89:2-38). Such recitals have generally been regarded as attempts to highlight the tragedy of the present by contrasting it with the glorious past.[62] For example, in Ps 44:2-9, the psalmist describes the entrance of Israel in Canaan as a victorious army led by Yahweh. In Ps. 77:12-21, the poet describes God's redeeming arm in the cosmic battle between the Sea and Yahweh which finally made Israel's passage

---

interest in the thological meaning of creation in Psalms among scholars before that period. However, H. J. Kraus has made a substantial study on the creation in the psalms in his book: *Theology of the Psalms* (Minneapolis: Augsburg, 1988).

[61] See R. J. Clifford, *Creation Accounts*, 152.

[62] See S. Mowinckel, *The Psalms I* (New York: Abingdon, 1967), 196-97; C. Westermann, *The Praise of God in the Psalms* (Richmond: John Knox, 1965) 35-57.

through that Sea, and the appointment of Moses and Aaron as leaders. Ps 89:2-38 describes Yahweh's victory over the Sea and his arrangement of the universe, which climaxes in the installation of the Davidic dynasty. Psalm 74 tells Yahweh's slaying of Leviathan and his orderly arrangement of the world. In these psalms, the psalmists depict the past glory to bring into contrast the present misery.

However, in most cases the recitals of the past in the laments are not pointing to a past to the origin of the world, but particularly to the period of Israel's origin, the creation of Israel as Yahweh's people.[63] For example, the description of the past in Ps 89 is not concerned with the original creation act of Yahweh. Rather, as Kraus has pointed out, here the statement about creation are polemical and confessional.[64] The real concern of the lament in Ps 89 is the defeat of the Davidic king by his enemies.

The Psalm begins with the poet's intention to sing "the steadfast love" of Yahweh (89:1). It praises his "faithfulness" and the incomparability of the Creator and Sovereign Lord over all that is created. All authorities and powers are subject to him only. From the description of creation and sovereignty of the Lord, the poet moves to the promise made to David and his dynasty. The covenant with David has installed the earthly rulers of the house of David as representatives of the universal rule of Yahweh. Irrefragable is the great basic promise. אמונה is the predominant term in vv.19-37. That is, his promise is not to be cancelled by any unforeseen incident.

Therefore, the main question of the lament is if God unconditionally promised worldwide sovereignty to the Davidic line when He created the world, why does the king now suffer defeat.[65] This psalm shows a clearly soteriological understanding of creation, that is, a connection between Yahweh's activities in

---

[63] See Richard J. Clifford, *Creation Accounts*, 155.
[64] H. J. Kraus, *Theology of the Psalms* (Minneapolis: Fortress Press, 1992), 62.
[65] See R. J. Clifford, *Creation Accounts*, 155.

creation and in salvation history. And the soteriological understanding of creation was by no means a discovery of Deutero Isaiah and a distinctive feature of that prophet.[66]

Similar understanding of creation can be found in other psalms also. In Ps 74, the language strongly suggests that the context is indeed of creation. Certainly in vv.15-17, with their references to divine mastery over the paired elements of the universe such as 'spring and torrents,' 'land and waters,' 'day and night,' 'moon and sun,' and 'summer and winter' ("You made them") must be taken as explicit reference to creation. But these elements are now threatened by the destruction of the Temple, which commemorates that creation. So the concern of the creation motif in this lament is not the origin of universe. Rather, the question is, would Yahweh let his enemies to destroy the symbol of creation?

The references therefore to the creation in the laments describe not just an event in the primordial period, but the moment of Israel's origin: the creation of Israel as Yahweh's people in his land. This act can be told in either historic or mythic style.

3.4.2. Hymns

The hymn is 'the song, which extols the glory and greatness of Yahweh as it is revealed in nature and history, and particularly in Israel's history.'[67] It invites the community to praise Yahweh for his deeds on its behalf. The typical hymn structure consists of invitatory description of the divine action introduced by כִּי ("for"), for which praise is to be given, and repetition of invitatory. The divine "deeds" mentioned in several psalms are the events that brought Israel into existence, that is, the Exodus and occupation of Canaan (Ps. 66:5-7; 105; 111; 114; 135; 136; 149). As in the communal lament, the events were sometimes described employing creation terminology.

---

[66] See. G. von Rad, *Old Testament Theology*, vol. 1, 138.
[67] O. Eissfeldt, *The Old Testament: An Introduction* (New York: Harper & Row, 1965), 105-6.

CREATION MOTIF IN THE HEBREW BIBLE

Psalm 136 is a good starting point from which to examine the hymn genre. It begins with the praise of the Creator (vv 4-9). Then suddenly changes to the theme of redemption. Consequently, some commentators divide the psalm into "creation" and "redemption." For example, von Rad wrote:

> Verses 5-9 deal with the creation of the world, and at verse 10 the psalm abruptly changes its course in order to recount the mighty deeds of Yahweh in history. In this psalm, therefore, the doctrine of creation and the doctrine of redemption stand side by side, yet wholly unrelated the one to the other. Because of the rigid form of the litany, nothing of particular interest emerges from this psalm with regard to the relationship between the two doctrines, which it embraces.[68]

However, the Hebrew syntax does not support such a division. For the psalmist, the origin of the people of Israel includes the marking of the physical environment and the bringing of Israel into the land.[69]

> [1] Praise Yahweh for he is good,
> ....
> [4] who alone did great wonders
> [5] who made the heavens through understanding,
> who spread the earth upon the waters,
> who made the great lights,
> the sun to rule the day,
> the moon and the stars to rule the night,
> [10] who smote Egypt through their first-born,
> [11] who brought out Israel from their midst,
> ....
> [21] and gave their land as a heritage,
> [22] a heritage to Israel his servant.

Here, creation and redemption are not given separate doctrines as von Rad suggested. The main concern of the psalmist here is the origin of the people of Israel. The creation of heaven and earth, and that of the sun, moon, and stars, are chapters in the story of

---

[68] G. von Rad, "The Theological Problem of the Old Testament Doctrine of Creation" in *COT*, 55.
[69] R. J. Clifford, *Creation Accounts*, 159.

the rescue of the people from Egypt, their journey through the Red Sea, and their taking of the land.[70] The same logic appears in psalm 135:

> [7] He it is who makes the clouds rise at
> the end of the earth;
> he makes the lightning for the rain,
> and brings out the wind from his storehouses.
> [8] He it was who struck down the first born
> of Egypt
> both human being and animal...

Here also, as in the case of Psalm 136, the description of creation of the world continues without interruption into the description of rescue from Egypt. Both of these psalms tell the story of Israel's emergence as a people. The story of the origin of Israel is told from both the historical and mythical perspective.

In most of the Psalms of the group, the praise of the Creator passes directly into praise of the Lord of history. God's activity in creation and direction of his works is the same as his activity in the history of the nations.[71] What is created and what occurs have not yet been separated from one another. Yahweh's lordship is praised in both. Thus, historical occurrences can frequently be spoken of in mythical pictures, which generally have also a cosmic significance.[72]

In the hymns examined so far, the key event is Exodus and taking the land of Canaan. However, it did not reduce the cosmic significance of the psalms. It praises God's powerful activity in creation as well as his work in the history of his people.

In the so-called enthronement psalms, which acclaim Yahweh as universal king, explicit reason for giving praise is Yahweh's creation. Universal kingship is based on Yahweh's sole creation

---

[70] R. J. Clifford, *Creation Accounts*, 159.
[71] C. Westermann, *The Praise and Lament in the Psalms* (Atlanta: John Knox Press, 1981), 127.
[72] C. Westermann, *The Praise and Lament...*, 127.

of the world. The basis for kingship is the victory over Sea that established the world (see Ps. 93). Yahweh's universal dominion results from his defeat of Flood or Mighty Waters, which would otherwise cover the earth. Once the floods are tamed, Yahweh issues his authoritative decrees. The real interest of these psalms is divine kingship. Yahweh's victory over cosmic elements shows why that kingship is absolute and universal.

Psalms 33 deals with the theme of creation from another angle. This psalm is a hymn. This song was probably used at the great Autumn Festival at which both the tradition of creation and salvation history were recounted and relived.[73] The reference to the 'new song' (v.3) is occasionally taken to mean that it was intended for the ritual of the renewal of creation at the turn of the year.[74] It begins with a customary call to praise Yahweh (1-3), which is followed by the main section, giving the reason for the same.

Verses 6-9 describe God's creation of the biblical three-tiered universe of the heaven, the waters, and the earth. This section begins with a statement of creation by word (v.6) and concludes in verse 9 with the point reiterated. Creation by God's word is only one mode of creation, but it is the most awesome and majestic. It asserts utter dependence of the world on Yahweh's speech. Therefore, in verse 8, the psalmist states the appropriate human response to God as Creator: the human race ought to fear the Creator God, who foils the plots of the nations in order to favor Israel (vv.10-15). Before God's creative power, all human actions, except faith and hope effects nothing (vv.16-19).

Therefore, Israel need not be anxious because God's rule is not in doubt and will not be challenged. The entire unit of Psalm 33 expresses complete confidence. It is this kind of confidence about God's governance of the creation that permits freedom from

---

[73] A. A. Anderson, *Psalms 1-72*, vol.1, New Century Bible Commentary (Grand Rapid: Wm. B. Eerdmans Publishing Co., 1972), 260.

[74] A. A. Anderson, *Psalms 1-72*, 260.

anxiety in Matt. 6: 25-33.[75] Israel's hope is not general or vague. It is focused on the steadfast love of Yahweh (v.18). The whole earth is full of that loyalty, but Israel is the one who grounds its specific expectations in that reliability found in the whole creation. So, Israel should see in the creation, a ground for hope in the Creator.

The hymn shows that the divine act celebrated in the liturgy is the moment of Israel's origin. It can be described either as the exodus or as a cosmogony. However, this does not limit its concern in the origin of Israel. Its creation theology is concerned with the sociological setting of the people of Israel.

An excellent expression of Israel's creation faith is found in Psalm 104, a hymn of an individual,[76] which has many affinities with the Genesis creation story. In composing this poem, the poet has drawn upon mythopoeic motifs known outside Israel. Indeed, at points this psalm displays striking resemblance in style and content to "The Hymn to the Aton," composed by the Pharaoh Akhenaton, the reforming Egyptian king of the fourteenth century B.C.E. who introduced a kind of monotheism based on the worship of the benevolent divine power symbolized by the sun disc.[77] Moreover, the poet has made use of the myth of the Creator's subduing powers of chaos, which was known in Mesopotamia from the fourteenth century B.C.E.

This well known Psalm is very closely related to Genesis 1. According to A. Weiser 'the relation of this nature-hymn to the story of creation in the first chapter of Genesis is like that of a 'colored picture to the clear lines of a woodcut.'[78]

---

[75] W. Brueggemann, *The Message of the Psalms: A Theological Commentary* (Minneapolis: Augsburg Publishing House, 1984), 35.

[76] H-J Kraus, *Psalms 60-150*, 297.

[77] B. W. Anderson, *Out of the Depths: The Psalms Speak for Us Today* (Philadelphia: The Westminster Press, 1983), 156.

[78] Artur Weiser, *The Psalms*, OTL (Philadelphia: The Westminster Press, 1962), 666.

This Psalm begins with an invocation addressed to the poet's נפש (soul or self). All the powers of one's being in their psychosomatic unity are invited to join in praising Yahweh. The invocation to praise Yahweh leads to the main body of the psalm (vv.2-30) which provides the motive for praise. The elaboration of the ground for praise is developed in seven strophes, which follow the sequence of the Genesis creation story. But, here the poet uses the ancient creation myth more freely than the Genesis account of creation. He uses the ancient creation myth about the conflict between the Creator and the powers of chaos, symbolized by the raging sea, insurgent waters or floods, or the monsters sometimes called Rahab or Leviathan (see Ps 89:10; 74:13-14). The earth is firmly established in the midst of primeval waters, but the waters appear to be wild, hostile and threatening. The waters symbolize the powers of chaos, which the Creator has to hold back.

This psalm begins with the heavenly activities of the creator God. (vv. 1-4), then speaks about the foundations of earth (vv.5-9). Verses 10-12 deal with the life giving irrigation of earth through brooks and rain, and links it with the placement of plants and animals within their environment (16-18). Verses 19-23 deal with the co-ordination of the creatures with their time-night and day. Verses 24-26 after an exclamation of astonishment at the multitude of Yahweh's work, occupy themselves once again with the sea and its inhabitants. Verses 27-30 describe the permanent dependence of all life upon Yahweh's creative activity.

Here the Psalmist is saying more than mere compilation of creatures and environment. He focuses on the meaningfulness of such a co-ordination. That is, 'in this world and its manifold spaces everything is well arranged ecologically', and 'everything fulfils its purpose in this world.'[79] Moreover this psalm indicates the radical dependence of all creatures upon the creator.[80] The powers of chaos are pushed back or tamed by integrating them to the

---

[79] Cf. H. J. Hermission, "Observations on the Creation Theology...," 123.
[80] Cf. vv.27-30.

ordered world. The implication is that if the creator's power were suspended, chaos would return. The cosmos is not an autonomous whole, governed by its own laws, but is completely dependent on the God who transcends it.[81] Here the creation verb ברא refers to *creatio continues*,[82] i.e., creation is not just an event occurred in the beginning, but is God's continuing activity of sustaining creatures and holding everything in being.

Another notable point is that it did not stress the supremacy of human being as in Ps.8, or the adversary nature of creatures like Leviathan (v.26). Instead, the poet stresses the equality of human beings and animals, which together depend upon the Creator.

Conclusion

Both in the hymns and laments the deeds of Yahweh in history and creation is recited and praised in close connection with each other. Ps 136 is an excellent example of this approach. The Creator God in the Psalms is not just a Supreme God, he is much more the Lord of history. The dichotomy suggested by "creation myth" and "salvation history" does not hold at least for the story of Israel's origins in several communal lament and hymns. The privileged moment of Israel's origin can be narrated in the form of myth or from historic viewpoint or bending of both.

The Psalms show a clearly soteriological understanding of creation, that is, a connection between Yahweh's activities in creation and in salvation history. Thus, as von Rad suggested, the soteriological understanding of creation is by no means a discovery of DI or a distinctive feature of the theology of DI.[83] The universal understanding of creation theology also is based on the history (see Ps 105:45; 135:12).

---

[81] B. W. Anderson, "Mythopoeic and Theological Dimension of Biblical Creation Faith" in *COT*, 13.

[82] B. W. Anderson, "Mythopoeic and Theological Dimension...", 14.

[83] See G. von Rad, *Old Testament Theology* vol. 1, 138.

The Psalms do not express the idea of *"creatio ex nihilo"*. Although the term ברא (create) contains implicitly the idea of a "creation out of nothing" (Ps 89:12, 47; 104:30; 148:5), as Kraus has rightly pointed out, 'it would be perhaps more appropriate to speak of a "creatio contra nihilun," if *nihil* includes the abyss of chaos, the primeval chaotic power.[84]

3.5. Creation in Wisdom Literature

The resurgent interest in the Wisdom Literature of the Bible in the late 1960s and early 1970s, persuaded biblical scholars to make a more comprehensive study about the theological importance of creation in the Wisdom Literature. Scholars in the past were inclined to find the God of Israel chiefly in the historical book of the Bible, and the Wisdom books appeared less revelatory of Yahweh. However, now the theologians are increasingly coming to appreciate the significance of wisdom for Yahweh religion and the significance of creation in wisdom.[85] Despite increasing scholarly interest in "creation theology," L. Perdue correctly notes that a "few have attempted to describe in comprehensive fashion the salient features of the sapiential understanding of creation."[86]

Wisdom instruction in Israel fits in many respects with the general West Asian environment. According to the Egyptian mythology, *Maat* (truth or justice) is constitutive order of creation

---

[84] H. J. Kraus, *Theology of the Psalms*, 63.

[85] One scholar whose writing typifies the changed outlook was the great Heidelberg theologian Gerhard von Rad. In his 1936 essay, "The Theological Problem of the Old Testament Doctrine of Creation," he saw creation as theologically significant only when joined and subordinated to the salvation history. However, in his later treatment, he corrected his misapprehension, and in his book *Wisdom in Israel* (1972) he assigned to creation much greater significance.

[86] L. G. Perdue, "Job's Assault on Creation," *HAR* 10 (1987) 295. Perdue himself attempts such a comprehensive description in *Wisdom in Revolt: Metaphorical Theology in the Book of Job*, Bible and Literature 29 (Sheffield: Almond, 1991). His survey of recent scholarship (on pp.13-22) lists four ideas that have been used to organize recent study of creation in Wisdom Literature: (i) anthropology (W. Zimmerli and W. Brueggemann), (ii) theodicy (J. Crenshaw), (iii) cosmology or world order (H.J. Hermisson), and (iv) cosmology-anthropology (G. von Rad).

established by the primeval creator deity to direct the harmonious regularity of the cosmos for all eternity.[87] *Maat* is also the constitutive order of society. We cannot deny out rightly its echo in Israelite wisdom. Still Israelite wisdom is distinct from other West Asian wisdom. According to Fohrer, "its uniqueness lies in two respects. In the first place, it was nationalized and made the common property of all Israel, so that it lost its connection with a particular class and became relevant to human life apart from all social restrictions. In the second place, it became ever more intimately associated with Yahwism.[88]

Thus, Israelite wisdom takes God and the meaning of God for human existence very seriously. But it does so in the context of its concern to understand and deal with the human problem. In this sense, we may say that wisdom in OT is anthropocetric in contrast to the theocentric approach of the other books of the Old Testament.[89]

It was once generally believed that the older Israelite wisdom was utilitarian and eudemonistic rather than religious.[90] How was such a prudential anthropocentric view, borrowed from neighboring people, be related to the belief of Yahwism? H. J. Hermission sheds light on this question by quoting W. Zimmerli: "The wisdom of OT says quite determinedly within the horizon of creation. Its theology is creation theology".[91] But we should not overlook the fact that Zimmerli gives a negative rather than a positive reason for this statement: "the God of Israel is no where mentioned in the older wisdom literature, and this gap is then filled "occasionally" by prediction of the creator".[92]

---

[87] George Fohrer, *Introduction to the Old Testament*, 306-7.
[88] George Fohrer, Introduction to the Old Testament, 310.
[89] J. C. Rylaarsdam, "Hebrew Wisdom" in *PCB*, 387.
[90] J. A. Emerton, 'Wisdom' in *Tradition and Interpretation*, edited by G. W. Anderson (Oxford: Clarendon, 1979), 216.
[91] Walther Zimmerli, "The Place and Limit of the Wisdom in the Framework of the Old Testament Theology," in *Studies in Ancient Israelite Wisdom*, edited by James L. Crenshaw (New York: Ktav, 1976), 316.
[92] H-J-Hermission, "Observations on the Creation Theology...," 119.

From time immemorial, there has been practical knowledge, based on experience, of certain laws governing the order of universe and the activities of daily life. Human need to make himself/herself master of his/her environment and control his/her own life within it makes it necessary for him/her to seek order and regularity in the manifold phenomena and events he/she encounters so as to fit smoothly into them.[93] Through this observation of natural phenomenon human being is trying to achieve true wisdom. This is evident in Proverbs 8, the great poem of wisdom, especially vv. 22-31, which gives the picture of creation somewhat broadly. But it does not speak of creation in the first place, but creation of wisdom before the world, and speaks about the superiority of wisdom. Proverbs 3: 19-20 also does the same thing, i.e., it stresses the significance of wisdom.

Each wisdom book devotes considerable attention to creation. However, in this section, we deal with creation in Proverbs and Job, not with all reference to creation in Wisdom Literature.

3.5.1. *Creation in the Book of Proverbs*

Proverbs has two cosmogonies: Prov 3:19-20 and Prov 8:22-31. These two main creation accounts occur within longer poems 3:13-26 and 8:1-36.[94] The creation accounts establish the authority of Woman Wisdom, especially over against Woman Folly. Prov 3:19-20 affirms that the world was created in wisdom and that wisdom is within the grasp of the insistent seeker. Proverbs 8:22-31 develops the same thought by personifying Wisdom and giving her a lengthy speech; intimately associated with Yahweh before creation, she can mediate alike intimacy to the human beings who court her (8:22-31).

---

[93] George Fohrer, *Introduction to the Old Testament*, 308.

[94] The three references to God the creator (and protector) of the poor person in Prov 4:31; 17:5; 22:2, and the more general reference to God the maker in Prov 16:4; 20:12; 29:14 will not be considered here as our interest is in cosmogonies rather than in every reference to creation.

3.5.1.1. Proverbs 3:19-20

This little cosmogony occurs within the longer unit of 3:13-26.[95] Six couplets precede God's creation in vv.19-20 and six couplets follow, thus making these two verses on creation central. The first six couplets declare that the finder of the wisdom will be blessed with life, wealth, honor, favor, peace, without explaining why. The explanation is only given in vv19-20: Yahweh built the world "by wisdom," and those who live "by wisdom" will enjoy the good things of that world. The second set of six couplets (20-26) exhorts "my son" (the conventional addressee in such instructions) to seek those gifts of life and live a life without fear. Thus, the two couplets on creation in the middle describe wisdom's vital role in the continuing life. Creation is not a once-for-all event locked in the primordial past, but rather continues in action. The Creator is the divine architect who designs and constructs the cosmos in the form of an elegant and well-planned building. Thus, the little poem on creation describes wisdom's role in the creation of the cosmos, emphasizing the tradition that leads to life, well-being, riches, and honor as it is grounded in the structures of the cosmos itself.[96]

This short description on creation resembles the traditions associating wisdom with creation, which are attested elsewhere in Mesopotamia and in the Bible. In the Sumerian Eridu tradition, Enki, the god of water and wisdom creates by bringing up water from the underworld to fertilize the earth through rivers and canals. The divine wisdom is closely associated with the power to create and sustain the cosmos and guide providentially both individual lives and human history (Job 38:36-37; Ps 104:24; Jer.10:12; 51:15).

---

[95] Scholars have no unanimity with regard to the delimitation of this unit. However, scholars like W. Zimmerli, R. B. Y Scott, Richard J. Clifford et al. consider vv. 13-26 a unit.

[96] See. Leo G. Perdue, *Wisdom and Creation: The Theology of Wisdom Literature* (Nashville: Abingdon Press, 1994), 82.

CREATION MOTIF IN THE HEBREW BIBLE 93

The manner of creation in Prov 3 (v.19f) is similar to that in Gen 2: 4-6. Earth is mentioned before heaven (v.19b, contrary to the order of the usual "heaven and earth") established. Heaven is similarly established over the earth. In v.3:20a, the waters are "broke open" to provide water for the earth. The themes of wisdom and of cosmic water fertilizing the earth are found in the Eridu creation tradition. This may be to suggest the essential nature of wisdom for a fruitful life in the world. Verse 20 says: "and the clouds drop down the dew." That is, God is the one who, by means of his divine wisdom, provides the cosmos with life-sustaining moisture. (See also Job 28:25-26; 36:27-28; 38:28; Ps 78:23)

Although the Bible associates creation with the divine attribute of power as well as wisdom (Jer 10:12; 51:15; 32:17; Ps 65:6), Proverbs prefer the association with divine wisdom in order to provide a rationale for the human quest for it.[97] The very wisdom by which Yahweh created the world is available to all who seek it. Wisdom thus mediates between the all-wise Yahweh and the human seeker.[98] Prov 3:19-20 affirms that the world was created in wisdom and that wisdom is within the grasp of the insistent seeker.

The general purpose of 3:19-20 does not differ from many ancient West Asian creation theologies, which explain an element of culture such as temple or king. However, the main purpose of this passage is the way of life.[99] Whoever finds wisdom will experience every good known to human beings such as long life, wealth, honor, beauty, and shalom, Yahweh intended for Israel and the human race, according to the confident outlook of the Book of Proverbs.

---

[97] Leo G. Perdue, *Wisdom and Creation*, 181.
[98] Leo G. Perdue, *Wisdom and Creation*, 181.
[99] However, some scholars think the main point of 3:19-20 is the praise of Yahweh in creation like in Psalm 104:24. Cf. P. Doll, *Menschenschöpfung und Weltschöpfung in der alttestamentlichen Weisheit*, SBS 117 (Stuttgart: Katholisches Bibelwerk, 1985), 50-51. The hymnic nature of this poem justify this view, however the context suggest that the main thrust of the hymn is to direct the way of life.

3.5.1.2. Proverbs 8:22-31

Proverbs 8 is a well-crafted section on Woman Wisdom, consisting of five related parts: 8:1-3 (The Sages Introduction to Woman Wisdom), 8:4-11 (Wisdom's Call), 8:12-21 (Wisdom's Providential Rule), 8:22-31 (Wisdom's Place in Creation), and 8:32-36 (Wisdom's Instruction of Life).[100]

In Prov 8:22-31, creation goes a step beyond Prov 3:19-20 by personifying wisdom, a quality traditionally associated with the divine act of creation and of cosmic order, and secondly by contrasting Wisdom with Folly or the wanton woman. Personification and contrast make chapter 8 an effective speech on how the search for wisdom brings with it every blessing.[101] This hymn of creation consists of two strophes that describe the origin of cosmos and the place of wisdom in creation.

One of the important theological metaphors in this first-person hymn of self-praise presents Yahweh as the divine parent. As the father and mother of wisdom, Yahweh 'procreated' her as the firstborn of creation. The term רֵאשִׁית in 8:22 echoes בְּרֵאשִׁית in Genesis 1. In the Genesis creation account, God creates the heaven and the earth primarily by means of the divine word that orders and structures the cosmos and brings into being the various types of living creature. In Prov 8:22, the term רֵאשִׁית points to wisdom as the firstborn of creation. Wisdom's priority in time fits with the ancient view that only the old can be wise. Being wise requires knowledge of reality from the very beginning. Only Wisdom can be completely wise, since she has seen it all from the beginning.

Verses 24-26 portray the condition before creation. In principle, the pre-creation condition can be described as nothingness. But, instead of telling the abstract concept of nothingness, the author lists the non existence of specific cosmic elements. This negative way of describing reality prior to creation does not suggest a *creatio*

---

[100] Leo G. Perdue, *Wisdom and Creation*, 84.
[101] R. J. Clifford, *Creation Accounts...*, 184.

ex nihilo, but that the present order of life was shaped out of an unformed, lifeless chaos.[102]

Verses 27-30 put the divine acts in an order slightly different from that of 3:19-20. Here God made firm the heavens, drew the circle of the horizon upon the deep (v.27), took from it water suitable for the human race by arranging rain and springs (v.28), set boundaries for the sea (29), and fixed the foundations of the earth (29c). The final section of this poem then returns to Wisdom's self-description of her activity. NRSV translates: "then I was beside him, like a master worker."[103] This portrays Wisdom as a pre-existent architect who designs and builds the cosmos. This is possible, since the imagery in verses 27-29 present the metaphor of Yahweh as the architect, and this is supported by Wisdom of Solomon 7:22.

Verses 30b and 31 are particularly important to understand the meaning of this poem. These two verses together emphasize the parity of Wisdom delighting in Yahweh, and wisdom delighting in the human race. As Wisdom is Yahweh's delight "daily" in v. 30b, so the youth is to wait at Wisdom's door "daily" in v.34. The affectionate relationship between Woman Wisdom and human being on earth is portrayed in verses 32-34, reflecting the affectionate relationship between Woman Wisdom and Yahweh in heaven. One might perhaps expect Wisdom to ground her authority on the fact that she has seen Yahweh create and hence can communicate to her clients the secrets of how the world works.[104]

The search for wisdom in this poem becomes more than performing or avoiding certain actions. Rather, one is to seek Wisdom herself. To court her is to touch a quality of Yahweh the creator, and to enter into a relationship with her is to receive every divine blessing. This cosmogony explains how life may have a

---

[102] L. G. Perdue, *Wisdom and Creation*, 90.
[103] The translation of this verse is disputed. The Hebrew word אָמוֹן also mean "little child"
[104] R. J. Clifford, *Creation Accounts...*, 184.

more profound meaning; it may be not only life in the sense of enjoyment of health, good name and family happiness, but also "life with" association with Yahweh.[105]

3.5.2. Creation in Job

Even a casual reader cannot miss the importance of creation in the Book of Job. The book contains many hymns to God the Creator (e.g., 9:4-13; 10:8-13; 12:13-25; 25:1-6; 26:5-14; 36:24-37:24). In addition to these, two lengthy speeches about creation is given in the so-called Yahweh speeches in 38:1-40:5 and 40:6-42:6. In a sense, creation is the main subject of the book.[106] However, the present study mainly focuses on the two Yahweh speeches which provide the most comprehensive witness to the creator and his creation in the Old Testament.

The tone of the creation accounts in this book differs according to who is speaking. For Job, creation of the universe is so closely linked to his own creation that God's randomness and injustice toward him is simply one more instance of God's randomness and injustice toward the world. He sees God's creation as a violent and careless manipulation of things and living beings (9:5-13; 10:8-13; 12:13-25). The pious Bildad sees only order and majesty in God's work (25:1-6; 26:5-24), and Elihu sees in the working of nature a basis for unquestioning awe (36:24- 37:24).

God's view of creation is given in the so-called Yahweh speech, which diverges from the perspective of all the human speakers, especially Job and his friends. However, the logic of the two divine speeches in chapters 38-41 has puzzled many scholars and

---

[105] Raymond C. Van Leeuwen, "Proverbs" in *NIB,* vol. 5 (Nashville: Abingdon Press, 1997), 10.

[106] Perdue argues that two patterns of creation have shaped the book: the cosmological pattern (found in Enuma Elish and the Ugaritic Baal cycle) with its sequence of battle, victory, kingship, judgment, and re-creation; and the anthropological pattern (found in Atrahasis) with its sequence of judgment (slavery), slavery and toil, revolt, fall, and judgment culminating in redemption. *Wisdom in Revolt: Creation Theology in the Book of Job,* JSOT Sup 112 (Sheffield: JSOT 1991).

provoked many rearrangements; none has won general assent. This study follows Norman Habel's analysis of them, which accepts the Hebrew text.[107] The divine speeches are not just and undifferentiated blast at Job; they are also addressing his desire that God appears in person to respond to the charge of governing the world arbitrarily and unjustly.

3.5.2.1. *The First Speech of Yahweh: 38:1-40:2*

The First speech opens with questions of challenge, and imperative in tone. The form of the speeches is that of a disputation combined with a hymnic description of creation.

This speech was given as an answer to Job's charges about God's arbitrary and capricious governance and his failure to care for his creatures, especially Job. God responds in the same legal idiom as that of Job's attack. The divine questions are legal in nature; "Who is this that darkens counsel...?", "Where were you when I...?", "Who placed...?" Where is...?" They equivalently ask who created the world, and resemble the questions in the great trial scenes of Deutero-Isaiah such as "Who has measured the waters in the hollow of his hand? (40:12); "Who has directed the spirit of Yahweh?" (40:13); "Who has stirred up one from the east?" (41:2); "Who declared it from the beginning that we might know?" (44:7). In Deutero-Isaiah the trial scenes summon the nations and their gods to a great trial to determine the real God. No doubt, all this rhetorical questions are pointed towards Yahweh, agreeing with the fact that Yahweh alone is God. In the book of Job also, these questions have the same intent: to remind Job that Yahweh is alone the sole Creator and the governing power.

The structure of the universe in the Yahweh speech is the same as it is in the traditional idea of creation. God's artisan-like building of the universe is divided into four spheres: the earth, sea, heavens, and the underworld. The use of building metaphor to describe

---

[107] Norman C. Habel, *The Book of Job: A Commentary*, OTL (Philadelphia: The Westminster Press, 1985), 517-74.

the creation of earth underscores its orderly planned design.[108] What is untraditional is the challenge these elements pose to Job.[109]

A general outline illustrates the point more clearly than any single verse. The first divine speech can be schematized as follows:

Where were you? or do you know about

A. the inanimate physical world (38:3-38)
   - the construction of the earth 38:4-7
   - the hemming in of the sea 38:8-11
   - dawn's role in ridding the earth of sinners 38:12-15
   - God's dominion over the underworld of death 38:16-18
   - the placement of light and darkness 38:19-21
   - the storehouse of earth's weather 38:22-30
   - the constellations controlling earth's destiny 38:31-33
   - the thunderstorms fertilizing the earth 38:34-38

B. the animal and the bird kingdoms (38:39-39:30)
   - the feeding of the lion 38:39-40
   - the feeding of the raven 38:41
   - the ibex and the hind 39:1-4
   - the wild ass 39:5-8
   - the ostrich 39:13-18
   - the horse 39:19-25
   - the hawk and the eagle 39:26-30[110]

---

[108] Norman C. Habel, *The Book of Job*, 337.
[109] R. J. Clifford, *Creation Accounts...*, 193.
[110] This outline is quoted from R. J. Clifford, *Creation Accounts....*, 193.

By answering Job's charges, Yahweh portrays the design of the universe. In 9:24, Job had accused that God does not distinguish between the wicked and the righteous, that the earth has been handed over to the wicked. God responds that dawn exposes the deeds done by the wicked during the night, but that he does not necessarily punish them (38:12-15). Job's assumption that human beings are the centre of the world is countered by Yahweh's question about the rain that falls where human beings do not live (38:26-27). Job had accused God of hunting like a lion (10:16). But for Yahweh even the lion is an example of his providence (38:39-40). Even the ostrich, proverbial for its stupidity, is so designed by Yahweh (39:13-18). All these remind that God's design does not operate exclusively for human beings or for a rational purpose. God's creation includes the useful, the strange, playful, and even the harmful. God creates for his inscrutable purpose; even Behemoth and Leviathan are admirable in the divine sight. God does not say that he always controls evil for the sake of human beings.

3.5.2.2. The second speech of Yahweh: 40:6-41:26

In this second speech, Yahweh develops the earlier theme that humans are not the centre of creation. Yahweh begins his disputation by defending his own justice:

> Will you annul my justice (מִשְׁפָּטִי)?
> Will you prove me wrong so that you may be in the right?

Job's innocence does not negate divine justice. Job's attack of divine rule is more than simply denying God's justice. He is attempting "to annul" (פרר) the righteous rule of God. The same verb is used to describe the "splitting" of the chaos monster in the battle preceding creation (Ps 74:13). Yahweh's מִשְׁפָּט is not confined to administering a rigid law of reward and retribution on earth. It is cosmic and it embraces the dimension of universal control.[111]

The descriptions of the two great beasts, Behemoth and Leviathan, in this speech are significant. What is the purpose of

---

[111] See, Norman Habel, *The Book of Job*, 562.

these two beasts in the book? These two beasts exemplify fearsome power that is beyond human knowledge or control,[112] yet they are allowed a place in God's universe. From the perspective of a human being, they fulfill no function. Yet they are part of God's creation and under divine control. For reason not stated, God allows them to exist despite their evil potential.

Thus, creation in Job is an act that an absolutely transcendent God does carry out in wisdom and justice. It cannot be searched out and summed up in traditional wisdom. The divine purpose behind the creation is inscrutable. Human beings cannot assume that they are the centre of creation. The anthropocentric perspective of the creation account of Genesis, the Psalm and Deutero-Isaiah is absent in Job.[113]

3.6. Conclusion

In common with all ancient West Asian literature, the biblical traditions show a profound interest in creation. Creation was a moment of enormous significance, revealing much about the world and God. In the light of ancient West Asian interest in creation, biblical scholars can no longer claim that creation came late to biblical consciousness, i.e., after Israel has discovered its God in history.

Biblical cosmgonies employ literary genres current in Mesopotamia and Canaan. Because cosmogonies occur in a great variety of works (Genesis, Psalms, Proverb, and Job), and in a great variety of genres (creation-flood epics, communal laments, hymns, prophetic disputations and announcement of restoration, wisdom instruction and speeches), it is difficult to formulate a single biblical perspective on creation. Biblical authors had diverse purpose in mind when they composed their creation accounts; their rhetorical strategies and aims must be determined before one can talk about their views on creation.

---

[112] R. J. Clifford, *Creation Accounts...*, 196.
[113] R. J. Clifford, *Creation Accounts...*, 197.

The Priestly creation story was given as a preface to the Yahwistic story for the exiles. It was intended to be an introduction to the redemptive history for the exiles, and to link its significance to the exilic community's practical living in the hostile world. J, with its creation narrative, unites a sense of historical cause and effect with a traditional respect for the privileged moment of creation.

Creation in Psalms is strongly determined by genre. Hymns and Communal lament are the main genres in which the creation motif occurs frequently. In both, the community holds up to God in prayer the originating moment of Israel, employing the historic language of Exodus-conquest and the mythical language of Yahweh's victory over the Sea. In the communal lament, the community appeals to God's honor: Will you let an enemy power destroy the people whom you have created and redeemed? In the hymn, the people praise Yahweh for generous actions, principally the great deed of creating Israel.

Wisdom Literature contains several creation motifs. God in Wisdom Literature is a creator God. Creation is the basis of order and regularity, and every thing in this creation is well arranged ecologically and everything has been created in this world with a meaningful purpose. According to Proverbs, the world was created in wisdom so that anyone seeking wisdom will grasp the secrets of life and prosperity in the world. Wisdom's emphasis on creation and providence is a valued resource for the believing community, which seeks to describe its faith in coherent and meaningful ways.

In the Book of Job, creation as understood by Job and his friends were negated by God's magnificent description of creation. Human being is not the center of the universe as Job thought. In addition, God did not divest the chaos monsters of all power at creation but let them roam free on a leash. Behemoth and Leviathan are as much a part of the world as the ordinary animals. According to the creation theology of Job, the world is not anthropocentric but theocentric, its secret lies hidden with God.

The theology of creation is an integral part of the faith of Israel. In sum, the God, whom Israel worships and to whom she bears witness, is the creator who originated the cosmos, who maintains this order in the face of threats from chaos, and who continues his creative activity in order to sustain the creation and holding everything intact.

CHAPTER FOUR

The Period of Exile:
A Socio-Historical Survey

In order to understand the theology of creation in DI and its significance, it is important to understand at first the socio-historical context in which DI and his community subsists. Therefore, before turning to the selected creation texts, we need to consider the social constituents of the exile itself.

4.1. Introduction

Of all the eras in Israel's history, the exilic period represents the most significant period. Its significance for the subsequent history can hardly be overstated. As Rainer Albertz has pointed out, 'here the religion of Israel underwent its most severe crisis, but here too was laid the foundation for its most sweeping renewal.'[1] Here began the dispersal of Israel among the nations and thus also its often painful Diaspora existence, lasting to the present.[2]

---

[1] See Rainer Albertz, *A History of Israelite Religion in the Old Testament Period; vol 2:From the Exile to the Maccabees* OTL (Louisville: Westminster John Knox Press, 1994), 369ff.

[2] It is difficult to delimit the exilic period historically. For the northern kingdom of Israel, the exilic period began in 732 and 722 B.C.E. with its conquest by the Assyrians. But the people deported from the northern kingdom have left almost no trace in subsequent tradition. Therefore, their history is lost. The Southern kingdom of Judah suffered substantial deportations by the Assyrians in 701 but remained in existence until the

Here, too, the religion of Israel opened itself for the first time to the nations, a development that made possible the subsequent appearance of Christianity. Nevertheless, recently significant doubts have been expressed about the whole question of the exile, whether we are dealing with a historical event or merely with a literary and theological construct.[3]

The first section of this study will attempt to reconstruct the history of the exilic period using the sporadic information given in the biblical narratives as well as the information collected form the cuneiform records and archaeological discoveries. Then it will undertake a comprehensive sociological analysis of the Babylonian exile. This will help us to examine the socio-political settings of the exile in which the theology of creation emerged.

---

punitive expeditions of the Neo-Babylonians in 597 and 587. Therefore it is usual to think that the exilic period begin with the destruction of Jerusalem and the final elimination of Judah as a state in 587 B.C.E, even though there was already a golah (group of exiles) in Babylonia in 597.

[3] The original 'doubter' was C. C. Torrey. In 1910, Torrey made a famous comment on exile, "which was in reality a small and relatively insignificant affair, has been made partly through mistake and partly by the compulsion of a theory, to play very important part in the Old Testaemnt." See his "The Exile and Restoration," in *Ezra Studies* (1910; reprint New York: Ktav, 1970), 285; See Robert Carroll, "Exile! What Exile? Deportation and Discoursed of Diaspora," in *Leading Captivity Captive: The Exile as History and Ideology*, edited by Lester L. Grabbe, JSOT Sup. Series 278, (Sheffield: Sheffield Academic Press, 1998). In this essay, Robert Carroll argues that exile and exodus are two aspects of a myth, which shapes much of the biblical narrative. He minimizes the historical event reflected in these concepts. See also P. R. Davies, *In Search of Ancient Israel* (Sheffield Academic Press, 1992); T. L. Thompson, *The Origin Tradition of Ancient Israel 1: The Literary Formation of Genesis and Exodus 1-23* (Sheffield: Academic Press, 1987); J. V. Seters, *In Search of History: History and Historiography in the Ancient World and the Origins of Biblical History* (New Haven: Yale University Press, 1983). Keith W. Whitelam, *The Invention of Ancient Israel: The Silencing of Palestinian History* (London and New York: Routledge, 1996). These scholars suggest that Israelite history begins after the rise of the Persian Empire, and any events previous to this, are questionable history at best.

Ackroyd's survey provides a solid starting point for any historical review of the 'Exile and Restoration.'[4] Moreover, the standard histories of Israel by Herrmann, John Bright, Soggin and others,[5] give us intelligible information about the Exile and its history. Therefore, the purpose of this chapter is not merely to reconsider details of history, instead, to focus politically and socially, in order to understand more precisely the social settings of the exile and its influence in the formation of a theology of creation.

4.2. Sources

It is a striking fact that the Bible does not contain a continuous account of the exilic period. Only the margins are recorded such as how the exile came about (2 Kings 24-25; Jeremiah 39; 2 Chronicles 36), and how it ended (Ezra 1 ff) together with a few isolated events such as the fall of Gedaliah and its consequences (Jeremiah 40:1- 43:7; 2 Kings 25:22-26) at the very beginning of exilic period and the pardon of Jehoiachin by Evil-Merodach in 562, the thirty-seventh year of his exile in 597 B.C.E. The book of Daniel adds a couple of dramatic episodes that Daniel and his friends are said to have experienced as Jews at the court of Nebuchadnezzar and his "son" Belshazzar (Dan.1-5). But these, too, do not form a continuous historical narrative; they do not write the history of the Babylonian *golah*. Moreover, its nature as folklore rather than a historical record and the scholarly suggestion of a much later date[6] of the book of Daniel has

---

[4] P. R. Ackroyd, *Exile and Restoration* (London: SCM, 1968). This work is still considered by many to be a major analysis of the exile.

[5] S. Herrmann, *A History of Israel in the Old Testament Times*, (Philadelphia: Fortress Press, 1975); J. Bright, *A History of Israel*, 3rd ed. (Philadelphia: Westminster Press, 1981); M. Noth, *A History of Israel*, 2nd ed. (New York: Harper & Row, 1960); J. H. Hayes and J. M. Miller, eds., *Israelite and Judean History* (London: SCM, 1977); Ralph W Klein. *Israel in Exile* (Philadelphia: Fortress Press, 1979); T. M Raitt. *A Theology of Exile: Judgment/ Deliverance in Jeremiah and Ezekiel* (Philadelphia: Fortress Press, 1977); etc.

[6] Though some of the traditions about Daniel seem older, its placing in the "Writing" section of canon, its historical problems, and the use of late Hebrew and Aramaic words by the writer, point to a date of composition

constrained us from using it as a reliable source for the construction of the exilic history.

Thus, the exilic period represents a huge lacuna in the historical narrative of the Hebrew Bible. Apart from a few brief references in Ezekiel to the Jews taken to Babylonia in 597 B.C.E., and in Jeremiah to the events in Judah immediately following the fall of Jerusalem, the exile is blank. Therefore, the historical reconstruction of this era faces almost insurmountable difficulties. Like the pre-monarchic period and the later Persian period (fourth century), the exilic period also remains historically obscure.

Our main source for the history of exilic period is the biblical history provided in II Kings, II Chronicles, Isaiah, Jeremiah, Lamentation, and Ezra-Nehemiah along with the relevant material from P stratum of the Pentateuch, the prophet Ezekiel and some Psalms that may be considered exilic or post-exilic.[7] This biblical data on exile will be assessed on the basis of the available cuneiform records of the Neo-Babylonian and Persian Empires.

There are however, a few extra-biblical written sources for the history of the Neo-Babylonian period. The Babylonian Chronicle confirms in essence the events surrounding the first deportation in 597. There is also a Babylonian record of royal rations of oil for "Jehoiachin, the king of Judah," his five sons, and thirteen other Judeans. These tablets cast interesting spotlight on a small fragment of the Babylonian *golah* that lived at the court of Nebuchadnezzar.[8]

However, we cannot use it uncritically. Materials, which have been edited and reworked over centuries, cannot be assumed to

---

in the second century B.C. E. See Victor H. Mathews and James C. Moyer, *The Old Testament: Text and Context* (Peabody, Massachusetts: Hendrickson Publishers, 1997, 256f.)

[7] A number of scholars (Niels Peter Lemche, Thomas L. Thompson, Robert Coote, Keith W. Whitelam, Philip Davies, and Robert Carroll et al.) have recently written on the problem of using the Old Testament for the reconstruction of the history and society of ancient Israel, especially the exilic history because it is very scanty in the Old Testament.

[8] *AENT,* 308.

THE PERIOD OF EXILE   107

have usable historical data without some sort of control. Of course, late compositions may have early material and may have preserved useful historical data. However, as they presently stand, these writings have a definite theological and moralistic function. They primarily stand to teach religious truth. Their success in doing so is one of the reasons they have been taken into the canon of both Judaism and Christianity.

4.3. The Assyrian Rise to Power

As Noth has suggested, the exile is correctly seen as the event in a series, which had begun already in the middle of the eight century B.C.E.[9] Therefore, the crisis faced by Judah really began with the threat of the Neo-Assyrians even before the Neo-Babylonian Empire. This threat has become sociologically, as well as historically important. Otzen has pointed out that the rise of Davidic-Solomonic Empire was largely possible because of the vacuum left by a declining hegemony and the emergent empire of the Assyrians in the North and East.[10] However, this situation changed entirely when Tiglath-Pileser III (745-727) had become king of Assyria. Tiglath-Pileser III is regarded as one of the greatest conquerors among the kings of Assyria. He had great successes in Syria and Canaan. He was also able to conquer Babylon.[11] He made Assyria a great world power.

In addition, three other factors played an important role in making Assyria a world power: the efficient organization of the Assyrian government and army, the fearful cruelties and 'punishments,' which the Assyrians inflicted on the peoples they conquered, and their deportation.[12] The main characteristic of

---

[9] See Martin Noth, *The History of Israel*, 2nd ed. (New York: Harper & Row, 1960), 289.

[10] B. Otzen, "Israel under the Assyrians," in *Mesopotamia* no. 7, edited by M. T. Larsen (Copenhagen: Akademisk Forlag, 1979), 251ff, cited by Daniel L. Smith *The Religion of the Landless* (Bloomington: Meyer Stone, 1989), 17.

[11] See J. Bright, *A History of Israel*, 3rd ed. (Philadelphia: Westminster Press, 1981), 270.

[12] H. Jagersma, *A History of Israel in the Old Testament Period* (Philadelphia: Fortress Press, 1983), 156.

their mode of government was strict control and efficient communications.¹³ The army was organized in such a way that troops were available at a very short notice and its equipment and weapons were modern for its time.¹⁴ The main aim of the cruelty and punishment that it practiced was to produce fear and terror. Their deportation policy was selective to the upper class of the conquered country and practiced in order to break the power and neutralize all possible opposition in the defeated country.¹⁵

The Assyrian royal inscriptions give us considerable information about the conquests of Tiglath-Pileser III. One of the first countries he defeated was the kingdom of Urartu, to the north of Assyria,¹⁶ inhabited by Hurrian population. His conquest also extended westwards, to include Syria and Canaan.¹⁷ The Assyrian rise to power was of decisive importance for further developments in Israel and Judah.

The so-called "Syro-Ephraimite War" brought about the direct interference of Assyrian power in Israel. Pekah, king of Israel, joined Edom and Demascus in an anti-Assyrian coalition, advanced against Judah. (2 Kings 16: 5-9). Ahaz, king of Judah, averted the threat by sending tribute to Tiglath-Pileser and asking him for help (2 Kings 16:7-9), and he became a voluntary vassal of Assyria. In all this, Ahaz acted against the pressing advice of the prophet Isaiah (Isa 7: 3-9). The Deuteronomic historian also criticizes this: "He [Ahaz] did not do what was right in the sight of the Lord his God..." (2 Kings 16:2).

Whether Tiglath-Pileser felt this as a reason to intervene or whether he already intended to do so is an open question. In any case, Tiglath-Pileser acted quickly; in 733/32 he captured

---

¹³ H. Jagersma, *A History of Israel...*, 156.
¹⁴ See H. W. F. Saggs, 'Assyrian Warfare in the Sargonic Period', *Iraq* 25 (1963), 145-46.
¹⁵ See Rainer Albertz, *Israel in Exile: The History and Literature of the Sixth Century B. C. E.* (Atlanta: SBL, 2003), 82ff.
¹⁶ J. Bright, *A History of Israel*, 270.
¹⁷ See *AENT*, 283.

Damascus and Samaria (the chronological details are disputed). The inhabitants of Israel were deported to Assyria and Tiglath-Pileser appointed Hoshea king over Israel in place of Pekah (see 2 Kings 15: 29-30). However, the biblical narrative does not tell whether Hoshea was appointed king by Tiglath-Pileser.

4.4. The End of Northern Kingdom

After the events of 733/32, Israel and Judah were vassals of the Assyrians. Moreover, Israel had lost substantial parts of its kingdom. Its history was not to continue much longer. 2 Kings 17:1-6 reports that Hoshea, the last king of Israel, again took part in anti-Assyrian coalition, and entered into negotiation with Egypt. He defaulted on his tribute payments. According to Daniel L. Smith, it was the last political decision of an independent northern king.[18] Shalmaneser V, the Assyrian king, thereupon undertook a campaign in his reign in 722. He captured Samaria, deported part of its population, and now made the whole of Israel into an Assyrian province. This brought the history of the northern kingdom to an end. However, there is some dispute as to whether it was Shalmaneser who conquered Samaria in 722, or whether Sargon II, when he claimed to deport 27,290 people in his conquest of this territory (*ANET*, 284). 2 Kings 17 reports the bringing of many peoples from various parts of the Assyrian empire in exchange for the deported Israelites. We have no idea what happened to these northern Israelites who were deported. The Bible contains no record of these Assyrian exiles.[19]

Even the legends surrounding these so-called "Lost Tribes of Israel" show that the Bible does not have any idea about what happened to the northern tribes after their deportation. Furthermore, attention quickly turns in the deuteronomic historical works to the Assyrian harassment of Judah.

---

[18] Daniel L. Smith, *The Religion of the Landless*..., 19.
[19] The reference in 2 Kings 17:6 is inadequate to make any valid conclusion. The late book of Tobit, though contains a story of Tobit who is deported by Assyrians, it has no historical value in this regard.

4.5. Judah's Movement to the Exile

We know nothing of the effect of the decline of the northern kingdom on Judah. Perhaps the Assyrians regarded Judah as a loyal vassal since King Ahaz had paid tribute. 2 Kings 16: 10-18 reports that after his meeting with Tiglath-Pileser, Ahaz had set up in the temple of Jerusalem an altar for which 'the altar in Damascus' had served as a model. It is often supposed here that the Assyrian state cult was installed in the temple of Jerusalem, and this is seen as a political gesture on the part of Ahaz.[20] But, Mckay notes that Uriah the priest made no protest about this new altar and thus assumes that the altar was simply a new design that pleased Ahaz and was not a form of worship imposed by Ahaz at the command of Tiglath-Pileser.[21] However, the literary context of deuteronomic historian's *condemnation* of Ahaz leads one to suspect that the removal of the old altar and the replacement with the new one certainly had something to do with the contact of Ahaz with Tiglath-Pilesr, and somehow it reflected his new political status in relation to the Assyrians.[22]

When Hezekiah, son of Ahaz, became king in 715 B.C.E., he planned to break the yoke of Assyrian control, but he was prepared to wait for the right moment. He reformed the religion (2 Kings 18: 4). For his religious reforms, he was highly commended in the book of Kings (2 Kings 18:3-7).

When Sargon II died, a number of nations in various parts of Assyrian empire revolted against Assyria. Hezekiah too made plans to shake off the Assyrian yoke and thought it was the right time for Judah to join the revolution. Thinking so, he refused to pay tribute to Assyria and formed an alliance with Babylon (2 Kings 20:12-13). The prophet Isaiah, however, rebuked Hezekiah for relying on foreign aid. He told him that Egyptian help was

---

[20] R. Rendtorff, *The Old Testament: An Introduction* (Philadelphia: Fortress Press, 1986), 49.

[21] John Mckay, *Religion in Judah under the Assyrians,* Studies in Biblical Theology No. 26 (London: SCM, 1973), 6-12.

[22] See Daniel L. Smith, *The Religion of the Landless...,* 19.

'worthless and empty' (Isa 30:1-7; 31:1-3), and Babylonia would one day rule over Judah (Isa 39:5-7).

In 701 Sargon's son Sennacherib, launched an attack on the rebelling nations, both within Palestine and across Jordan.[23] Judah suffered severely in this attack. We can read the record of these events in 2 Kings 18: 13-16. According to this passage, Hezekiah stripped the temple treasures to provide the tribute, which Sennacherib demanded. 2 Kings 18:17- 19:37 probably describe another revolt led by Hezekiah which might have been put down by Sennacherib.

Hezekiah probably spent the last 15 years of his life rebuilding his devastated country. Some ten years before his death, he made his son Manasseh co-regent.

The next two kings of Assyria, Esarhaddon and Ashurbanipal, set about the task of conquering Egypt. Esarhaddon captured Memphis in 671 B.C.E. and gained control of the delta region of Egypt. Ashurbanipal went further and captured and destroyed Thebes in 663 B.C.E. Assyria's power was then at its peak, but only for a short period.

For most of this time, Manasseh was king in Judah (687-642 B.C.E). The Bible records of Manasseh are exclusively concerned with cultic matters and are completely negative (2 Kings 21:1-18). He is depicted as a great 'heretic king'. Here all that is said about him serves in every detail as a negative foil for the subsequent reform by Josiah.[24] It is hardy possible to make a historical evaluation of this information. The only historical statement we

---

[23] Sennacherib had the story of his attack on Judah inscribed on a stone prism, which is now in British museum. Part of the inscription says: "And Hezekiah of Judah, who had not bowed beneath my yoke, forty of his cities and numberless small towns in their neighborhood I besieged and took; 200,150 people young and old, male and female, horses, beasts of burden, sheep, camels, cattle and flocks without number I took from them and accounted as spoil." See *ANET*, 288; B. Oded, "Judah and the Exile" in *Israelite and Judean History*, edited by John H. Hayes and J. Maxwell Miller (London: SCM, 1977), 449.

[24] R. Rendtorff, *The Old Testament: An Introduction*, 50.

are left with is that Manasseh had an unusually long reign (fifty-five years!)[25]

Manasseh's son Amon, followed him as king (2 Kings 21:19-26) and carried on the same policies as his father, and became the victim of a palace intrigue (v.23). Thus at the age of eight Josiah, Amon's son, became the king. With him began the last phase of the history of the kingdom of Judah. At the center of the detailed report about Josiah (2Kings 22:1-23:30) stands the great cultic reform. According to the story, it was sparked of by the discovery of 'the book of the Torah' (2 Kings 22:8) in the renovation work in the temple. The reference here is without doubt to Deuteronomy.[26]

Josiah's reform stood in a wider political context. It took place at a time when the Assyrian empire was collapsing. Josiah eventually exploited this chance to consolidate and extend his rule. According to McKay, Josiah's reform of the cult was primarily concerned to remove elements of the Assyrian cult from Yahweh worship.[27]

Despite the deuteronomic historian's tributes to the reforms of Hezekiah and Josiah, the text continues to document a steady decline. The description of Josiah's reforms occupies a considerable detail, but 2 Kings 23: 26ff. concludes by indicating that the reforms were not enough to overcome the evil of Manasseh.

---

[25] 2 Chro. 33:11ff. reports the deportation of Manasseh to Babylon; this moves him to repent, so that after his return he instigates a restoration of the legitimate Yahweh cult. This narrative is probably to be understood as a midrashic explanation of the fact that so sinful a king could have such a long and untroubled reign (cf. R. Rendtroff, *The Old Testament: An Introduction*, 51). It is improbable that there is a historical background to it (cf. B. Oded, "Judah and the Exile," 456).

[26] There is considerable doubt as to whether this account is historical. In its present form, the report is a thoroughly deuteronomic stamp, so it is hardly possible to make a historical reconstruction of the details of the cultic reform and its context. See Rendtorff, *The Old Testament: An Introduction*, 51.

[27] See, John McKay, *Religion in Judah* ..., 28ff.

The description of Josiah's unsuccessful campaign at Megiddo, has given rise to speculation over the exact circumstances of his death. Perhaps he wanted to prevent the Assyrian power being strengthened with the help of the Egyptians, or he feared an Egyptian domination in the wake of that of Assyria. The Bible is silent about his purpose. However, Josiah's action becomes more significant in the context of the empire. Seeing the threat of a growing Babylonian- Median alliance, Egypt undoubtedly saw an opportunity to secure the coveted Palestinian trade routes and land by shoring up the failing strength of the Assyrians. According to Malamat, this was intended to preserve a small Assyrian power as a buffer against the advancing Median- Babylonian alliance.[28] Malamat goes even further in suggesting that Josiah's action was a sign that there was a broad strategic plan or military alliance between Judah and Babylon.[29]

This action by Josiah, when combined with earlier Jewish contact between Merodach- Baladan II and Hezekiah, may be a significant factor in the exilic social alignments and conflicts evident in the book of Jeremiah and in the behavior of the prophet himself.[30]

The defeat of King Josiah by Pharaoh Necho at Megiddo in 609 B.C.E. was a pivotal moment in the latter years of the kingdom of Judah: national prosperity and high hopes for a renewed Judean Empire dissolved into incessant turmoil, with Judah caught in a political bipolar system between Egypt and Babylon until it finally fell in 586 B.C.E.[31] Though Jehoahaz, son of Josiah, was appointed by the 'people of the land,' soon Pharaoh Necho removed him and appointed his brother Eliakim in his place, renaming him

---

[28] A. Malamat, "The Last Wars of the Kingdom of Judah," *JNES*, 9 (1950), 218.
[29] A. Malamat, "The Last Wars...," 223.
[30] Daniel L. Smith, *The Religion of the Landless...*, 20.
[31] A. Malamat, "The Last Years of the Kingdom of Judah," in *Archaeology and Biblical Interpretation: Essays in Memory of D. Glenn Rose*, edited by Leo G. Perdue, Lawrence E. Toombs and Gary L. Johnson (Atlanta: John Knox Press, 1987), 287.

Jehoiakim, as a demonstration of Egyptian superiority. Moreover, Necho imposed a heavy tribute on the country (2 Kings 23: 31-35).

4.6. The Rise of the Neo-Babylonian Empire

The rise of the Neo-Babylonian Empire toward the end of the seventh century B.C.E. was anything but a foregone conclusion. The later years of Ashurbanipal are marked by a steady decline of Assyrian Empire, and the power relationship shortly changed in favor of the Babylonians. Eventually, Assyria lost her grip on Judah. In 605, the Egyptians once again encountered the Chaldean army and, in this battle, the crown prince Nebuchadnezzar defeated the Egyptians at Carchemish. The Egyptians therefore had to give up their claims over the area of Syria and Palestine. Judah was thrown into consternation by this turn of events. In turns, Jehoiakim transferred his allegiance to Nebuchadnezzar and became a vassal of the Babylonians (2 Kings 24:1).

4.7. The End of Judah

Jehoiakim died in 598. His son Jehoiachin, eighteen years old (2 Kings. 24:8), had reigned only three months when Nebuchadnezzar undertook another campaign against Jerusalem in 597 (2 Kings. 24:10). Jehoiachin voluntarily surrendered to Nebuchadnezzar, and the Chaldeans took their first group of exiles. While this initial group was small,[32] it is important to note that it was the king and the aristocracy who were removed, in an attempt to remove leadership and the potential for revolt.[33]

---

[32] The numbers pose a problem. According to 2 Kings 24:14, the number of exiles taken at this time was 10,000; then in v. 16 the number 7000 and 1000 craftsmen were added to it; by contrast Jer 52:28 gives the number 3023. These are possibly two groups of deportees, since Jer 52:28 speaks of the seventh year of Nebuchadnezzar, while 2 Kings 24:12 speaks of the eighth year. Thus the figure could be understood as a round number for the 3000 deportees of the first group, directly after the capture of the city and the second group of about 7000, which followed some time later (cf. Malamat, "The Last Years...," 133 f.)

[33] Daniel L. Smith, *The Religion of the Landless...*, 21.

Then, Nebuchadnezzar placed Jehoiachin's uncle Mattaniah as a puppet ruler of the Babylonians and changed his name to Zedekiah (2 Kings 24: 17). At this time, there emerged a series of political, ideological, and theological splits among the Jewish communities with regard to the Babylonian rule. This can be seen from Jeremiah's warning against a defection from the Babylonians (Jer 27), and from his controversy with the prophet Hananiah (Jer 28). In a letter to those who had been deported to Babylon, Jeremiah also warned them to prepare for a long time in exile (Jer 29).

However, Zedekiah was not wise enough to pay attention to Jeremiah's warning. Probably because of his fear of pro-Egyptian ministers,[34] he sought to rebel against Babylon, which led Nebuchadnezzar to besiege Jerusalem. This time, Jerusalem suffered severe destruction. Zedekiah attempted to escape from the city and fled, probably hoping to find shelter with Baalis, the king of Ammon,[35] but was captured and suffered brutal punishment (2 Kings 25:7). We hear nothing further of his fate.

Many of the inhabitants of Jerusalem including the military, court, and temple officials were captured and brought before Nebuchadnezzar and executed (25:18-21). The temple was destroyed and many of the religious equipment of worship were carried away into exile with the people. This exile, as recounted in 2 Kings 25:11ff. and Jer. 52:15ff., was more general than the surrender of Jehoiachin. Only some of the "poorest of the land" were left to be "vinedressers" and "plowmen" according to the text.

Nebuchadnezzar then appointed Gedaliah as the governor, who chose Mizpah as his administrative center (2Kings 25:22; 2 Chro 36:20). The ruined site of Tell en-Nasbeh, situated about 12 k.m. north of Jerusalem, is generally identified with the biblical Mizpah.[36] However, after only a short time he was assassinated

---

[34] See, B. Oded, "Judah and the Exile," 472.
[35] B. Oded, "Judah and the Exile," 475.
[36] See Hershel Shanks, ed., *Ancient Israel* (Washington, D.C.: SPCK, 1988), 148.

by 'a captain of force' named Ishmael (2 Kings 25:25). The report ends with the information that thereupon 'all the people' and the captains of the forces fled to Egypt for fear of the Babylonians (v. 26). After this, however, the Bible is relatively silent about the historical events until Cyrus.

From this historical review, there are a number of issues that are of particular significance for a sociological analysis, most specifically:

1. The number of Judeans deported to Babylon.
2. The socio-political and economic conditions of the exiles.
3. Neo-Babylonian impact on the religion of the Israelites.
4. The fate of the Judean left behind.
5. Impact of the exile in general.

4.8. Number and Dates of Deportations

While 2 Kings 24-25 reports two Babylonian deportations, 2 Chronicles 36:6-7 assume a third deportation, during the reign of Jehoiakim, when Nebuchadnezzar carried off the king and some of the temple vessels. Daniel 1:1 dates this deportation more precisely in the third year of Jehoiakim. In addition, Jer 52:30 mentions yet another deportation of 745 Jews by Nebuchadnezzar in the twenty-third year of Nebuchadnezzar (582).

There is no doubt about the deportation in 582; it is probably best understood as a punitive action carried out by Babylon for the murder of Gedaliah. But a deportation in the time of Jehoiakim, especially prior to the battle of Carchemish, in which Nebuchadnezzar defeated Egypt in 605, is historically most unlikely. Moreover, according to the Babylonian Chronicle, Nebuchadnezzar did not come to Judah until the following year.[37] The Babylonian Chronicles mention only one conquest. Chronicle BM 21964 reads as follows:

---

[37] See, A. K. Grayson, *Assyrian and Babylonian Chronicles* (Locust Valley: Augustin, 1975), 15 f.

Verse 11: Year 7: in the month of Kislev (November/ December), the King of Akkad mustered his troops and marched to Hatti (Syria/ Palestine). (v.12) He besieged the city of Judah and on the second of Adar (February/ March) he took the city and captured the king. He appointed a king of his choosing there, took heavy tribute and returned to Babylon.[38]

In these verses the king of Akkad refers to the Babylonian King Nebuchadnezzar. In Assyrio- Babylonian practice, the regnal years of kings were counted as beginning with the New Year in spring (Nisan).[39] "Therefore, the seventh regnal year of Nebuchadnezzar ran from spring 598 to spring 597. Adar is the last month of this regnal year. The capture of Jerusalem on the second day of Adar therefore corresponds approximately to March 16, B.C.E., in our calendar."[40]

The date of the second deportation is still disputed. The majority of scholars formerly presumed the date of the second deportation in 587. However, today an increasing number of scholars are inclined to date it in 586. Albertz cites three reasons for this uncertainty. First, the text of the Babylonian Chronicle breaks off in the year 594/593, so that we have no extra-biblical data to verify the date of the second deportation. Second, the Bible gives contradictory dates. According to 2 Kings 25:8 (cf. Jer 52:12) the capture of Jerusalem took place in the nineteenth year of Nebuchadnezzar. But Jer 52:29 dates the second deportation in his eighteenth regnal year. Finally, the synchronization of Babylonian and Judean chronologies is fraught with problems. Since a detailed debate on the issue is beyond the scope of this study, the present study follows the recent scholarly view as given below:

---

[38] D. J. Wiseman, *Chronicles of the Chaldaean Kings (626-556 B.C.E.) in British Museum* (London: British Museum, 1956, plates v, xiv- xv, pp. 66- 75, cited by Bob Becking, "Ezra's Re-enactment of the Exile" in *Leading Captivity Captive: The Exile as History and Ideology*, edited by Lester L. Grabbe, JSOT Sup Series 278 (Sheffield: Sheffield Academic Press, 1998), 43.

[39] See Rainer Albertz, *Israel in Exile*, 78.

[40] Rainer Albertz, *Israel in Exile*, 78.

118   EXILE AND THEOLOGY OF CREATION

Rainer Albertz reconstructs the dates of the three deportations in the following chart:[41]

The Deportations of Judah		
First Deportation	2 Adar of the 7th year Of Nebuchadnezzar	16 March 597
Second Deportation	Wall breached: 9 Tammuz Destruction: 7 or 10 Av of the 18th year of Nebuchadnezzar	29 July 587 ca. 25 August 587
Third Deportation	23rd year of Nebuchadnezzar	582

4.9. Number of Judeans deported to Babylon

Unfortunately, we do not have adequate information on this. Moreover, the Old Testament gives contradictory numbers of those deported. According to the Chronicler, the entire surviving population of Judah and Benjamin were deported into exile (2 Chro 36:20), and the land lay empty of inhabitants until the return of exile (2 Chro 36:21). But many scholars do not think this statement historically accurate.[42]

First, let us consider the numbers themselves. 2 Kings 24: 14 says that there were 10,000 captives, but then in v. 16, it list 7,000 "men of valor", and 1,000 craftsmen. Jer 52:28ff. lists the following: in Nebuchadnezzar's seventh year, 3023 Jews; in his eighteenth year, 832; and in the twenty-third year, 745, yielding a total of

---

[41] Rainer Albertz, *Israel in Exile*, 81.
[42] See for example, Hans Barstad, *The Myth of the Empty Land: A Study in the History and Archeology of Judah During the "Exilic" Period* (Oslo: Scandinavian University Press, 1996). He looks at earlier scholarship in question; the biblical evidence, the archaeological evidence, the evidence form Transjordan, and the relationship between Neo-Babylonian Empire and Judah, and he concludes that while there were deportations from Judah, the bulk of the population remained in the land; the archaeology shows no significant break in settlement or culture, and although there was a return, it was not nearly as large as depicted in Ezra- Nehemiah.

4,600. On the other hand, the *Golah List* of the return suggests the number of those who returned as 42,360 (Ezra 2:64; Neh 7:66).

The book of Kings, as a theological assessment of the exile, states that "so Judah went to exile out of its land". Here the author of the Book of Kings gives us an impression that the history of Judah ceased with the exile. However, the account cannot completely hide the fact that the deportations left some people behind in Judah, even if only they were the insignificant "poorest people of the land" (2 Kings 24:14; 25:12).

The Book of Jeremiah gives us another picture. According to Jeremiah, besides the poor, there were influential and educated individuals such as Gedaliah, Baruch, Jeremiah and a large number of officials in Judah or returned from their places of refuge (Jer 40:7-8, 11-12). Of course, we are told that most of these members run away to Egypt after the murder of Gedaliah (Jer 43:5-7). However, the text does not say that the land lost its entire population.

Secondly, although archaeology shows that several cities were destroyed, the destruction was not as extensive as was once believed. However, the settlement in the hill country of Judah was reduced to small villages.[43]

Moreover, the Near Eastern documents show that even the Assyrians, who developed the mass deportation as a strategy for exercising their imperial power[44] never carried off the entire population, instead Assyrian deportation was very selective.[45]

Scholars generally agree that Babylonians followed the Assyrian policy in their dealing with their defeated nations. Indeed, there is evidence that the Babylonians were even more selective

---

[43] See B. Oded, "Judah and the Exile," 478.
[44] See B. Oded, *Mass Deportations and Deportees in the Neo-Assyrian Empire* (Wiesbaden: Reichert, 1979), 19-20.
[45] B. Oded, *Mass Deportations...*, 47.

than the Assyrians.⁴⁶ They deported only those groups that served the military, economic, and political interests of the empire. Such selectivity can also be seen in the biblical account (2 Kings 24:14, 16; 25:11).

Many scholars view the deportations as very limited in extent. Noth gives a classic statement of this position:

> Certain though it is that very important developments in life and thought took place among those deported to Babylon, which were to influence the whole later history of Israel, nevertheless even the Babylonian group represented a mere outpost, whereas Palestine was and remained the central arena of Israel's history. And the descendants of the old tribes who remained in the land, with the holy place of Jerusalem, constituted not only numerically the great mass but also the real nucleus of Israel.⁴⁷

On the other hand, scholars have cited archaeological evidence to support the claims of the biblical traditions: assuming extensive destruction in Judah and deportation of substantial numbers, they emphasize the Babylonian exile for the subsequent life of Israel. Smith, for example, has estimated the number of exiles as almost half of the population.⁴⁸ Albright argues, on the basis of archaeological remains, that the population of Judah in the eighth century was approximately 250,000, and it fell roughly half to that number between 597 and 586, and then surely we can find a reasonable middle ground.⁴⁹ But once it is granted that a body of people were exiled large enough to form large "communities" of disaster and exile victims, then specific numbers become less relevant.

4.10. Condition of Judah during Exile

As our focus is on the Babylonian exile and its impact upon DI, the situation in Judah is not our main concern. However, every event that happened in Judah has its effect on the people lived in exile. We can assume that the exiles were very eager to know the

---

[46] Daniel L. Smith, *The Religion of the Landless...*, 30.
[47] Martin Noth, *The History of Israel*, 296.
[48] Daniel L. Smith, *The Religion of the Landless...*, 32.
[49] Albright, cited by Daniel L. Smith, *The Religion of the Landless...*, 32.

conditions of their homeland and every piece of information from the homeland had created some psychological effect on the life of exiles (cf. Neh. 1:2-11). Therefore a short description about the condition of Judah is essential.

For the period immediately following the destruction of Jerusalem in 587, we can draw from relatively contemporary sources in Jer 40:7- 43:3 and Lamentation 1-2; 4-5. These sources, however, give us a totally dark picture of the situation of those who were left behind in Judah. Jeremiah's narrative describes an opportunity for rapid improvement of the survivors' living conditions in cooperation with the Babylonians. The account however, in 2 Kings 25:1-26 is more negative than the corresponding narrative in Jeremiah. Since the account in 2 Chronicles 36 is very distant from the events and shaped by theological interests, it cannot be regarded as a legitimate historical source.

The Babylonians had a clear interest in consolidating the situation in war-torn Judah. Their punitive measures were aimed primarily at the groups and institutions that had supported the revolt against Babylon. But, the "pro-Babylonian" group enjoyed the favor of Babylonians. For example, Jeremiah, who demonstrated against the policy of revolt against Babylon (Jer 27-28), was released from prison by a Babylonian officer (Jer 39:13-14), and even offered a generous living in Babylon, which he nevertheless refused. More important than this was Babylonians' appointment of Gedaliah as the governor of Judah (Jer 40:7). Gedaliah seized this opportunity and built his capital at Mizpah. His primary goal was to provide bread and jobs for the remaining population as soon as possible. In this he had the support of Babylonians, who assigned to the poor the abandoned property of the deported upper classes (Jer 39:10). Babylonians thus made a serious attempt to rebuild Judah under their supervision. The installation of the landless on the properties of the large landowners (Jer 39:10; 40:10) indicates that it was in the interests of the Babylonians occupying power to consolidate the situation

122 EXILE AND THEOLOGY OF CREATION

as soon as possible in the land which had been devastated by the war.

Different groups of the population judged the Babylonian policy of occupation quite differently. The reports in Lamentations of extreme famine extending even to cannibalism in Jerusalem (Lam. 1:11; 2:12, 20; 4:4, 10), raping of women (5:11) and forced labor (5:13), probably relate to local phenomena limited to a particular place and time, but on the other hand, one can see a different attitude toward the catastrophe. The majority of the people who remained in the land were positive about the division of property and even justified it theologically. (See Ezk 11:15; 33:24) For them the exile was Yahweh's judgement on the exploitation of the upper class and often even a *de facto* liberation from debt. Those who were often labeled as the 'poor of the land' would have enjoyed more political influence under Babylonian authority than under Davidic rule, and formerly property-less peasants became landholders.[50] Gottwald believes that, with most of the officials in exile, the pre-monarchic village tribalism (which had been suppressed by monarchy) 'was able to re-emerge as the dominant force in organizing and preserving Palestinian Jewish identity throughout the exile.'[51] If Gottwald means a return of the hypothetical egalitarian society of the twelfth and eleventh centuries by this that can hardly be the case; as too many centuries had elapsed, and the Babylonian would not have allowed it. However, it would be correct to say that village norms took greater prominence (vis-à-vis urban norms) in the formation of a new social structure in Palestine.[52]

Therefore, we can assume that under the somewhat loose Babylonian administration, despite occasional confrontations, the land, which had been devastated by war, soon recovered

---

[50] P. Ackroyd, *Exile and Restoration*, 23.
[51] Norman K. Gottwald, *The Hebrew Bible: A Socio-Literary Introduction* (Philadelphia: Fortress Press, 1985), 425.
[52] Jeffrey A. Fager, *Land Tenure and the Biblical Jubilee: Uncovering Hebrew Ethics through the Sociology of Knowledge*, JSOT Suppl.155, (Sheffield: Sheffield Academic Press, 1993), 46.

economically.[53] As the Babylonians did not import a foreign upper class, as Assyrians did in the case of Samaria, the people of Judah could evidently even develop a limited degree of self- government based on elders. For the majority of small farming families, domestically the situation seems even to have had become easier for many.

However, the political condition in Judah was not so favorable to them. The military weakness and legal uncertainty in Judah at the time of the exile thus led to a constriction and a penetration of the area of Judahite settlement and to a constant confrontation with foreigners from the surrounding states, whose political and economic influence the people of Judah usually had to accept with clenched teeth, since they had no possibility of retaliation. Although they still lived in their own land, those who remained behind had to a large degree lost their territorial and social integrity.[54]

Gedaliah and his supporters saw the breakdown of structures of national government and deportation of the upper class as a great opportunity to establish in Judah a less stratified society, based on the deuteronomic brotherhood ethics. However, Gedaliah's policy evoked bitter response among the deportees who were the former owners of the properties (See. Ezk 11:14-21; 33:23-29).

The Book of Chronicles, with its emphasis on the land "enjoying its Sabbaths" (2 Chronicles 36:21), suggests that the land was completely desolate. In some measure, this is supported by archaeological evidence. It would seem that in turn the legitimacy of Yahwism was also threatened. In response to the disaster, many returned to older indigenous cults (See Jer chapter 44; esp. vv 16-18). Even among those who retained a belief in Yahweh at all, many turned to a syncretistic religion, which included Canaanite as well as Babylonian elements.[55]

---

[53] R. Albertz, *A History of Israelite Religion*...372.
[54] R. Albertz, *A History of Israelite Religion*..., 373.
[55] See G. Fohrer, *History of Israelite Religion* (Nashville: Abingdon Press, 1972), 309-10.

Yet Yahwism did not die in Palestine. The condition of the temple and the temple cult is not at all clear for the exilic period, but it seems evident that some sort of religious activity occurred at the site.[56] According to the ancient theory, the site was sacred regardless of the presence of the temple; therefore, sacrifice would have still been appropriate at the sacred site and probably still offered.[57] However, Yahwism, for the reason that there was no official priesthood, was weakened without the official structure.

4.11. Israel in Babylonian Exile

A reconstruction of the history of Israel in the Babylonian exile is possible only within very narrow limits. The first reason for this is due to the scant record of the exile in the historical tradition of the Bible, probably for theological reasons. Babylonian and Egyptian sources cannot fill this lacuna, because what was left in this period was too marginal in the eyes of the great powers to merit more than casual mention in passing.

Our main source in this regard is the indirect information in Ezekiel and Jeremiah. For the exiles of 597, Jeremiah 27-29 and the book of Ezekiel furnish important information. 2 Kings 25: 27-30 give some information about the early years of the exile after the destruction of Jerusalem in 587/586. From the later period, only the pardon of Jehoiachin by Amçl- Marduk in 562 is mentioned (2 Kings 25:27-30 ∥ Jer 52:31-34). Texts such as Ps 137, Ezk19, and Isa 40 provide some insight into the annoying psychological state of the Babylonian exiles of the later period. Jer 43:8- 44:30 gives some information about the Egyptian *golah*.

There are a few extra-biblical written sources for the history of the Neo-Babylonian period. The Babylonian Chronicle confirms in essence the events surrounding the first deportation in 597. There is also a Babylonian record of royal rations of oil for "Jehoiachin, the king of Judah", his five sons, and thirteen other Judeans. These tablets throw interesting light on a small fragment

---

[56] P. Ackroyd, *Exile and Restoration*, 25-29.
[57] See G. Fohrer, *History of Israelite Religion*, 310.

THE PERIOD OF EXILE

of the Babylonian *golah* that lived at the court of Nebuchadnezzar.[58] But the problem with the "ration list" is that we have no way of determining for certain the number in Jehoiachin's entourage, and thus we are not able to decide whether the portions are generous or not. With such a slim and uncertain evidence, one cannot go along with a confident view.

4.11.1. Social Situation of the Babylonian Exile

There is a little evidence of the conditions under which the exiles lived. However, the indirect evidence from Ezekiel and Jeremiah suggests that during the early years the exiles enjoyed a reasonable degree of freedom. The main feature of the situation of the exile was that the Babylonians settled them all together. Expect for Jehoiachin and his small household, the majority of those deported in 597 were settled in Tel-abib by the river Chebar in the vicinity of Nippur (Ezk 1:2; 3:15). Later other towns were built,[59] probably to accommodate an influx of Judeans from the later deportations of 587 and 582.

The exiles lived in their various towns grouped together either by families (Ezra 2:59) or occupation; despite having no function, the priests and other members of the temple staff constituted independent groups (Ezra 2:36ff; 8:17). Besides priests and prophets, elders played a leadership role on the model of premonarchic society (Ezk 8:1; 14:1; 20:1). The "*elders of golah*" (זקני הגולה) to whom Jeremiah addressed his letter may have constituted a leadership council.

Evidently, they were able to some extent to order their common life and thus maintain the traditions they had brought with them.[60] When Jeremiah calls on the exiles to build houses, plant gardens and have families (cf. 29: 5f.), his word suggests that these things were possible for them and they took advantage of these

---

[58] E. F. Weidner, ed., 'Jojachin, König von Juda in Babylonischen Keilinschriften', in *Mélanges Syriens offerts à Monsieur René Dussaud* (Paris: J. Gabalda, 1939), 924-31; *AENT*, 308.

[59] Tel-melah, Tel-harsha, Cherub- addan, Immer (Ezra 2:59), Casiphia (Ezra 8:17).

[60] Rold Rendtorff, *The Old Testament, An Introduction*, 57

possibilities. In his analysis of the conditions of exile, Noth suggests that:

> ...the exile were not "prisoners" but represented a compulsorily transplanted subject population who were able to move about freely in their daily life, but were presumably compelled to render compulsory labor service.[61]

In another classical work on Israelite history, (*Israelite and Judean History*, ed. by Hayes and Miller) Bustenay Oded writes:

> There is no clear and explicit evidence that the Mesopotamian exiles lived under conditions of suppression or were subjected to religious persecution at any time during the years 586-538 B.C.E.... One gets the impression that they had a certain internal autonomy and that they enjoyed the freedom to manage their community life.[62]

Also we see that the Babylonian *golah* at the end of the exile was in a position to make a sizable financial contribution to Jerusalem (Zech 6:10-11; Ezra 2:69; 8:30). Moreover the fact that only a limited number were prepared to return to Judah show that most of the Babylonian *golah* had found a way to make a good livelihood during their distant exile.[63] Often these factors initiate scholars to make a hasty generalization of a reasonable freedom they enjoyed in Babylon.

However, there are signs of different opinions along the way. In his *Studies in the Book of Lamentation* (1954), for example, Gottwald anticipated a different attitude to the exile that would emerge more fully at a later time:

> If the enduring memory of events and their impact upon succeeding generations is the major criterion of historical importance, then there can be no doubt that the sequence of happenings from 597 to 538 were among the most fateful in all Hebrew-Jewish history. It is far wide of the mark to recognize in the sixth century BC the severest test which Israel's religion ever faced?[64]

---

[61] M. Noth, *The History of Israel*, 296.
[62] B. Oded, "Judah and the Exile", 483
[63] Cf. Josephus, *Antiquities*, 11.9.
[64] Norman K. Gottwald, *Studies in the Book of Lamentation* (London: SCM, 1954), 19.

Thus, the scholarly opinions remain mixed or often ambiguous regarding the situation of the exiles. Smith-Christopher has illustrated an excellent example of this ambiguity from Bright's influential *History of Israel*. "Although we should not belittle the hardships and the humiliation that these exiles endured, their lot does not seem to have been unduly severe...,"[65] and yet two pages later, he writes: "When one considers the magnitude of the calamity that overtook her, one marvels that Israel was not sucked down into the vortex of history along with the other little nations of western Asia..."[66] This ambiguous statement is shared in many of the recent works on the impact of the exile on biblical literature. Even in Ackroyd's work, which is still considered by many to be the major analysis of the exile, one can find this ambiguity in assessing the impact of exile. In his assessment of the conditions of the exiles in Babylon, Ackroyd writes:

> ...Here the indications are of reasonable freedom, of settlement in communities-perhaps engaged in work for the Babylonians, but possibly simply engaged in normal agricultural life - of the possibility of marriage, of the ordering of their own affairs, of relative prosperity.[67]

Yet a few lines later, he acknowledges that 'the *uncongenial nature* (italic mine) of the situation should not, however, be understated.'[68]

The *Murasu* archive gives some evidence of the exilic condition. It is frequently pointed out that many Jewish names appear in the Murasu Archive from Nippur, texts that were found in 1893, and already being analyzed in print by 1898. As these are business documents that appear to show Jews to be involved in commerce, it was quickly concluded that life in exile was obviously not so bad. But as Smith-Christopher has rightly pointed out, since this text reflects the Persian period, how much one can assume this to be a reflection of the earlier Neo-Babylonian period? Zadok

---

[65] J. Bright, *History of Israel*, 345.
[66] J. Bright, *History of Israel*, 347.
[67] P. R. Ackroyd, *Exile and Restoration*, 32.
[68] P. R. Ackroyd, *Exile and Restoration*, 32.

challenges any assumptions about an image of comfortable Jewish communities in exile. According to Zadok, 'the highest positions in the Achaemenian administration of Babylonia were held by Persian and to some extent by Medes. Jews were largely minor functionaries. Nehemiah, who held a senior position, was an exception.' [69]

In 1938, Weissbach discussed a cuneiform inscription of Nebuchadnezzar II which read, in part, as follows:

> ...the lands of Hattim, from the upper sea to the lower sea, the land of Sumer and Akkad, the land between two rivers ... the rulers of the Lands of Hattim across the Euphrates where the sun sets, whose rulership, at the bidding of Marduk my Lord, I overcome, and the mighty Cedars of the mountain of Lebanon were brought to the City of Babylon, the whole of the races, people from far places, whom Marduk my Lord delivered to me- *I forced them to work* on the building of Etemenanki- *I imposed* on them the brick- basket....[70]

According to Smith-Christopher the phrase "*I forced them to work*" refer to corvee labor, and the phrase "*I imposed on them the brick basket*" implies strong terms of subservience.[71] Further, Weinfeld suggests that the term "*tupsikku*" used for the 'forced labor' is related to the Hebrew term סבל ("bearing burdens"; see 1 Kings 11:28)[72] It is significant how often labor is associated with rule over varied people in the Neo-Babylonian inscription.

Jer 51: 34-35 and similar passages in DI warns us not to overlook such evidence when considering the impact of the Babylonian exile. In this connection, J. M. Wilkie argues that we may need to reassess the attitude toward the treatment of the exiles

---

[69] R. Zadok, *The Jews in Babylonian During the Chaldean and Achaemenian Period According to the Babylonian Sources* (Haifa: Haifa University, 1979), 87.

[70] F. H. Weissbach, *Das Hauptheiligtum des Marduk in Babylon* (Leipzig: Hinrichs, 1938) 46-47, cited by D. L. Smith Christopher, "Reassessing the Historical and Sociological Impact of the Babylonian Exile," in *Exile: Old Testament, Jewish, and Christian Concept*, edited by James Scott (Leiden, New York, Köln: Brill, 1997), 24.

[71] D. L. Smith Christopher, "Reassessing the Historical...," 24.

[72] M. Weinfeld, *Social Justice in Ancient Israel and in the Ancient Near East*, (Philadelphia: Fortress, 1995), 85.

THE PERIOD OF EXILE

in the light of Deutero-Isaiah's concept of the *suffering* servant. He writes:

> ...there is independent evidence to suggest that Second-Isaiah's language is neither metaphorical nor at variance with the actual conditions, but is an accurate description of conditions which he knew only too well. [73]

The blurred memories of the historical circumstances described in the book of Daniel[74] also indicate the opportunities and dangers that the Babylonian *golah* experienced. It reflects a typical experience of the exilic community.

As Oded has pointed out, 'there is no clear and explicit evidence' for oppressive measures Israel faced during the exile (see fn. 62). Nevertheless, there is some indirect evidence that Nabonidus attempted to achieve a greater religious uniformity throughout the empire, which was unpopular among the Babylonians and oppressive to the exiles.[75] The narrative in Daniel 3 may actually be recollections of oppressive measures taken by Nabonidus and projected back onto Nebuchadnezzar. Moreover, Deutero-Isaiah's polemic against idols may reflect the pressures felt by the Jewish community to conform to Nabonidus's religious programme.[76] Deutero-Isaiah also makes many allusions to the harsh treatment being suffered by the exiles (40:2; 41:11-12; 42:7, 22; 47:6; 49:9, 13, 24-26; 51:7, 13-14, 23).

Another sobering judgement of the impact and experience of exile comes from a brief consideration of the harsh vocabularies used frequently in association with the Babylonian exile. For example:

---

[73] J. M. Wilkie, "Nabonidus and the Later Jewish Exiles," *JTS* 2 (1951), 40.

[74] Even though the stories recorded in the book of Daniel are not an integral part of Israel's historical traditions, and relatively late (Klaus Koch, *Das Buch Daniel*, pp. 55-76), as part of oral traditions, it throws some light on the social situations of the exilic period.

[75] See P.R. Ackroyd, *Exile and Restoration*, 37.

[76] Cf. J. M. Wilkie, "Nebonidus and the Later Jewish Exiles," 41-42.

1. מוסר n.m., from אסר "to tie, imprison" is usually translated "bonds" in Nah 1:13: "And now I will break off his yoke from you and snap the *bonds* that bind you." Significantly, of the Babylonian exile in Isa 52:2: "Shake yourself from the dust, rise up, O captive Jerusalem, loose the bonds from your neck..." and Ps 107:14: "He brought them out of darkness and gloom, and broke their *bonds* asunder."

2. זק "fetter" (always in plural זקים); Nah 3:10: "Yet she became in exile, she went into captivity ... all her dignitaries were bound in fetters..."; Isa 45:14 (of foreigners coming as prisoners, a reversal of fortune motif): [they] shall come over in chains and bow down to you.."; Ps 149 echoes the treatment of the dignitaries:"...to bind their kings with *fetters* and their noble with *chains* of iron" (See Jer 40:1).

3. נחשתיק "bronze fetters" from the root נחשת, "bronze/ copper," is used in Jer 39:7 to refer to the bonds on Zedekiah (cf. 2 Kgs 25). 2 Chr 36:6 speaks of such fetters on Jehoiachin. Finally, Lam 3:7 speaks of a siege and *chains* in reference to the post-event reflections on the conquest of Jerusalem.

Based on the above set of words describing the trauma experienced by the exile, and observing the frequent biblical motif that relates to providing "sight to blind" and the "release of prisoners" as a metaphor of exile, Smith asserts that contemporary assessment of the exile must not simply dismiss this imagery as purely metaphorical with no historical basis.[77]

4.11.2. *Sociological Development during the Exile*

During the exile, Israel underwent profound social changes, which had far-reaching consequences for the subsequent history of Israel and the further development of Israel's religion. The fall of Jerusalem monarchy and the destruction of Jerusalem were a severe blow to the official Jerusalemite theology of King and temple.

---

[77] Smith-Christopher, "Reassessing the Historical...," 31.

Unlike those who remained in Judah, the Babylonian *golah* had undergone the terrible experience of forcible displacement. They had experienced a humiliating social uprooting. They had lost not only their homeland but also their real property and their generally influential position. The sense of having been uprooted and dispossessed against their will kept alive their hope to return and revise the facts of history.[78]

There was also a sense of bitterness toward those left behind. The helpless exiles had been robbed of their property (Ezk. 11:15; 33:24) and their claim to leadership. They had been struck by God's judgement. But more distressing was the attitude of the people who left in Judah. They had clearly written the deported off. Many were quite ready to admit their transgressions; they suffered an overwhelming burden of guilt. How great this burden of guilt and loss of self-confidence must have been for many of the exiles is clear from the way that the prophet Ezekiel or his disciples exercised what amounted to pastoral ministry among them, promising them that their property and positions of leadership would be restored (Ezk 11:16-21) and showing them how personal repentance and return offered a way to escape the burdensome guilt of their parents (Ezk 18).[79]

The problems afflicting the Babylonian exiles were primarily political, psychological, and religious. The political problem had to do with the person Jehoiachin. When he was deported to Babylon in 587 at the age of eighteen, along with his mother and household, the Judean exiles, (most of whom were supporters of religious nationalism) quite naturally recognized him as their leader even in a foreign land. His imprisonment must have been a severe shock to the Babylonian *golah*; the Judeans had lost not

---

[78] We may possibly understand in the light of this basic mood the decision of the Babylonian *golah*, unlike the Egyptian *golah*, not to organize its cult permanently abroad by building a temple; probably there were tendencies in this direction within it, but they were abruptly rejected by the Ezekiel circle (cf. Ezk.20:32). Thus they prevented the total integration into Babylonian society, and nurtured the hope of return.

[79] Rainer Albertz, *Israel in Exile*, 105.

only their political representative at court but also their most important symbol of hope. When Jehoiachin disappeared from the public life of the capital, the party of religious nationalism lost its last support. How oppressive this political dispossession must have been during the first half of the exilic period can be heard in Ps 89, a shattering exilic lament for the king.[80]

The psychological problems are evident in Ps 137: the initial wistful homesickness for Jerusalem was threatening to disappear and had to be kept alive by self- imprecations not to forget Jerusalem (137:1-6). There was also a depressing sense of helplessness, of inability to influence the course of political events, which exploded in a violent desire for vengeance on the victorious Babylonians and their opportunistic Edomite allies (137:7-9).

In addition to political and psychological problems, there were religious problems. Their hope for a speedy return from the exile had proven deceptive. The last spark of hope had been extinguished by the imprisonment of Jehoiachin. Yahweh appeared simply to have disregarded his people's rights (Isa 40:27), to have turned his back on them (Isa 50:1), and forgotten his own city (Isa 49:14). In contrast, the symbols and images of the Babylonian gods were paraded through the streets in magnificent processions, accompanied by the rejoicing of the crowd (Isa 46:1-2); they obviously ruled over human society and world history, while Yahweh seemed unwilling or unable to intervene in history. In the domain of political history, Yahweh appeared to have been so distant.

These factors set the exiles in complete perplexity. James Newsome describes the situation by listing three typical forms of the response: (1) some people capitulated to the Babylonian

---

[80] Psalm 89 incorporates extensively the theology of the Jerusalem temple and kingship, and it laments the end of Davidic monarchy. Even though some scholars dates this psalm to the post-exilic period, this lament is immediately understandable when we realize that Jehoiachin probably languished in prison from 582 to 562 in consequence of the murder of Gedaliah. The lengthy lament for the king in Ps 89 thus looks for the release of Jehoiachin in whom exiles placed great hope.

theology and joined their captors in their worship and prayers (see Isa 44:9-20; and Ezk 20:32); (2) others submerged into a denial of self; (3) and the third group stood suspended between hope and despair, not wanting to give up the old formulas of faith, yet neither able to derive meaning or succor from them.[81]

The extreme derision of DI towards Babylonian culture and religion implies that assimilation to the conqueror's way of life and worship exerted a strong impact on his audience. This frontal attack on all things Babylonian may further imply that, over the decades, some Judahites had been drawn into the mainstream Babylonian life, possibly in commerce or government service, and were therefore satisfied with their conditions, a situation that legends of Daniel 1-5 may distantly reflect.

However, the majority of exiles did not assimilate or give up their hope. First of all, as mentioned above, they had the chance to live together in certain towns. They lived in locations in families (Ezra 2:59) or according to professional groups (Ezra 8:17). Here Levites, Priests and other former temple officials- despite their lack of function- formed their own groups (Ezra 2:36ff). Along with the priests and prophets, elders took over functions of leadership (Jer. 29:1; Ezk. 7:1; 14:1; 20:1). They also capitalized on specific survival strategies.

Survival Strategies

The first step towards this survival strategy was the revival of the decentralized forms of organization along kinship lines. Among the Israelites of the exilic period, the family or the family association became the main social entity.[82] Relics of tribal organization, which had never been completely forgotten, were revived. The elders again became significant and took over the limited local and political functions of leadership alongside priests and prophets.

---

[81] James D. Newsome, *By The Waters of Babylon: An Introduction to the History of Theology of Exile* (Edinburgh: T & T Clark, 1979), 72.

[82] See Rainer Albertz, *A History of Israelite Religion...*, 375

As a result of this sociological development, the family became more important in the religious sphere. This shift from nationhood to family influenced their theological thinking also. When they were in the homeland, their relationship with Yahweh was based on God's saving act in history. But, when the family became the primary social entity, the relationship with Yahweh was based, not on God's saving act, but on God's creation of each individual. (see Ps. 22:9-10; 71:5-6; 119:73; 138:8; Job 10:3,8-12; Isa 43:1; 44:1, 24; 45:9; 51:13). This new understanding of Yahweh as the Creator enabled them once more to sense Yahweh's presence, protection and support. Because this piety was rooted in creation, the historical catastrophe of the exile was not a mortal blow. Thus, finding a new basis for confidence and hope that the historical and political catastrophe did not mean that Yahweh had rejected his people (Isa 64:7-8; 49:21), the Deutero- Isaiah group drew on the primordial personal relationship with God in order to build confidence in Yahweh. Thus, God's relationship with Israel in God's act of creation was made the foundation for their message (Isa 43:1; 44:2, 21, 24; 54:5).

The other survival strategies were religious and ceremonial in nature. To secure the identity of every individual male belonging to the *golah* and as a token of his membership in the Judean ethnic group, the ritual circumcision of infants was introduced (Gen 17:12; 21:4; Lev 12:3). Circumcision was originally an ancient rite practiced by the Egyptian and by most of the ancient Semitic, except the Babylonian and the Assyrians.[83] Therefore, the Babylonian *golah* took it as their confessional badge to declare their membership in the community of exiles and their fidelity to the ancestral religion.[84] Thus, from the exilic period onward, circumcision became such an accepted hallmark of Jewish faith that it could be required from converts (Judith 14:10).

---

[83] See J. P. Hyatt, "Circumcision" in *IDB* vol.1, 631.
[84] Rainer Albertz, *Israel in Exile*, 107.

THE PERIOD OF EXILE 135

Another important strategy was their Sabbath observance.[85] Since the traditional form of worship such as the offering of first fruits, sacrificial meals, and sacrificial vows, could not be performed in a foreign land without the temple, an alternate religious observance had to be invented. So, as a substitute, it was probably the theological reformers of the Babylonian *golah* who enjoined familial observance of the Sabbath every seven days.[86] Thus, the *golah* found a regular act of worship that could be observed by families without the temple and far from their homeland. This regular rest from labor on a particular day was also a highly visible external confessional badge of the Judean ethnic group.

It is remarkable that the theological reformers of the exile evolved only ritual and religious survival strategies that did not need a cultic center. Unlike the Egyptian *golah*, the Babylonian *golah*- as far as we know- never built a temple in their foreign land.[87] There may have been tendencies in this direction. But Ezekiel and his disciples brusquely rejected them (Ezk 20:30-32). Therefore, we cannot say that the synagogue worship originated in Babylonian exile; the earliest evidence of them is much later.[88]

The most momentous theological innovation of this period was the discovery of monotheism by the Deutero-Isaiah group

---

[85] The origin and history of the Sabbath have still not been fully explained. However, there is much to suggest that in the pre-exilic period the Sabbath was the Israelite new moon festival (2 Kgs 4:23; Is. 1:13; Hos. 2:11: Am. 8:15). The pre-exilic Sabbath was largely part of the official cult and had ended with the destruction of the Jerusalem temple (Lam.2:6) See, R. Albertz, *A History of Israelite Religion...*, 408.

[86] Rainer Albertz, *Israel in Exile*, 108.

[87] Rainer Albertz, *Israel in Exile*, 109.

[88] The earliest inscriptions mentioning a synagogue are from Hellenistic Egypt and date from the third century B. C. E.; the first building that can be identified as a synagogue was built on the island of Delos in the first century. The earliest synagogue discovered in Palestine date from the first half of the first century C. E. See Lee I. Levine, *The Synagogue in Late Antiquity* (Philadelphia: American School of Oriental Research, 1978); Lester L. Grabbe, "Synagogue in Pre-70 Palestine: A Reassessment," *JTS* 39 (1988): 401-10.

(Isa 41:4, 23-24, 27-29; 43:10-13; 44:6, 8; 45:5-6, 14, 18, 21-22; 46:9; cf. 48:12 and the Deuteronomists (Deut 4:35, 39; 2 Sam 7:22; 1 Kgs 8:60). Probably the collapse of the Judean state and the theological problem arose as the consequence of the collapse, might have motivated Israel to think in that direction, which eventually initiated their thinking on a sole Creator.

Structure and Function of the Exilic Community
Early Israel had carried over from its nomadic past a social structure consisting of families, clans and tribes. Settlement involved certain weakening in the old kinship constitution of society. However, family and clan structure were maintained even after the settlement. The clan elders also continued. The group was characterized by 'organic solidarity.'[89] Worship in Yahweh remained as the powerful socially binding influence on the solidarity of the group. With the introduction of the monarchy and urbanization this social solidarity further weakened. The social center of gravity was shifted towards cities and rich members of the society. Yahweh became the God of the state rather than the God of the tribe. A professional priesthood emerged and thus the cult became separated from the life of the primitive group.[90] The simple, joyful, natural worship of the family grouped around its patron God declined.[91] Deportation marked another transition. From the moment of deportation, Israel became a people without land.

Diaspora Community
The loss of the state and the associated deportations and emigrations led to an irreversible disintegration of Israel's territorial integrity. It became a people without a country and appeared as an outcast people who live in the towns of others. The exile marked the beginning of Israel's life in the Diaspora.

---

[89] A. D. H. Mays, *The Old Testament in Sociological Perspective* (London: Marshall Pickering, 1989), 80.
[90] A. D. H. Mays, *The Old Testament in Sociological...*, 81.
[91] A. D. H. Mays, *The Old Testament in Sociological...*, 81.

However, Babylonian *golah* saw their diaspora condition as an opportunity and a demand for a radical renewal of Yahwism along the line of the Josianic reform, that is, an opportunity to impose exclusive and an iconic worship of Yahweh.[92] Since their identity and survival were threatened by the diaspora condition, they were forced to innovate new survival strategies, as noted above, such as Sabbath, circumcision, dietary laws etc. These survival strategies, coupled with the impressive theological structures created by the DI community might have given rise to self-assurance among the exile.

Family

As we noted above, the loss of centralized political power led to a strengthening of decentralized forms of organization based on kinship. In the Israel of the exilic period, the family became the main social entity.[93] However, the family during exile was not the extended social group that can be observed in the patriarchal period. The family had transformed itself. To the extent that its mobility had increased, it had lost its primitive character and some of its political, economic, and cultic distinctiveness. In addition, the traditional older mores had weakened. The power of the father was less absolute, and the women tended to assert more influence.[94]

The family became the foundation for an effective preservation, not only for maintaining the race but also for moral

---

[92] Rainer Albertz, *Israel in Exile*, 135.
[93] See Rainer Albertz, *A History of Israelite Religion...*, 375.
[94] For the study of the rights and influence of women in this period, we have the case of Zelophahad's daughters in the Priestly Code (Num 27:1-10; 30:1-12). In the epilogue of the book of Job, we see Job's daughters receiving a part of the inheritance along with their brothers (Job 42:15). In Prov. 31:10-31, the mistress of the house appears as a morally and socially independent person. This conception of virtues and social dignity of women is much closer to the concepts current in Babylonia. See Antinin Causse, "From an Ethnic Group to a Religious Community: The Sociological Problem of Judaism," in *Community, Identity and Ideology: Social Science Approaches to the Hebrew Bible*, edited by Charles E. Carter and Carol L. Meyers (Indiana: Eisenbrauns, 1996), 99.

education. In the pre-exilic period, family religious observations had long flourished freely alongside the official religion of Yahweh. But after the institution of monarchy, and especially, following the Josianic reform, the role of the family in religious matters weakened.[95] But during the exile, in the absence of official religion, the family piety played a supportive and substitutionary role that contributed substantially to the overcoming of this crisis.[96]

Elders

The leadership of elders was part of the structure of the old tribal organization. During the time of exile this old tribal structure took on new life and the elders one more became a significant force and took on limited functions of local political leadership along side the priests and prophets. Elders were at this time a permanent institution in the Orient.[97] They were charged with directing the group, with representing it before the pagan authorities, and with judging between members in case of conflict. Their role was more extensive due to the lack of a national organization and the fact that the great states only intervened with their lives from afar and this solely for taxes and recruitment of forced labor or military service made all the difference.[98]

Mixed Group

During the period of exile, it became more difficult to maintain the cohesion and purity of the clans. We can imagine how many non-Jewish exiles and some native poor were assimilated into Judaism. In the list of Ezra 2 and Nehemiah 7, for instance, it is explicitly stated that certain groups sought their genealogical titles in vain: "they could not prove their families or their descent, whether they belonged to Israel" (Ezra 2:59-63; Neh 7:61-65). The frequent mention of the issue of mixed marriage also confirms

---

[95] See Rainer Albertz, *A History of Israelite Religion in the Old Testament Period: From the Beginnings to the End of Monarchy*, vol. I, (Louisville, Kentucky: Westminster/ John Knox Press, 1994), 186ff.
[96] See Rainer Alberts, *Israel in Exile*, 136.
[97] Antonin Causse, "From an Ethnic Group...," 98.
[98] Antonin Causse, "From an Ethnic Group...," 98.

this (Ezra 9-10; Neh 13:23-27). This gives us sufficient reason to think that the mixed community had caused social tension among them as a result of the conflicting interest of the different population. This mixed nature of the community also made them to reflect on the nature of their God in a wider perspective: not only as a redeemer of a specific community, but as the creator of the whole humanity.

Following the deportation and emigration, the solidarity of the population weakened and consequently Israel led to ally themselves with pagan families.[99] The Murašû documents and the Elephantine papyri are conclusive in this regard. There were at that time some fathers who had foreign theophoric names, while the sons, Hebrew names, or vice versa.[100]

The loss of state also influenced their attitude to other nationalities. The result was two different attitudes towards these foreign neighbors. On the one hand, strict separation from the foreign nations was preached. On the other hand, the "survivors of the nations," who like Israel had been victims of imperial Babylon, were invited by the Deutero- Isaiah group to share the deliverance that Yahweh was about to bring for his people (Isa 45:20-25); thus they occasioned a momentous opening of the national religion of Israel towards universalism. Without denying the faith in Yahweh, these theologians enlarged the horizons of the faith community beyond it borders, even crossing those of race, color, ethnicity and space to open its door for other people.

---

[99] The deportation of the Assyro-Chaldean Period had established in the region of Mesopotamia many remnants of a people who were brought in to compensate for the depletion of the original population that the conquest had created. In addition, the fact that Babylon was a capital city and that the cities of the Egyptian Delta were very active from an international business standpoint must have greatly enhanced international contact and the mixing of the races. (See Antinin Causse, "From an Ethnic Group," 100)

[100] See Antonin Causse, "From an Ethnic Group...," 100.

4.12. Conclusion

The period of exile marks a deep rift in the history of Israelite religious thinking. With it the previous religion of Israel became involved in its most serious crisis, but in it the foundation stone for the most far-reaching renewal of their religious thinking was also laid. The experience of exile as well as the social, economic, and political context of the exile was the decisive factor for their religious rethinking, especially in their notion of God and their worldview. This brief review of the history of exile provides with us a number of important religious and sociological responses to those events that are highly important for our investigation in the concept of creation in Deutero-Isaiah.

CHAPTER FIVE
Introduction to Isaiah 40-55

5.1. Introduction

Deutero- Isaiah[1] is the name given to the anonymous author of Isaiah 40-55. Since the Greek word *deuteros* (δευτερος) means "the second," the designation "Second Isaiah" also is in use. In this study, the name "Deutero Isaiah" (abbreviated to DI) has been used, in order to bring out the artificiality of the name given to the text.

As long ago as the twelfth century, Ibn Ezra had suggested the possibility of different authorship for the book of Isaiah. However, the credit for identifying the distinct origin of chs.40-66 is generally assigned to J. C. Döderlein[2] (1775) and J. G.

---

[1] The identification of Isaiah 40-55 as an independent literary unit composed by an author other than the eighth-century prophet Isaiah son of Amoz is a hypothesis of historical criticism. However, some of the recent scholars criticize the use of the term "Deutero-Isaiah." For example, Coggins criticizes the very use of the term "Deutero- Isaiah." He believes that the identity of Isa 48:22 and 57:21 is sufficient argument against treating chapters 40-55 as a separate unit. He goes on to claim that the impossibility of assigning a date or geographical location to the author of the work means that the term "Deutero-Isaiah" should not be used. See Richard J. Coggins, "Do We Still Need Deutero-Isaiah?" *JSOT* 80 (1998), 77-92. Unfortunately, Coggins makes no contribution to the question of how to account for the clear stylistic, linguistic, and theological emphasis of this section than by positing a distinct author or authorial group.

[2] J. C. Döderlein, *Esaias*, (1775; 3rd ed. 1789) XII-XV.

Eichhorn[3] (1783). Eichhorn also was the first to identify chapters 40-66 as from a prophet of the exilic period. He put forward a definite theory that chapters 40-66 are an independent work, the work of an anonymous prophet who lived towards the end of the Babylonian Exile in the middle of the sixth century B.C.E.

In 1892, B. Duhm suggested further divisions in the book.[4] Not only did he propose that chapters 1-39 were a literary compilation rather than the work of one author, he also made a division between chapters 40-55 and 56-66. Chapters 40-55 were dated from around 540 B.C.E., while the Servant Songs and chapters 56-66 reflected a later setting, the period after the return to Jerusalem. His methodology was similar to that of the source critics who analyzed the Pentateuch in the late 1800s. However, the conservative scholars, continued, and still continue, to defend Isaiah's authorship of the entire book.

Most of the scholars today accept Döderlein's and Eichhorn's division in matters of the historical background of the text. Duhm's basic division also finds wide acceptance. A variety of arguments have been put forward to delineate the sections more precisely. According to Whybray, the main arguments supporting this division may be grouped under three headings.[5]

1. Anonymity

The name of Isaiah never occurs in the last twenty seven chapters of the book. In the earlier chapters, it occurs sixteen times: four times in chapters 1-13, twice in chapter 20, and ten times in chapters 37-39. Of these occurrences, three are in editorial headings (1:1; 2:1; 13:1) which clearly intended to claim Isaiah's authorship for the following oracles. On the other hand, the total cessation of

---

[3] J. G. Eichhorn, *Einleitung in das AT* III (1783), 76-97.
[4] B. Duhm, *Das Buch Jesaia*, 4th ed. (Gottingen: Vandenboeck & Ruprecht, 1922).
[5] See R. N. Whybray, *The Second Isaiah* (Sheffield: Sheffield Academic Press, 1995), 2.

such references after chapter 39 suggests equally strongly that the chapters 40-66 stand outside of Isaiah-ben- Amoz's authorship.

2. Style

Obviously, a full appreciation of the stylistic characteristics of a literary text is not possible through the medium of a translation, though in the case of Isaiah 40-55 even an English translation conveys something of the change of mood, which occurs at the beginning of chapter 40. The author certainly has some key phrases in common with his eighth-century predecessor, but these may be accounted for by a common Judean religious tradition.[6] But in general, there is an unmistakable note of exultation and confidence which runs through these chapters and marks them out as quite distinctive. Its use of phraseology, vocabulary and imagery, and its use of characteristic literary forms and stylistic devices; all these show a distinct authorship of this portion.

3. Historical Situation

Since the end of the eighteenth century, it has been increasingly recognized that all literature is to a large extent a reflection of the period in which it is written, and has been influenced by the circumstances in which the authors lived. In the OT, it is particularly true of the words of the prophets, who were not primarily authors but men who believed themselves to have been called to proclaim urgent messages to their contemporaries. Therefore, it is particularly important to set them, as far as possible, against their historical backgrounds.

The most obvious indication of a sixth-century date is provided by the occurrence of the name Cyrus in 44:28 and 45:1. There can be no possible doubt that this person, who is described in this passage (44:24-45:7) and also –without being specifically named – in other passages (e.g. 41:2, 25; 42: 6(?); 45:13(?); 46:11; 48:15) as a king and a great conqueror raised up by Yahweh to rescue

---

[6] R. N. Whybray, *The Second Isaiah*, 2.

Yahweh's people from captivity, is the sixth-century Persian king Cyrus the Great, the founder of the Persian Empire.

However, the sixth century date does not depend on these two references alone. It is a simple fact that the content of the prophet's message from start to finish is quite inappropriate to the circumstances of the eighth century B.C.E., but entirely appropriate when seen as a message to Jewish exiles in Babylon in the sixth century. It is clearly addressed to a group of people who have been exiled from their homeland by a conquering power, which is also referred by name: Babylon. In four passages (43:14; 47:1; 48:14, 20) Babylon is spoken of by name in these terms, and this historical situation is confirmed in numerous other passages.

A comparison with other exilic literature may help us to get a more precise date of this work. In the book of Jeremiah, the fall of Jerusalem comes towards the end (Jer 39). In Ezekiel, it constitutes the midpoint toward which everything moves and from which everything evolves.[7] But the book of Deutero-Isaiah looks back on it from the very outset. To DI, God's judgement on Jerusalem lies in the past, while now a new era of God's mercy and favor has dawned (40:1ff). Therefore, the central focus and turning point of the book is the fall of Babylon (Isa 47) and it concludes with the miraculous resurrection of Zion (49-54). Thus, the book of Deutero-Isaiah is the only prophetic book of exilic period that contains nothing but prophecy of salvation. This is because it dates from the end of the exilic period and the beginning of the postexilic period.

With the identification of Isa 40-55 as an independent literary unit composed by an author other than the eighth-century prophet Isaiah, the problem of unity becomes a heated issue of arguments. The primary issue is whether Deutero-Isaiah was conceived from the outset as a continuation of Proto-Isaiah or originated as an

---

[7] Deuteronomic edition of Jeremiah places the fall of Babylon at its very end (Jer. 50-51); but the book of Ezekiel, strangely, does not even mention it.

independent work that was linked subsequently with Proto-Isaiah, either earlier[8] or later.[9] The former possibility is suggested by the absence of any superscription in Isa 40 and many stylistic and material affinities, such as between Isa 40 and Isa 6;[10] the latter is suggested by the clear compositional linkage of 40:1-2 with 52:7-10 and 40:6-8 with 55:10-11.[11] One possible solution is that the individual or group we call "Deutero-Isaiah," considering themselves the late disciples of Isaiah (cf. the affinities between 50:4-9 and 8:1-4, 16-18; 30:8-10),[12] initially composed a separate document, which at a later redactional stage was linked to the extended Isaiah tradition of Isa 1-32.[13]

The relationship between Deutero-Isaiah and Trito-Isaiah is another problem. Elliger assumed that Trito-Isaiah was a disciple of Deutero-Isaiah who not only composed Isa 56-66 but also edited Isa 40-55.[14] However, this view of origin of DI has been abandoned by later research inasmuch as scholars have serious doubts about 'Trito- Isaiah' as a specific historical figure. A detailed discussion on this issue is beyond the scope of this study.

5.2. The Unity of the Book of Isaiah

To say that historically speaking the book of Isaiah has derived its origins, not only from the eighth-century prophet (Proto-Isaiah) but also from the exilic and post-exilic (Deutero-Isaiah and Trito-Isaiah), marked an important contribution to our understanding of the character and the theological motivation of the various sections of the work. However, the simple assignment of chapters1-

---

[8] U. Berges, *Das Buch Jesaja: Komposition und Endgestalt*, Her BS 16 (Freiburg: Herder, 1998) proposes a fifth or fourth century date.

[9] O. H. Steck, *Gottesknecht und Zion: Gesammelte Aufsätze zu Deuterojesaja* (Tübingen: Mohr Sieback, 1992) proposes third century date.

[10] H. G. M. Williamson, *The Book Called Isaiah: Deutero-Isaiah's Role in Composition and Redaction* (Oxford: Clarendon, 1994), 30-40.

[11] See Rainer Albertz, *Israel in Exile...*, 380.

[12] See Williamson, *The Book Called Isaiah*, 94-115.

[13] See Rainer Albertz, *Israel in Exile...*, 378.

[14] K. Elliger, *Deuterojesaja in seinem Verhaltnis zu Tritojesaja*, BWANT 63 (Stuttgart: Kohlhammer, 1933). 217f, cited by R. Albertz, *Israel in Exile...*, 379.

39 to Proto- Isaiah, 40-55 to Deutero-Isaiah and 56-66 to Trito-Isaiah and thus linking specific chapters to specific period do not solve the problem entirely. A variety of sections in Proto-Isaiah can be assigned to a later period for showing signs of having been shaped by the post-exilic theological concerns raised in chs.40-66. While eighth-century Isaiah does not disappear entirely, there nonetheless remains a great uncertainty about the assignment of material to this date and figure (e.g. ch.34,35 etc.). This is the case of even the most well known chapter 11. Why should Isaiah 11 be seen as the eighth-century material when its very outlook envisions a shoot growing out of the stump, an obvious reference to exile?[15] On the other hand, Isaiah 58 echoes the very strongest social criticism voiced in Proto-Isaiah. Several issues like this persuaded biblical scholars to reject the tripartite paradigm of Duhm, which dominated for the greatest part of the twentieth century.

However, the suggestion of the single authorship for all the 66 chapters is an oversimplification. With the exception of certain conservative perspectives, the unity of Isaiah is not understood on the basis of authorship. In order to explain the unity of Isaiah, scholars have made use of the variety of exegetical methods developed since 1970s. For example, especially in English-language scholarship, there has been a tendency to reassert the unity of the book of Isaiah on literary, structural and occasionally theological rather than authorial grounds and to minimize the distinctions and difference among the three major sections of the book.

For example, Ronald Clement, in an article on *Interpretation* in 1982, proposed a view of the unity of the book of Isaiah based on the relationship between prophecies of the historical Isaiah and their later interpretation after the destruction of Jerusalem.[16] For

---

[15] As Sweeney argues, we should not overlook the integral role of Isa 11 to the conceptual project of Third Isaiah. See M. A. Sweeney, "The Reconceptualization of the Davidic Covenant in Isaiah," in *Studies in the Book of Isaiah: Festschrift Willem A. M. Beuken*, edited by J. Van Ruiten and M. Vervenne (Louvain: Leuvan University Press, 1997), 41-61.

[16] Ronald E. Clement, "The Unity of the Book of Isaiah," *Interpretation* 36 (1982), 117-129.

Clement, this is a matter of identifying the motif, which appears throughout the book and finding in chs 40-66 indications of development of the theme present in chs.1-39.[17] He proposed a view of the unity of the book of Isaiah based on the relationships between the prophecies of the historical Isaiah and their interpretation after the destruction of Jerusalem. Within chapters 1-39 there are references to Babylon (13:1-14:23, 39), so that the supposed distinction between First and Second Isaiah is not razor sharp. Instead, we find that the book as a whole deals with the political fortunes of Israel from the eighth, and all the way to the fifth centuries B.C.E.[18] This led Clement to conclude that 'the overall structure of the book shows signs of editorial planning and that, at the stage in its growth, attempts were made to read and interpret the book as a whole.'[19]

Rolf Rendtorff's studies on the unity of the book of Isaiah focus on the text itself rather than on diachronic considerations about the redactional process by which the book was given its form.[20] He asserts that 1-39 and 56-66 were shaped and edited with reference to 40-55. However, Rendtorff accepts that the treatment of major themes in the First Isaiah is quite different in Second Isaiah. Roy F. Melugin took the absence of a superscription and call narrative to imply that the section was never intended to stand alone, but was conceived from the beginning as a continuation of 1-39.[21]

Brevard S. Childs does not deny that Isaiah 40-55 was originally addressed to the Hebrew exiles in Babylon by an

---

[17] R. E. Clement, "The Unity of the Book of Isaiah," 120.
[18] R. E. Clement, "The Unity of the Book of Isaiah," 120.
[19] R. E. Clement, "The Unity of the Book of Isaiah," 120.
[20] R. Rendtorff, "The Book of Isaiah: A Complex Unity-Synchronic and Diachronic Reading," in *New Visions of Isaiah*, edited by R. F. Melugin and M. A. Sweeney, JSOT Supl. 214 (Sheffield: Sheffield Academic Press, 1996), 32-49.
[21] Roy F. Melugin, *The Formation of Isaiah 40-55*, (Berlin: Walter de Gruyter, 1976), 176.

unnamed exilic prophet dating from the sixth century. But based on its present canonical shape, the elimination of historical allusion from ch. 40-66, and the absence of a superscription, he argues to read the whole book as one canonical text. In his view, Second Isaiah derives its canonical meaning exclusively from its connection with First Isaiah and cannot be grasped theologically apart from it. While it is certainly possible to read Isa 40-55 theologically with reference to Isa 1-39, however we explain the connection, we must question the proposition that these chapters only make sense theologically when read in this way.[22]

In order to highlight its canonical unity, Childs minimizes or disregards the historical reference, either directly or indirectly, that these chapters do in fact contain.[23]

H. G. M. Williamson holds a more strong position on the issue of the connection between ch 1-39 and 40-55. According to Williamson, not only the pervasive influence of First on Second but for the latter's editing and expanding of the former. Both were therefore intended to be read as one text.[24] He argues that Second Isaiah announces the fulfillment of the plan announced in First Isaiah, that the Second Isaiah cannot be understood theologically without First Isaiah, and that in fact it was never circulated independently of First Isaiah.[25] Most of the Williamson's study is taken up with cross-referencing terms and phrases occurring in both parts of the book to demonstrate the influence of the First on the Second. There is no doubt the author of Isa 40-55 was familiar with Isaiah's pronouncements, but he was also familiar with the pronouncements of other early prophetic figures.

According to Christopher Seitz, there were earlier Isaianic traditions, which existed, independent of the book as it now is.

---

[22] J. Blenkinsopp, *Isaiah 40-55: A New Translation with Introduction and Commentary*, AB vol.19A (New York: Doubleday, 2002), 48.
[23] J. Blenkinsopp, *Isaiah*, 49.
[24] H. G. M. Williamson, *The Book Called Isaiah*, 240.
[25] H. G. M. Williamson, *The Book Called Isaiah*, 240.

But Isaiah 40-55 and 56-66 were never literary complexes which once existed apart from chs.1-39. Isaiah 40-55 contains no call narrative of its own; 40:1-8 is only a commissioning of the prophet 'Second Isaiah' but rather a transition between traditions concerning the epoch of Isaiah to a new time following the exile of Babylon.[26] Seitz is also a historical-critical interpreter. Yet his approach is not as much focused on the socio-historical setting of Isaiah 40-55. Moreover, the kind of unity, which is upheld now by scholars, belongs to a relatively later stage in the book's compilation.[27]

In sum, the recent scholarly discussion once again seriously began to think about the unity of Isaiah. Of course, it is not a simple unity but a highly complex one. Yet scholars have now begun to realize the complexity of this unity and to interpret it. The methodological approaches are different. Nevertheless, the progress made in the understanding of the book of Isaiah as a whole during the last decades is remarkable. However, in our interpretation we shall follow the socio-historical approach, which gives due weight to diachronic as well as synchronic approaches, to deal with the chapters 40-55.

5.3. Literary Questions of Isaiah 40-55

1. The Text

The Hebrew text of Deutero Isaiah is comparatively well preserved. According to James Muilenburg, "The Hebrew text of Second Isaiah has been transmitted exceptionally well. Its superior value is shown by the way in which it has preserved parallelism and metrical construction and also by the fact it generally yields

---

[26] Christopher Seitz, "Isaiah 1-66: Making Sense of the Whole'" in *Reading and Preaching the Book of Isaiah*, edited by Christopher Seitz (Philadelphia: Fortress Press, 1988), 109-112.

[27] Certain striking expressions such as "Holy One of Israel," "justice and righteousness," "blind and deaf" "former things" and "new things" and motifs such as election of Zion and David etc., led many scholars to recognize the inherent unity of the book of Isaiah. They try to explain this unity through tradition-historical or redaction historical methods.

a satisfactory sense. It is not flawless, but the number of corruption is small."[28] IQIs[a] agrees almost word for word with the MT. The differences between MT and IQIs[a] are mainly orthographical.[29] The Septuagint (LXX) version of the book of Isaiah has been preserved in an astonishingly large number of manuscripts. The translation initially reflects the interpretation current in the Greek-speaking Jewish community in Alexandria from the third century B.C.E. onwards.[30] The Targums, the Syriac translation, and Vulgate are all part of the interpretative tradition.[31]

2. *Form-Critical Study*

No serious student of the Old Testament can deny the contributions of form criticism to the Old Testament scholarship. In his short history of the literature of Israel, published in 1906, Gunkel stressed the necessity of examining the literary genres or types, their proper character and, if possible, their history.[32] Especially concerning the prophets, he indicated the importance of an exact delimitation of the small unit and its exact *Sitz im Leben*. The pioneer in applying the from-critical method in the study of Deutero Isaiah was H. Gressmann.[33] He claimed that in the study of the prophets we must give up the "book" as a basic unit, because the prophetical "books" consist of short utterances, rarely longer than one chapter.[34] Therefore, the first task of the form-critic, according to Gressmann, is to delimit the literary unit.

---

[28] James Muilenburg, Isaiah: Chapters 40-66, *IB* vol.5 (Nashville: Abingdon Press, 1956), 414; See also C. C. Torrey, *The Second Isaiah: A New Interpretation*, Edinburgh: T&T Clark, 1928), 206-7.

[29] Klaus Baltzer, *Deutero Isaiah: A Commentary on Isaiah 40-55* (Minneapolis: Fortress Press, 2001), 2.

[30] See I. L. Seeligmann, *The Septuagint Version of Isaiah* (Leiden: Brill, 1948).

[31] Klaus Baltzer, *Deutero Isaiah*, 3.

[32] H. Gunkel, "Die Israelitische Literatur," *Die Orientalischen Literaturen* (Leipzig, 1906), 52, cited by A. Schoors, *I Am God Your Saviour: A Form Critical Study of the Main Genres in Is XL-LV*, VT Sup 24, Leiden: Brill, 1973), 1.

[33] H. Gressmann, "Die literarische Analyse Deuterojesajas," *ZAW* 34, 1914, 254-297.

[34] H. Gressmann, "Die literarische Analyse.", 258, cited by A. Schoors, *I Am God Your Saviour.*, 5.

INTRODUCTION TO ISAIAH 40-55

The very important contribution to the form-critical analysis of Deutero Isaiah came from J. Begrich.[35] He underlines the necessity of making out the literary units. After having listed the literary units and enumerated the literary types of DI, he proceeds to a detailed analysis. He distinguished 70 units in DI.[36] The types most frequently attested are the oracle of salvation or oracle of grant, such as it was given in the cult after the lament and before the assertion of confidence.[37] Next to the oracle of salvation, he studies the trial speech (*Gerichtsrede*). In a brief outline of Israelite lawsuit, Begrich gives the different trial speeches and their setting. Another category he identified was 'disputations.' The aim of a disputation consists in convincing somebody and in invalidating his objections. This genre, as well as the foregoing one, is a prophetic imitation of living forms of speech taken from daily life.[38]

Even in recent studies of Isaiah 40-55, the form-critical approach prevails. Antoon Schoors's study is a good example of the form-critical approach of DI.[39] Other major works include those by C. Westermann, R. Melugin, and R. N. Whybray.[40]

---

[35] J. Begrich, *Studien zu Deuterojesaja*, BWANT 77 (Stuttgart: Kohlhammer, 1938).

[36] Different scholars follow different point of view regarding the demarcation of the unit. For the delimitation of units by different form-critics, see A. Schoors, *I Am God Your Saviour*, 30-31.

[37] See A. Schoors, *I Am God Your Saviour*, 20.

[38] A. Schoors, *I Am God Your Saviour*, 22.

[39] A. Schoors, *I Am God Your Saviour: A Form Critical Study of the Main Genres in Is XL-LV* (1973).

[40] Claus Westermann, *Isaiah 40-66: A Commentary* (OTL, Philadelphia: Westminster) and "Sprache und Struktur der Prophetie Deuterojesajas," in *Forschung am Alten Testament: Gesammelte Studien*. TBü 24 (Munich: Kaiser, 1964); R. E. Melugin, *The Formation of Isaiah 40-55*, BZAW 141 (Berlin: de Gruyter, 1976); R. N. Whybray, *Isaiah 40-66* (NCBC; London: Marshall, Morgan & Scott / Grand Rapids: Eerdmans, 1981)

The principal types have been enumerated as the oracle of salvation and the proclamation of salvation, disputation and trial speech, hymn and thanksgiving psalm.[41] Scholars generally accept that a valuable interpretation is difficult, if not impossible, without a precise knowledge of the genre. However, DI uses these genres with a considerable freedom.

However, the form-critical questions about the "smallest unit" and its *Sitz im Leben* alone will not help us to get into the fuller implication of DI's creation theology. There is an integrating major or "umbrella" genre, which can absorb the different genres to which the smaller units belong. Westermann, for example, wrote: "Isaiah 40-55 is not a collection of single fragments belonging in each given case to different speech genres; it is a meaningful whole which has grown up out of these speech forms."[42] In the case of such composite genre too, the question about the text's literary structure and function must be set in a social context, in order to understand DI's creation theology.

3. Structure

The structure of a text can provide important clues to the meaning, especially when they are presented in the traditional forms of expression. However, the identification of structure of DI is not an easy task. One reason for this is they underwent several redactions and therefore often underwent restructurings.

In its present form, these chapters constitute a unity in which the beginning and the end interlink. The prologue in 40:1-11 affirms that the divine word articulated in what follows will come true, and the epilogue repeats this promise of its infallible realization. The language also shows correspondences.

However, some commentators think that chapters 40-48, which are bracketed with their own conclusive passage (48:20-22), form

---

[41] Joseph Blenkinsopp, *Isaiah 40-55...*, 65. A Schoors, *I Am God Your Saviour*, 29.
[42] C. Westermann, *Sprache und Struktur der Prophetie Deuterojesesaja*, 167.

a separate section, which is quite different in theme and tone from 49-55, in which we hear no more about Cyrus and the fall of Babylon, and no more satire is directed against foreign deities and their devotees.[43] In 40-48, the focus is on Jacob/Israel, while in 49-55 Jerusalem/Zion is in the foreground. The usage of the term עֶבֶד (servant) also is significantly different in the two sections. With the exception of 42:1-4, use of עֶבֶד in 40-48, whether singular or plural, always refers to the people, or at any rate, never to an individual (41:8-9; 42:19; 43:8-10; 44:1-2, 21, 26; 45:4; 48:20), where as in 49-55 it is generally acknowledged that an individual figure is indicated (49:1-6; 50:4-11; 52:13-53:12).[44]

Based on the marked contrast between these two parts, some commentators concluded that the two sections must have come from distinct authors.[45] Carol Stuhlmueller explained the distinction in terms of stages in the prophetic career.[46] Joseph Blenkinsopp considers this division as the result of different stages of redaction.[47] Several of the recent commentators have noticed the structural significance of 52:11-12 but have drawn different conclusions from it. Plamondon considers 40:12-52:12 as a unit presenting four successive stages in the restoration of Israel.[48] Antti Laato finds five subsections in 40:3-52:12.[49]

However, a number of scholars think that Chapters 40 and 55 form a kind of framework for the book of Deutero Isaiah.[50] According to Westermann, 'chapters 40-55 show such clear sign

---

[43] See J. Blenkinsopp, *Isaiah 40-55*, 59.

[44] J. Blenkinsopp, *Isaiah 40-55*, 60.

[45] See Thomas K. Cheyne, *The Prophecies of Isaiah*, vol.2 (London: Kegan Paul, Trench, 1882), 178.

[46] See Carol Stuhlmueller, "Deutero-Isaiah (Chaps.40-55): Major Transitions in the Prophet's Theology and in Contemporary Scholarship," *CBQ* 42, (1980), 1-29.

[47] See J. Blenkinsopp, *Isaiah.*, 61.

[48] P.-H. Plamondon, "Sur lechemin du salut avec le IIe Isaie," *NRTh* 104 (1982)241-66, cited by Joseph Blenkinsopp, *Isaiah*, 61.

[49] See Antti Laato, "The Composition of Isaiah 40-55," *JBL* 109 (1990), 207-28.

[50] See for example, C. Westermann, *Isaiah*, 28; Muilenburg, *Isaiah*, 385.

of a deliberate, orderly arrangement. The whole is set within the framework of a prologue (40:1-11) and epilogue (55:6-11), which are in turn related in content.'[51] Chapter 40 announces the theme: comfort for Israel as God's people. The new exodus is promised, and it is with this promise that chapter 55 then ends (vv. 12-13). The decisive point is the reliability of the divine Word of God communicated through the prophet. Here 40:8 at the beginning corresponds to 55:11 at the end. The entire final chapter (55:1-13) was meant as a summary of the message of chapters 40-54. The division into two or more sections is confusing. Nevertheless, as C. R. North has rightly pointed out, 'following the prelude the theme is that Yahweh as Creator; next Yahweh as Lord of history; and finally, Yahweh as Redeemer of Israel and Zion' shows a broad continuity in the thinking of the prophet.[52]

4. Rhetorical Criticism

Rhetoric is the art of persuading by the effective communication of a message in a particular situation. It involves developing an argument that articulates the speaker's intention and does so by deploying strategies for engaging the interest and emotions of the speaker's public and persuading them to accept the message.[53] It was James Muilenburg, who used rhetorical analysis extensively in the commentary on Deutero-Isaiah.[54] Another notable contribution to the rhetorical study of DI came from Yehoshua Gitay.[55] He described the system as exploring the act of communication among the speaker, speech, and the audience. Hence, he proposed that DI made a public address to the Jewish exiles in Babylon, seeking to persuade them of divine activity on the international scene and so alter their religious attitude. To accomplish this goal, the prophet used various arguments and

---

[51] See C. Westermannn, *Isaiah* , 28.
[52] See C. R. North, *The Second Isaiah: Introduction, Translation and Commentary to Chapters XL-LV* (Oxford: The Clarendon Press, 1964), 9.
[53] Joseph Blenkinsopp, *Isaiah 40-55*, 61.
[54] James Muilenburg, *Isaiah*, 381-773.
[55] Yehoshua Gitay, *Prophecy and Persuasion: A Study of Isaiah 40-48* (Bonn: Linguistica Biblica, 1981).

employed numerous stylistic devices. Of the three kinds of persuasive discourses,[56] the judicial best characterized his speech.

DI begins his rhetoric by representing himself and his associates as authorized to address his public audience, and the source of authorization is indicated right from the beginning ("says your God," Isaiah 40:1). And also at the very outset, he makes it clear that his message is about a new intervention of the God of Israel, one leading to a reversal of fortune for a beaten and dispirited people (40:9-11). In keeping with the established rhetorical procedures in using the argument from authority, the speaker goes on to establish the credentials of the one authorizing and does so by claiming for Yahweh a preeminent and an incomparable status vis-à-vis other deities, in the first place as the creator of the world (40:12-26).[57] DI asks several rhetorical questions to call the attention of the exiles to the Creator and His creative power.

5.4. Socio-Historical Setting of Isaiah 40-55

It has been increasingly recognized that all literature is to a large extent a reflection of the period in which it was written, and has been influenced by the circumstances in which the authors lived. In the Old Testament, this is particularly true of the words of the prophets, who were not primarily authors in a purely literary sense, but men who believed themselves to have been called to proclaim urgent messages to their contemporaries. Therefore, in

---

[56] Phyllis Trible describes three kinds of rhetoric: judicial rhetoric, deliberative rhetoric and demonstrative rhetoric. Judicial rhetoric, focused on justice, and belonged to the law court. Through artful words, the speaker sought to persuade the audience to make a right decision about the past events. Deliberative rhetoric, focused on expediency, belonged to public assembly. Through artful words, the speaker sought to persuade the audience about future events. Demonstrative rhetoric, focused on adulation, and belonged to public ceremony. Through artful words, the speaker sought to move the audience to praise individuals in the present. See Phyllis Trible, *Rhetorical Criticism: Context, Method, and the Book of Jonah* (Minneapolis: Fortress Press, 1994), 8.

[57] See Joseph Blenkinsopp, *Isaiah 40-55*, 62.

studying the prophetic books, it is particularly important to set them, as far as possible, against their socio-historical context.

As we have already discussed, the socio-historical settings of exile in detail is set in chapter 4. Here we review only the main features of the sociological situation in which DI or his community functioned.

The downfall of the state of Judah with the end of monarchy and the destruction of the temple in Jerusalem left behind a social torso, which one could hardly still call Israel. Several thousands of Judeans were deported to Babylon in several stages. Many others fled to Egypt and probably to other countries also. The Babylonian exile was thus a severe crisis. Those who were deported to Babylon experienced a deep social uprooting. They had lost not only their homes but also their land and social status, which was usually influential. They had been torn away from their clans or even families and were deprived of the solidarity provided by their kinsfolk. They had thereby lost not only their prominent positions but also their property. Moreover, their own people in Judah had written them off.

By human standards, this dispersed people 'without a shepherd' i.e., without a king, could not survive. They could really only go under and lose itself in the giant empire of the Babylonians, as those settled by the Assyrians in their empire after the conquest of Samaria. Fortunately, this did not happen in the case of Judeans exiles. They could preserve their identity at least in part. This came about mainly because they were settled together (Ezk 3:15). This fact of living together was decisive, since experience shows that those emigrants who are forcibly deported like to maintain protected groups, which, when they exceed a certain critical mass, have chances of preserving their culture over a long period.[58]

---

[58] Erhard S. Gerstenberger, *Theologies in the Old Testament*, translated by John Bowden (Minneapolis: Fortress Press, 2002), 208.

INTRODUCTION TO ISAIAH 40-55

As we noted above in chapter 4, the elders appear as leaders of the group of exiles.[59] Elders were at this time a permanent institution in the Orient.[60] They were responsible for directing the group and judging between its members in case of conflict. Also they were responsible for representing the people before the pagan authorities. Due to the lack of national organization, their role once again becomes prominent. Thus, the old village self-administration, which was customary in Palestine, came to the fore, but now was limited from above by the Babylonian imperial administration.

Along with the civil authority of the elders, a spiritual leadership also was formed, composed of men of priestly origin and the guild of scribes. This elite stratum succeeded in gathering the traditions of the people together and developing them in written form, which hitherto had been predominantly oral.[61] Thus, as a religious community in the Babylonian exile, they had ample opportunities to focus on their God in the new environment.

Despite all the disappointments, priests and other functionaries of the monarchy maintained their orientation towards Yahweh, which created an identity in the upheaval of the turbulent times. That means, while the national, monarchial level of society had collapsed under the supervision of the mighty Babylonian empire, this could not be regained. So, for the newly arising communities, which sociologically were more like family clans, belief in Yahweh took on a fundamental significance and provided meaning in this context.

---

[59] See Jer.29:1, where the elders are named before the priest and prophets; Ezk. 8:1 and 14:1, where elders of Israel gather together in the house of the prophet and seat themselves before him.

[60] Antonin Causse, "From an Ethnic Group to a Religious Community: The Sociological Problem of Judaism," in *Community, Identity and Ideology: Social Scienc Approaches to the Hebrew Bible*, edited by Charles E. Carter and Carol L. Meyers (Indiana: Eisenbrauns, 1996), 98.

[61] E. S. Gerstenberger, *Theologies in the Old Testament*, 209.

A sociological analysis of this exilic community needs to consider three factors. First, *Socio-economic factors*: Socio-economic factors are the organization of work and the distribution of its products between productive workers and those who enjoy the profits. The "social rootlessness"[62] of the exiles made them dependable on their foreign lords for all their needs. Daniel L. Smith-Christopher highlights a number of details in an inscription purporting to cite Nebuchadnezzar's boasts of the "the whole of race, people from far place, whom Marduk my Lord delivered me- I forced them to work on the building of Etemenanki- I imposed on them the brick-basket..." (See above chapter 4). This is possibly true, as contemporary assessments of the exile do not simply dismiss this imagery as purely metaphorical with no historical basis. Instead, it should be considered as an accurate description of the condition of exiles. The "poor and needy" in Isa 41:17 also need to be considered as a portrayal of the socio-economic condition of the exiles. The social rootlessness thus correlated the socio-economic stress the exiles underwent during their Babylonian exile. This socio-economic factor had a crucial role in formulating the life and thinking of the exilic community, especially in their thinking on creation and worldview. The evolution of their creation theology could be viewed as a definite reaction to the state of rootlessness they experienced in Babylon. In their understanding within the context they were living in, the land, which is an important ingredient for supporting life, is the creation of Israel's God. Thus, the theology of creation indicates the socio-economic tension behind its formulation.

Secondly, *socio-political factors*: The socio-political factors include the structure of the government in Babylon and its treatment of the exiles: imposing its will and overcoming the opposition of the exiles by force. We do not have any direct evidence of the Babylonian treatment of deportees. Nevertheless, the power of the Babylonian empire was clearly a part of everyday

---

[62] This phrase is taken from Gerd Theissen's *Sociology of Early Palestinian Christianity*, translated by John Bowden (Philadelphia: Fortress Press, 1978), 33.

life of the exiles. Some scholars presume the condition of exiles as slaves.[63] We do not have any direct evidence to argue that the Jews were 'slaves' in Babylon. However, the dismissive statement that the Jews were not slaves can be a hasty generalization. In his book, *Slavery and Social Death*, Patterson while making a symbolic analysis of slavery reviews the structure of slave relationship using data from over forty different slave systems from all over the world and in different periods. Common to all is the significance of symbolic institutions:

> The symbolic instruments may be seen as the cultural counterpart to the physical instruments used to control the slave's body. In much the same way that ...whips were fashioned from different materials, the symbolic whips of slavery were woven from many areas of culture. Masters all over the world used the special rituals of enslavement upon first acquiring slaves: the symbolism of naming, of clothing, of hairstyle, of language, and of body markers. And they used, especially in the more advanced slave systems, the sacred symbols of religion.[64]

Patterson's symbolic analysis shows that the economy is not the only or the predominating factor. According to Patterson, slavery is, in essence, removal of identity and "social death."[65] Indeed, we have important hints that the exiles did face symbolic aspects of slavery in Babylon.

The collective conscience and the feeling of social unity have been gravely weakened by the fact that the exiles lacked a territorial base and had been tossed about and scattered by political crisis. The socio-political factors, which caused a tension between

---

[63] It is often suggested in studies of Babylonian Exile that the exiles were not slaves. This argument is usually accompanied by reference of late biblical texts that mention economically prosperous Jews who prefer to stay in Babylon because of their success in Babylonian life or the generous contribution of exiles to the temple construction (Ezra 2:68-69). However, recent studies on 'slavery' made many scholars to reassess the condition of the Babylonian exile. See Daniel L. Smith, *The Religion of the Landless*, 38-41.

[64] Orlando Patterson, *Slavery and Social Death* (Cambridge: Mass, 1982), 8, cited by Daniel L. Smith, *The Religion of the Landless...*, 40.

[65] Daniel Smith, *The Religion of the Landless...*, 40.

the structure of the government and the exilic community, added the longing for the absolute rule of Yahweh as the sole creator of whole universe.

Thirdly, *socio-cultural factors*: The socio-cultural factors include all values, norms and traditions that give a group self-awareness and identity. Since the identity and the survival of the exiles in Babylon were threatened, they were responsible for many innovative religious and ritual safeguards such as Sabbath, circumcision, dietary laws etc. (chapter 4). These innovations, coupled with the impressive theological structures created by the DI community, may have given rise to self-assurance.

5.5. Domicile of Deutero Isaiah

The place where these chapters were written cannot be determined with certainty. Yet the Babylonian location for the author of Isaiah 40-55 still continue to be a default position in the commentary traditions since the late eighteenth century. Perhaps one of the early commentators who suggested the Babylonian setting of Deutero Isaiah was de Wette.[66] He argued that the political conditions reflected in this part of the book of Isaiah reveal that they did take place in Babylon.

Another scholar favoring Babylonian background for Deutero Isaiah was Knobel.[67] Knobel believed that DI most probably lived in Babylon. He built his assumption on the prophet's apparent knowledge of the conditions of the exiles, a knowledge which could only be available to someone who lived among the exiles himself (Isa 56:9ff; 57:3ff; 58:2ff; 65:3f). Knobel's second argument is that DI refers to the ill-treatment in a way, which obviously shows that it was brought upon him by the exiles themselves (Isa 50:4-5).

---

[66] W. M. L. de Wette, *Lehrbuch der historisch- kritischen Einleitung* 1. T. Berlin (1833), 261.
[67] A. Knobel, *Der Prophetismus der Hebräer*. Zweiter Theil. (Breslau, 1837), 347.

INTRODUCTION TO ISAIAH 40-55

Kuenen also believed that DI must have lived in Babylon. He came to this conclusion because of the prophet's intimate knowledge of the details of life among the exiles in Babylon.[68] Kuenen finds support for his assumption above all in the following texts: Isa 40:27; 45:9-10; 46:6-7; 49:24; 56:3ff; 57:5ff; 58:2ff; 62:6-7; 65:4ff; and 66:1-5.

With Dillmann we are introduced to a whole series of reasons in favour of the Babylonian setting of DI.[69] Dillmann's major argument is the prophet's knowledge of the Babylonian circumstances and the conditions of the exiles. DI's knowledge of Babylonian life, according to Dillmann, is clearly to be seen from Isa 43:14; 46:1ff; and 47, as well as from the descriptions of the production of statues in 40:19f; 41:6f 44:9ff; and 46:6f. It is also obvious, according to Dillmann, that the author of Isa 40-55 is quite familiar with Palestinian conditions. Thus he refers to Jerusalem (40:9; 44:26), the cities of Judah and Lebanon (40:16), and to cedar, cypress, acacia, and wild olive trees (41:19; 55:13). All this, however, is no more than what one could expect from a pious patriot, whose thoughts and minds were always contemplating on Zion.

However, some critical scholars do not assume a Babylonian setting for DI. Duhm, for example, suggests Phoenicia or the region of the Lebanon, probably on the ground of Isaiah 40:16, as the location of DI. Ewald, Marti, and Hölscher also opposed the Babylonian setting of DI.[70]

Perhaps the most important assault against Babylonian domicile of DI came from Hans Barstad.[71] Barstad thinks that the notion of the Babylonian background of DI is a fundamental error. He attributes the dominance of the Babylonian setting to two main

---

[68] A. Kuenen, *Historisch- kritisch onderzoek*. Tweede deel. (Leiden, 1863), 108.
[69] A. Dillmann, *Der Prophet Jesaja*. (Leipzig, 1890), 355- 356.
[70] See J. Muilenburg, Isaiah: Chapters 40-66, 397.
[71] Hans M. Barstad, *The Babylonian Captivity of the Book of Isaiah: "Exilic" Judah and the Provenance of Isaiah 40-55* (Oslo: Novus forlag, 1997).

factors: scholars believed they had to assert such a setting to prove the Deutero-Isaian thesis; they did not sufficiently take into account the poetic and metaphoric language of the prophet. His statement of the latter factor is worth quoting:

> the moment one starts to interpret the different poetic holy war texts of Isa 40-55 literally, one puts a false construction on them. Just as the address to Zion/Jerusalem to wake up and put on garments in 52:1 should not be taken literally, so the appeal to go out in 52:11 does not refer to any literal going out of the exiles from Babylonia. The allusion is rather to the going out from Jerusalem in holy war (cf. 52:1-2; 52:7-8, and 52:11-12 all of which belong together) in a strictly *metaphorical* way (Italics in the original).[72]

Barstad shows convincingly that the case for a Babylonian setting is weak. But his reservation on the method of showing the weakness of one argument over others does not necessarily prove the competing argument.

According to Kalus Baltzer, 'Jerusalem is most probably the place where DI's work was composed.' He thinks, if the place was Babylon, it is surprising that so little is said about Babylon's concrete situation, and there is so little local color in the text.[73] Moreover, according to Baltzer, 'the author seems to be familiar with Jerusalem's geographical position and incorporates it into his text.[74] But his argument based on DI's familiarity with Jerusalem's geographical position is not valid, because he was taken from Jerusalem.

Several passages give us an impression that the prophet talks about Babylon from a distance (43:14; 48:20; 52:11). This is also not a valid argument for a non-Babylonian home of the author. The perspective of exile in Babylon as a foreign territory and Jerusalem as the spiritual centre may be the reason for such expression.

---

[72] Hans M. Barstad, *The Babylonian Captivity of the Book of Isaiah*, 71.
[73] Klaus Baltzer, *Deutero Isaiah*, 23.
[74] Klaus Baltzer, *Deutero Isaiah*, 24.

INTRODUCTION TO ISAIAH 40-55

Sellin very strongly supports the Babylonian domicile. He presents us with a series of arguments in support of a Babylonian setting of DI. In support of his argument Sellin is able to point to DI's intimate knowledge of events in Babylon in the year 538 B.C. (with reference to Isa 43:14), to his knowledge of Babylonian religion and astrology (with references to Isa 40:19f; 41:6f.; 44:9ff.; 46:1; 47:2f), but above all to the prophet's language, which shows such a strong Babylonian influence that not only did its user live in Babylon, but he must even have been born and raised there.[75]

It is true, as Koole has suggested, 'the place where these chapters were written cannot be determined with certainty.'[76] However, the evidences for a Babylonian setting of Isa 40-55 are several. The exiles are mentioned explicitly in Isa 43:14; 47:1 and 48:14, 20. The prophet often addresses himself directly to the exiles: 40:1, 27f; 41:8-10, 12-16; 43:1ff, 10; 44:8; 46:3, 12; 48:1ff, 20; 51:1ff; 52:1ff, 12. The prophet is also acquainted with the approaching conquest of Babylon by Cyrus (41:2-4, 25; 44:28; 45:1-4,13; 46:11), and he never gets tired of describing the production of idol statues, in order to warn the exiles from being allured to worship deities other than Yahweh (40:19f; 41:7, 19; 42:17; 44:9-17, 19f; 46:6f). Also the producers of idol statues are addressed directly by the prophet (40:18, 25). Further, he is acquainted with Babylonian astrology (47:13), and he challenges the gods of Babylon to trials (40:21, 41:2f, 43:9). In turn, the very fact that Babylon is mentioned in several passages is especially important (See Isa 43:14 Ch 47 etc). As Whybray has pointed out, 'his familiarity with the Babylonian scene establishes beyond doubt that he was one of the exiles in Babylon.[77]

The theological view of DI also betrays to the Babylonian setting. It is felt that, the theology of creation and the notion of monotheism etc., are possible only in a non-Palestinian setting. In

---

[75] E. Sellin, *Einleitung in dsa Alte Testament*. 3 neu bearb. (Aufl., 1920), 96.
[76] Jan L. Koole, *Isaiah Part III* (Kampen-The Netherlands: Kok Pharos Publishing House, 1997), 13.
[77] R. N. Whybray, *The Second Isaiah*, 8.

fact, DI's theological views are more appropriate to the Babylonian setting.

5.6. The Community of Deutero-Isaiah.

The literary section, which is preserved in the chapters 40-55 of the book of Isaiah, is anonymous and without the usual introduction[78] about the author or the time in which he carried out his work. The term "Deutero- Isaiah" clearly shows the artificiality given to the text. Who lies behind that designation? Is it a single person or a community?

The Book of Deutero-Isaiah is remarkably ambiguous. However, as Robert R. Wilson has pointed out, using the evidence of the texts themselves, the community of Deutero-Isaiah can be reconstructed with reasonable clarity, and this reconstruction in turn helps us to read in a more sophisticated way the text that the community treasured.[79] Already, this hypothesis was put forward by Michel that there is not a single person but a whole 'prophetic school' behind this book.[80] In this connection, Rainer Albertz has pointed out: 'certainly in my view one can still talk of a prophet of salvation, Deutero-Isaiah, who shapes the quite distinctive poetic and emphatic language of the book, but he did not stand alone; he was the head of a group, which discussed the content of his message with him, reflected on its theological presuppositions and consequences internally, and continued writing into the post-exilic period.'[81]

Of course, it is hard to determine such a group, which raised its voice during the last days of the exiles, before the downfall of the Babylonian empire in 539. However, as we have noted above,

---

[78] For the usual introduction, see Isa 1:1, Amos 1:1; Jer. 1:1; Ezk1:1; Hos 1:1 etc

[79] Robert R. Wilson, "The Community of the Second Isaiah," in *Reading and Preaching the Book of Isaiah*, edited by Christopher R. Seitz (Philadelphia: Fortress Press, 1988), 69.

[80] D. Michel, "Deuterojesaja," *Theologische Realenzyklopädie* 8 (1981), 527, cited by Rainer Alberts, *A History of Israelite Religion*, 414.

[81] Rainer Albertz, *A History of Israelite Religion*, 414.

INTRODUCTION TO ISAIAH 40-55

there are indications that it was a group, rather than an individual, who was called to function as God's agent of the new revelation. The very beginning of the portion of this book begins with such an indication:

> Comfort ye O comfort (נַחֲמוּ נַחֲמוּ) my people
>   says your God.
> Speak "(דַּבְּרוּ) tenderly to Jerusalem,
>   and cry (קִרְאוּ) to her
> that she has served her term .... (Isa 40:1-2)

Here, the imperatives "comfort" (נַחֲמוּ), "speak"(דַּבְּרוּ) and "cry" (קִרְאוּ) are not singular imperatives and therefore cannot be addressed to an individual prophet. Rather they are plural imperatives and addressed to an unidentified group, which is to be the agent of God's salvation. [82] Who are the members of this group? Some commentators interpret it as a heavenly council, God's advisory committee made up of lesser deities that do God's will.[83] But this cannot be correct because DI's strong monotheistic approach does not allow any room for such a council (See 40:13-14). It is also unlikely to think that God is addressing the entire people of Israel, given the fact that this group is to be the agent of salvation for all of Israel. We are therefore forced to conclude that God is speaking to a particular group, and it makes sense to assume that God is addressing the disciple of Second Isaiah, the group that treasured these oracles and saw itself playing an important role in realizing the prophecies that the book contains.[84]

Wilson examines the Fourth Servant Song (Isa 52:13-53:12) and finds evidence for the existence of a community. Because of the traditional Christological interpretation of this passage, Wilson says, 'it has sometimes not been noticed that for six verses in the

---

[82] See Robert R. Wilson, "The Community of the Second Isaiah," 54.

[83] F. M. Cross suggested that the words are directed to members of a supposed divine council, such as appears in 1 Kgs. 22:19-21; Job 1:6; Dan.7:9. See his, "The Council of Yahweh in Second Isaiah," *JNES* 12 (1953), 74-77. Some commentators interpret this group as the heavenly council (Jer.23:18), i.e., God's advisory committee made up of lesser deities that do God's will.

[84] Robert R. Wilson, "The Community of the Second Isaiah," 54.

middle of the song (53:1-6), the text takes the form of a confession in which a group admits that it did not understand the meaning of the servant's suffering: 'Who has believed what *we* have heard? ...surely he has borne *our* grief and carried *our* sorrows.'[85] Usage of these plural pronouns in this Servant Song also clearly indicates the presence of the prophet's community. So, in Isaiah 40-55, DI is not an individual prophet who is dealing with the issues of the exile, rather DI is a community reflecting the exilic problems collectively.

Both of the above passages point to a community who struggled with DI in their task of communicating their distinctive message to the exiles. Therefore, if we want to understand the words of the prophet, we must understand something of the community of DI who discussed the issues with DI and who collected and passed on those words to us. However, the task of reconstructing the community is not an easy one. DI does not say anything explicitly about such a community. Neither do we have any extra biblical evidence. However, the political and religious conditions during the time of DI can provide a helpful background against which to examine the book in order to see what clues it might provide about the nature of the prophet's community.

Based on the prophet's familiarity with the Psalms, Westermann connected this community with temple-singers,[86] but probably also the cult prophets. The sovereign way in which it deals with all the important religious traditions[87] suggest a profound theological education; the prominent place with the Zion tradition (40:2, 9-11; 41:27; 44:26, 28; 46:13) occupies in its thought further points to the circle of those who formerly served in the Jerusalem temple.[88] In short, by 'Deutero Isaiah' we understand

---

[85] Robert R. Wilson, "The Community of the Second Isaiah," 55.

[86] C. Westermann, *Isaiah*, 8.

[87] This community knows the traditions of creation of the world (40:22, 26, 28; 44:24; 45:6 etc.) and of the human being (42:5; 43:1; 45:12; 49:5. etc.), of the primeval history (51:9f; 54:9), the Patriarchal history (41:8f; 43:27; 51:1f), the Exodus (43:16f; 51:9f; 52:12).

[88] Rainer Albertz, *A History of Israelite Religion*, 415.

a community of theologians gathered around a master who came from circles of descendants of the temple singers and cult prophets of the Jerusalem temple with their nationalistic attitude.[89]

It is possible to assume that this community was inspired to bring about this prophetic message by its study of scripture. Their meditation on the traditions of hymns helped them to see Yahweh as the sole creator and the lord of the world history. These reflections on the traditions had probably given this community a surprising insight into the plan of Yahweh behind the rise of the Persian king Cyrus and a different, and a radical worldview at that.

Thus, the *structure of the DI community* was determined by the interaction of three factors: (1) their exilic condition, (2) their devotion to the study of old traditions, (3) and their unique way of interpretation of the old traditions on the basis of the current political scenario.

The Social Location of the Community

According to Wilson, the literature produced by the Deutero-Isaiah community suggests two important features of the group's location within the social spectrum of the Babylonian exile.[90] First, the group clearly saw itself as a minority within the exilic community. An indication of this minority status can be seen in the tone of the book, which makes heavy use of the language of exhortation. The reader gets the clear sense that the group is trying to convince its audience of a theological and political position that most of the exiles do not accept. The rhetoric of persuasion permeates the literature, a fact that suggests that the DI community was arguing for a minority point of view.[91]

Another indication of the community's minority status can be seen in the references to persecution that appear periodically in

---

[89] Rainer Albertz, *A History of Israelite Religion*, 415.
[90] R. R. Wilson, "The Community of the Second Isaiah," 61.
[91] R. R. Wilson, "The Community of the Second Isaiah," 62.

the book. These references to persecution are usually taken to be allusions to oppression by the Babylonians. But Wilson assumes that these references are related to the friction caused by the community's unsuccessful attempts to convince other exiles of its description of the way that God intends to bring about a return to the land.[92]

Community of DI as a Prophetic Movement

Following this assumption, one could say that the DI community as a prophetic movement promised a miraculous divine intervention in Israel's favor. The redemption from Babylonian exile is described in terms of God's past act of salvation of the Exodus tradition. Thus, the main task of this community was to prophesy deliverance from the Babylonian exile.

As mentioned earlier, this group was inspired to bring forth its prophetic message by its study of scripture. The tradition of hymns taught them that Yahweh continues as the Lord of world history, who humbles the mighty and exalts the lowly (Isa 40:23, 29; cf. e.g. I Sam. 2:4-8). From their study of the scripture, they learn that Yahweh rules world history according to a mysterious plan (Isa 5:19; 8:10; 14:24, 26, 27; 29:15; 30:1), giving his people periods of judgement and salvation (6:11; 8:17f.; 14:24-26), and even using foreign powers to implement his plan (5:25ff.; 10). Sensitized by this prior theological knowledge, in its reflections on where the hand of God could be recognized in its time, the group was inspired to the surprising insight that Yahweh was at work in the spectacularly victorious course of the Persian king Cyrus.[93] This group was convinced that Yahweh had raised Cyrus to execute his plan for the sake of Israel, so that he could liberate his people from captivity in Babylon and rebuild Jerusalem. With this conviction, the prophetic community of DI preached its message to the fellow exiles.

---

[92] R. R. Wilson, "The Community of the Second Isaiah," 62.
[93] Rainer Albertz, *A History of Israelite Religion*..., 415.

However, the interpretation of the tradition by the community of DI was not acceptable to their fellow exiles. Yahweh might have used foreign kings for his act of judgement upon his people (Isa 10:5ff; Jer. 27:6). But the choice of a foreign king as his "anointed" to save Israel had no support in the tradition. According to the Jerusalem kingship theology, only a member from the Davidic dynasty could do this. Thus, the message of the DI community was not only politically incredible but also theologically highly offensive.[94] Thus, the community's view about the Persian king, Cyrus as God's anointed drew criticism from other exiles. Although other exiles would eventually come to accept this point of view (cf. Ezra 7:25-26; Neh 6:1-19), it was controversial at a time when nationalist hopes were still strongly held by many of the exiles.

Community of DI as a Resistance Movement

It is seen however that, the community of DI and the other Israel in exile share the same traditions and same faith. Both were part of the same social system. Yet they stand in opposition and in tension because of their divergent perception of reality. The idea of being rescued by a Gentile king must have been radical enough to evoke serious resistance (see 45:9-13 in response to such resistance). The DI community's worldview arises from an alternative perception of reality. Therefore, they describe other exiles as blind and deaf people who want to neither see the signs of the time nor hear the word of God, which interpret them (42:7, 16, 18-20, 23; 43:8). Because of their unprecedented perception of reality, they were persecuted by their fellow Israelites as well as by their Babylonian lords. In this sense, the community of DI was the 'exiles among the exiles.'[95]

Thus, the Deutero Isaianic community considered itself as a special group, which God had set apart from the rest of exiles for

---

[94] Rainer Albertz, *A History of Israelite Religion*, 416.
[95] In the Servant Song, the 'servant' sometimes is considered as 'the servant among the servants.'

a particular task. They considered themselves as the group 'who know righteousness' of God and as the 'people who have Yahweh's law in their hearts' (Isa 51:7). In contrast, their persecutors are described as those 'who had forgotten Yahweh, their Maker' (Isa 51:13). This claim from the DI community obviously evoked opposition from the other exilic group. However, in the face of this opposition, the DI community is exhorted not be discouraged by persecution because their enemies are transitory, even if they pose themselves as strong, since God's salvation is eternal. (Isa 51:7-8).

As a resistance movement, the members of the DI community also set themselves against the Babylonian hegemony. It is evident in their criticism about the Babylonian gods (see Isa 46:1-2). Many commentators think that this was intended to be a specific prediction of the fall of Babylon.[96] They proclaimed the sole rule of Yahweh and his absolute sovereignty. Therefore, when other exiles were attracted to the Babylonian cult, in view of its splendor, the DI community resists it strongly.

Community of DI and Priestly Tradition

Another feature of the DI community was its strong link with the priestly tradition.[97] Scholars have often noted the theological links between DI and the priestly layers of the Pentateuch. Both sources share similar traditions about creation, the period of ancestors and the Exodus. And both sources use the same vocabulary and tend to use the same terms to discuss technical and theological issues. Both share the belief that God dwells in Israel in the form of the divine glory (כבוד).[98]

---

[96] See John S. Oswalt, *The Book of Isaiah. Chapters 40-66*. (Grand Rapid. Michigan: Wm. B. Eerdmans Publishing Company, 1998), 228.

[97] For a detailed discussion of the linguistic and theological links between Deutero Isaiah and Priestly tradition, see Carroll Stuhlmueller, *Creative Redemption in Deutero-Isaiah* (Rome: Biblical Institute Press, 1970), esp. pages 96-97; 156-57.

[98] For a discussion of this motif, see C. Stuhlmueller, *Creative Redemption*, 95-98.

DI's extensive use of the literary form of 'salvation oracle' also point towards its connection with priestly tradition. This type of oracle is usually thought to have been used in Israel's cult, where it was delivered by a priest to worshipers who had brought a complaint or a request to the temple. After the worshiper presented the complaint, the priest would respond with a salvation oracle, assuring the sufferer that God would hear the complaint and grant relief.[99]

Moreover, the community of DI shared with the priestly tradition a deep concern for the cultic purity of the restored Jerusalem and the people who would be allowed to enter it.[100] This concern, to which the Priestly writer and Ezekiel also devote much attention, can be seen most clearly in the oracle directed to Zion:

> Awake, awake,
> put on your strength, O Zion!
> put on your beautiful garments,
> O Jerusalem, the holy city;
> for the uncircumcised and the unclean
> shall enter you no more. (Isa 52:1)
> ....
> Depart, depart, go out from there!
> Touch no unclean thing;
> go out from the midst of it,
> purify yourselves,
> you who carry the vessels of the Lord. (Isa 52:11)

The exilic Israel is exhorted to leave Babylon and return to Jerusalem as a purified community. Only as a purified community, its members become eligible to carry the temple vessels, which were taken from Jerusalem by the Babylonians. These concerns

---

[99] C. Stuhlmueller, *Creative Redemption*, 19-28.
[100] R. R. Wilson, "The Community of the Second Isaiah," 65.

for cultic purity and for the sanctity of Jerusalem show that they belonged to the priestly group. However, as Wilson has pointed out, there were many priestly groups in the exilic and post-exilic period with the concern for cultic purity. (cf. Ezk 40-48; Zech. 14:20-21). And these groups often differed in their views in terms of the degree of purity which was to be maintained. Therefore, it is impossible to identify with any certainty the specific priestly group to which members of the DI community belonged. According to Wilson, it may be that the community represented some branch of the Aaronide priesthood, but further research must be done on this question before any conclusions can be reached.[101]

Although DI provides only a few hints about the social location of the community that produced these oracles, the book is much more explicit about the religious and political programme of the community. The community advocated a return to Zion and a restoration of life in the land. While other exiles think that such a return was impossible or unnecessary, the DI community argued that God required such a return and that God was powerful enough to make such return a reality. It was affirmed thereby that, the pagan deities or rulers cannot thwart Yahweh's decision to act on behalf of his people in exile. As Yahweh is the Creator, even natural forces of the cosmos as well as the world rulers, are at his disposal in bringing out his plan. However, limiting their programme to the 'return to the homeland' will be an imperfect understanding of the community. As the socio-historical analysis of the passages show an integration of different exilic groups into a harmonious living with a renewed worldview and a vision for the mission was also their programme. It was through the creation theology, the community of DI developed this message.

Thus, creation theology was an integral part of their proclamation. The socio-historical context of the exile was a decisive reality for the Deutero-Isaianic community in formulating their theology of creation. Most of the scholars however, who have

---

[101] R. R. Wilson, "The Community of the Second Isaiah," 65.

reflected on the theology of creation have failed to note the socio-historical circumstance in which DI community present their message: the historical traditions that are reflected in their message, the immediate concern of their message and the sociological factors, which led them to formulate the theology of creation. Therefore, a fresh study of the passages that describe the creation in the socio-historical context of exile is required.

CHAPTER SIX
An Exegetical Study of Selected Passages with Creation Motif

6.1. Exegetical Study of Selected Passages with Creation Motif

In this section we will undertake a detailed socio-historical exegetical study of the relevant texts. In the process of expounding the text, all available models of Historical criticism such as text-critical, form-critical, literary-critical and traditio-historical factors are taken into account along with the sociological critical approach.

6.1.1. Hope on the Creator

Text: Isaiah 40:12-31

12 Who has measured (the) waters[a] in the hollow of his hand
 and marked off[b] the heavens with the span[c] of his hand,
 and enclosed the dust[d] of the earth in a measure[e],
 and weighed mountain in a balance,
 and the hills in the scales?

13 Who has directed the spirit of Yahweh
 or[a] instructed him as his counselor?[b]

14 Whom has he consulted for his enlightenment,
 and who taught him in the path of justice
 and taught him knowledge[a]

and showed him
and^b made him known the way of discernment?

15 Behold, nations^a (are) like a drop from a bucket,
they are reckoned as dust on the scales^b.
Behold, the islands weigh^c as a fine dust.

16 ^{a}And Lebanon does not suffice for a fire
nor^b are its beasts enough for a burnt offering^a.

17 All the nations (are) as nothing in his presence,
they are accounted by him as less than
nothing^a and emptiness.

18 Then^a, to whom will you liken God?
or (with) what likeness compare to him?

19 An image^a that a craftsman casts,
and a smith overlays with gold,
and casts^b for it silver chain.

20 When one sets up^a an image
chooses wood that will not rot,
seeks out a skillful craftman
to set up an image that cannot move.

21 Do you not know?
Have you not heard?
Has it not been told you from the beginning?
Have you not understood (from) the foundation^a of the earth?

22 He who sits above the circle of the earth,
and its inhabitants are like grasshoppers;^{a}
he stretches out (the) heaven like a curtain,
spreading it out like a tent to dwell in;

23 who brings the princes to naught,
and makes the rulers of the earth as nothing.

24 Hardly are they planted,
hardly are they sown,
hardly has their stem taken root in the earth,
when he blows upon them and they wither,
and the tempest will carry them away like chaff.

25 And with whom will you compare me.
that I should be like him?
says the Holy One.

26 Lift up your eyes on high
and see! who created these?[a]
he brings out their host by number
all of them he calls by name
because he is great in strength,[b]
mighty in power,
not one is lacking.

27 Why do you say, O Jacob,
and speak,[a] O Israel
My way is hidden from Yahweh,
and my right is disregarded by my God?

28 Do you not[a] know?
Have you not heard?
An everlasting God is Yahweh,
Creator of the end of the earth
He will not grow weary,
and will not become faint;
His understanding is unsearchable.

29 He gives strength to the weary
and to him, who has no power,
he multiplies strength.

30 But youths may be faint and be weary,
and choice young men[a] will surely fall.

AN EXEGETICAL STUDY OF SELECTED PASSAGES... 177

31 But those who wait for Yahweh will renew (their) power;
they shall go up (with) wings like eagles,
they shall run and not be weary,
they shall walk and not be faint.

Textual Notes

12 a. Instead of MT's מים 1QIs^a reads מי ים ("water of the sea"). Most commentators are agreed that MT's מים is preferable as the harder reading. The emendation ימים ("seas") has frequently been proposed. But the assonance מים וסמים in MT is surely intentional.

12 b. Most interpreters render as תכן "to measure". G. R. Driver thinks this is wrong: the basic meaning of the root *tkn* is "to adjust"; there is no place in the Hebrew Bible where the word means "to measure", and modern translators have uncritically followed the ancient versions.[1] However, the parallelism in this verse suggests a corresponding word in this place.

12 c. 1QIs^a has "his span," but the other versions agree with MT.

12 d. The word עפר "dust" is missing in LXX, Aqu., Symm., Theod.

12 e. The word translated "measure" is שלש ("a third part," it is probably a third of an ephah. Childs translated it "basket." See B. S. Childs, *Isaiah*, (2001), 305.

13 a. LXX, Syr, and Vg repeat the interrogative pronoun "who" (και τις) "who has been his counselor." See *BHS*.

13 b. Lit. "man of his counselor" (ואיש עצתו) So Watts translates here "his personal counselor." See John D. W. Watts, *Isaiah 34-66*, 84.

14 a. This line is missing in LXX. This could be a gloss (but if so an early one; cf. 1QIs^a) See R. N. Whybray, *The Heavenly*

---

[1] See A. Schoors, *I Am God Your Saviour: A Form Critical Study of the Main Genres In Is.XL-LV*, VT Sup 24 (Leiden: Brill, 1973), 247.

Counselor in Is 40:13-14 (SOTS Monograph 1, 1971), 10 n. 1, and R. F. Melugin, "Deutero-Isaiah and Form Criticism," *VT* 21 (1971) 326-37.

14 b. LXX inserts here τις "who."

15 a. LXX πάντα τὰ ἔθνη "all the nations"

15 b. 1QIs^a has מזנים which can mean "cloud," instead of MT's מאזנים. It is possible that the *'alep* was omitted by error. The versions support MT.

15 c. MT's יטול "he takes up." The LXX and Syr read as plural יטלו "they are lifted up." This fits the context better. The final *waw* may have been assimilated to the following word. (See C. R. North, *The Second Isaiah*, 81).

16 a-a. This verse does not perfectly harmonize with vv. 15 and 17. It may be a later addition. (See Westermann, *Isaiah 40-66*, 51)

16 b. LXX inserts παντα "all"

17 a. MT has a preposition מן before אפס "nothing." In this place 1QIs^a have כאפס "like nothing." Many commentators have accepted 1QIs^a as the original reading. However, many recent commentators consider MT's reading (מאפס) is harder and hence the more probable one. See Joseph Blenkinsopp, *Isaiah 40-55*, 189.

18 a. Lit. 'and'

19 a. Contrary to MT the ה in הפסל ought probably to be understood not as an article but as an interrogative particle. See NRSV "An Idol? - A workman cast it"

19 b. The use of צורף as a verbal- participle so soon after the noun-participle create a problem. *BHS* suggests יצרף, however, makes no difference in meaning.

20 a. המסכן תרומה, one of the most difficult expression, perhaps wisely omitted in LXX, Syr and Vg. Reading of מסכן as "impoverished" ("the one too poor to make a gift") is syntactically impossible, and an impoverished person would not hire a skilled craftsman. See Joseph Blenkinsopp, *Isaiah 40-55*, p. 189. Sidney Smith identifies *amsuchan* with Akkadian *musukkanu*, 'mulberry,' and translates: 'The wise artificer chooses mulberry of the offering, a wood that will not rot; he seeks to secure it to the cast figure, so that it will not tumble.' Childs also translate it as 'mulberry wood.' (See, *Isaiah: A Commentary*, 304).

21 a. MT's מוסדות is supported by LXX, Syr, Vg, and Tg. The emendation as per *BHS* is not necessary. (Cf. John N. Oswalt, *The Book of Isaiah*, 64).

22 a. According to Delitzsch, one reason for the usage of the word כחגבים (grasshoppers) here was its assonance with חוג (circle).

26 a. LXX πάντα ταυτα "all these"

26 b. אמיץ, "mighty" is an adjective and is somewhat difficult to interpret in this sentence since there is no noun for it to modify. *BHS* suggests emending to the noun form אמץ (might) on the basis of versions and 1QIs[a].

27 a. LXX και τι (and why). So *BHS* suggests ולמה ת. However MT is supported by other versions.

28 a. LXX καὶ νῦν (and now). *BHS* suggests ועתה

30 a. נערים speaks of young people in general, while בחרים speaks more particularly of young men specifically selected and trained for military service (See Judges. 20:15; I Sam 24:2; Jer 51:3; Ezk 23:6) (See John N. Oswalt, *The Book of Isaiah 40-66*, 71)

Form, Structure and Setting

Scholars do not have a consensus with regard to the unity of this passage. Gressmann and Mowinckel have considered these verses as a unity.² But Kohler, Elliger, and Begrich have viewed them as a collection of three or four originally separate speeches.³ Westermann also considers that these verses are a unity; however he differs from them by accepting with minor changes Begrich's form critical units as smaller parts of the larger poem.⁴ The crucial difference between Begrich and Westermann is whether these verses are a collection of separate speeches or a long poem based on imitation of speech form, which can be identified by their structure.⁵ Muilenburg views these verses as a poem containing seven strophes (vss12, 13-14, 15-17, 18-20, 21-24, 25-27, 28-31).⁶ Westermann agrees with Muilenburg that vv.12-31 is a literary unity, but not on the basis of strophe. He views the entire poem as an imitation of the structure of the hymn of praise (*Lobpsalm*) with a dual structure which emphasizes on the one hand Yahweh's ability to deliver (vv.12-26), and his desire to save the other (vv.27-31).⁷

The main proof of the unity of this passage, according to Westermann, is the 'mutual relationship of the sections' (12-17; 18-24; 25-26; 27-31). Each section begins with rhetorical questions. However, only the final section, vv.27-31, is introduced by a true disputation.⁸

The unity may be observed in several ways. J. N. Oswalt highlights the thematic continuity of the passage in order to prove its unity.⁹ First of all there is a unity in content. Let us analyze the

---

² Hugo Gressmann, "Die literarische Analyse Deuterojesajas", *ZAW* 34 (1914), 264; Sigmund Mowinckel, "Die Komposition des deuterojesajanichen Buches," *ZAW* 49 (1931), 90.

³ Ludwig Köhler, *Deuterojesajas Stilkritisch Unterucht* (Giessen: Alfred Töpelmann, 1923), 111; K. Elliger, *Deuterojesaja in seinem Verhaltnis zu Tritojesaja* (Stuttgart: W. Kohlhammer, 1933), 225ff.; Begrich, *Studien zu Deuterojesaja*, TB 20 (Munich: Chr.Kaiser, 1963, Reprint of BWANT 77, Stuttgart: W. Kohlhammer, 1938), 42.

⁴ C. Westermann, *Isaiah 40-66: A Commentary* (Philadelphia: Westminster, 1969), 48-9.

⁵ R. F. Melugin, "Deutero-Isaiah and Form Criticism," *VT* 21, (1971), 330.

⁶ J. Muilenburg, *Isaiah: Chapters 40-66*, IB vol. V., 434.

⁷ Westermann, "Sprache und Struktur," 127-132, cited by Melugin, "Deutero Isaiah and Form Criticism," *VT* 21, (1971), 328.

⁸ C. Westermann, *Isaiah*, 48.

⁹ John N. Oswalt, *The Book of Isaiah Chapter 40-66*, NICOT (Grand Rapids: Eerdmans, 1998), 58.

AN EXEGETICAL STUDY OF SELECTED PASSAGES... 181

first section of this poem. The prophet asks a series of questions (vv.12-14), following which he draws a conclusion (vv. 15-17). The mental picture elicited by the questions contributes to the unity of these verses.[10] The appeal is to Yahweh's majestic size and wisdom. Who besides Yahweh could measure the waters in the hollow of his hand? Or who is wise enough to be his teacher? Expected conclusion is that the nations are nothing before Yahweh. The stylistic unity is also seen in the questions introduced by מי and the conclusion by הן.

However, the style and subject change with the next unit. In the previous unit the prophet asks questions without clear designations. But here the prophet addresses the hearers directly: "Have you not known...? Also the focus is no longer the nations, but the "gods". The tone changes to mockery: "...set up an image that cannot move" (19-20). Then appeals to what his hearers have already known about Yahweh (21-24).

The unit, which begins with v.25 is almost identical in style with the previous unit: "with whom will you compare me." But here the speaker is not the prophet. The speaker is now Yahweh himself. Moreover the tone of mockery is absent in this unit.

In vv. 27-31 we could see another shift in style. Once more the prophet becomes the speaker and the addressee is change from plural to singular: "you (singular) say, O Jacob" (תאמר יעקב). Here the focal point is no longer the 'nations' or the 'gods,' but Jacob, the people of Israel and the *power* and *willingness* of Yahweh to save his people. Indeed these verses are arguments against Israel's complaint that Yahweh has ignored their cause.

Where can we find the unity of this passage? Melugin has rightly pointed out that 'the entire passage is a series of arguments for faith in Yahweh.'[11] In each case the prophet based his arguments on Israel's knowledge of Yahweh as Creator. Yahweh's depiction as the ruler of the nations and his superiority over the gods and

---

[10] R. F. Melugin, "Deutero Isaiah and Form Criticism," 329.
[11] R. F. Melugin, "Deutero Isaiah and Form Criticism," 329.

182   EXILE AND THEOLOGY OF CREATION

the heavenly hosts are all affirmed by the fact that he is the Creator God. With a series of rhetorical questions DI asserts that the Lord is the sovereign ruler of the nations and the sole Creator without any pantheon and therefore Israel can trust him without any hesitation.

With regard to the *Gattung* of this passage, most form critics are unanimous in regarding Isa 40:12-31 as a disputation. Melugin divided this passage into four sections; vv.12-17; 18-24; 25-26 and 27-31. Each section begins with rhetorical questions. However, according to Westermann, only the final section, vv.27-31, is introduced by a true disputation. The three preceding sections headed by rhetorical questions simply prepare the way for the disputation proper in vv.27-31, which has a concrete historical setting, and only in the light of the fourth section, one can properly set and understand the function and meaning of the first three sections.[12]

Vv. 12-17 are a series of rhetorical questions introduced by מי. The disputation concludes with an assertion introduced by הן. Disputations with questions introduced by מי along with other forms of rhetorical questions are typical of wisdom.[13] For example, in Job 41:1ff. (HB.40:25ff.) the rhetorical questions are designed to show human impotence against Leviathan (Job 41:1-8), followed by a conclusion introduced by הן (41:9). This type of disputation speech was adopted by the wise men and made into a wisdom genre. In both Job 38ff. and Prov.30:4, the rhetorical questions function to show that mortal human is nothing compared to Yahweh the Creator.

Thus, Isa 40:12-17 reflects both the form and the content of the wisdom genre: 'Who but Yahweh could measure the waters in the hollow of his hand? Who has enough wisdom to be his teacher?' On the basis of its similarity with Job 38 and Prov. 30:4,

---

[12] See Westermann, *Isaiah*, 48.
[13] R. F. Melugin, *The Formation of Isaiah 40-55*, BZAW 141 (Berlin and New York: Walter de Gruyter, 1976), 32.

Melugin concludes that, 'Isa 40:12-17 is a genre at home in Wisdom circles.'[14] However, its similarity with the rhetorical questions found as a stylistic form of hymns is not to be overlooked, as the question in Isa 40:12-17 is disputational, rather than an element of praise.[15]

The next two sections, vv.18-24 and 25-26, are given in a stereotyped structure. The form is as follows:

1. The question "To whom will you liken God/ me? (v.18, 25)
2. Sarcastic description of the manufacture of idols (v.19-20)
3. The prophet's hearers are asked to remember what they have long known through the cult, sometime by means of rhetorical questions (v.21), sometimes through imperative (v.26)
4. What they are to remember is expressed in the participial style of the hymn (v.22)[16]

However, DI uses the structure with certain freedom. In vv. 18-24, the prophet is the speaker. But in the next section Yahweh becomes the speaker. Another variable is the use of a hymn. DI arbitrarily adopted a hymn style well known to him and incorporated it within the framework of a disputation speech. He first employs the hymnic participial style as a point of agreement between him and his opponents, proceeding then to a new-undeniable assertion of the disputed matter by means of a parallel clause in the same style.

Finally, verses 27-31 bring the disputation to a climax by confronting the Jewish community in exile explicitly with their questions of doubt and proclaiming boldly the sole sovereignty of God and God's abundant grace that was made available to those who believe Yahweh's power.

---

[14] R. F. Melugin, *The Formation of Isaiah*..., 33.
[15] In the hymn, rhetorical questions have always an element of praise; never are they attempts to convince doubters. (See R. F. Melugin, 'Deutero-Isaiah and Form Criticism,' 333).
[16] Melugin, *The Formation of Isaiah* ..., 33

This disputation was formed as a response to the complaint stated in v.27. According to Westermann, this one is the 'disputation proper,' and only in the light of this disputation one can properly understand the function and meaning of the entire passage. The complaint is in the style well known from the individual lament psalm, and the disputation is structured in liturgical style as an argument against the cultic complaint. In order to persuade his opponents that their complaint is not justified, DI appeals to what they have always known from the cult: "Do you not know, have you not heard?" The disputation then proceeds in the style of the "expression of confidence" found in the individual lament psalm (Ps 25:8; 102:13). This was used to express faith in Yahweh's redeeming love, and it is taken from its original setting and made the content of the prophet's 'argument' against the complaint.[17]

It is very difficult to determine the exact nature of the *Sitz im Leben* of the passage. According to Begrich, the disputations in DI are independent units composed as imitations of speech-forms used in everyday situations of dispute.[18] One reason for this position was his belief that the circumstance of the exiles made oral preaching impossible.[19] If DI did not dispute with the people face-to-face, his disputation speeches would necessarily be literary imitations of the speech-forms occurring in real life. And for him, the forms of disputation speeches have their original setting in the everyday world and the prophet consciously imitated these non-prophetic disputational speech forms, much as they sometimes imitated priestly *tôrâ*.[20] Melugin identified this passage as a disputation against Jacob's specific complaint in v.27.[21] The complaint is similar to that found in the psalm of community lament.[22]

---

[17] Melugin, *The Formation of Isaiah* ..., 35.
[18] Begrich, *Studien zu Deuterojesaja*, 49.
[19] Begrich, *Studien zu Deuterojesaja*, 97.
[20] R. F. Melugin, *The Formation of Isaiah*. 28.
[21] R. F. Melugin, *The Formation of Isaiah*, 35.
[22] See C. Westermann, *Isaiah 40-66*, 59.

Thus the disputation becomes an argument against the cultic lament. However, to limit the text to its cultic setting will not help us to understand it properly.

What is its socio-historical setting? Almost all form-critics agree that 40:12-31 is dominated by the genre of disputation. However, Westermann's analysis seems more plausible that only vv.27-31 constitute a proper disputation and that the preceding oracles consist of rhetorical questions with the flavor of a disputation. They simply prepare the way for the one true disputation which has a concrete historical setting. That is, the exiled "Jacob" complains that their rights have been forgotten by God. Thus this text helps us to recover the socio-historical setting. So, as Westermann has pointed out, v.27 forms the real focus of the entire unit, wherein the deported Jewish population described as residing in Babylon in the late 540s, and inheriting a shaming identity as defeated Israel, and rejected by God, is conveying its traumatizing story by liturgies of lament.

Socio-historical comment focusing on the creation motif

As a starting point proper to a socio-historical exegesis, this study begins focusing attention on the socio-historical context which is implied in the text of DI.

In brief, DI addressed a deported Judean population resident in Babylonia in the late 540s. At this moment in time, the community of DI encountered the exilic community reinforced by a story of trauma and rejection that left it with little hope for the future.

The hope for a return from the exile had been extinguished with the passing of the years. Yahweh appeared simply to have disregarded his people's rights (Isa 40:27), to have turned his back on them (50:1) and forgotten his own city (49:14). The symbols and images of the Babylonian gods were paraded through the streets in magnificent processions, accompanied by the rejoicing of the crowd (46:1-2); they obviously ruled over human society and world history. But Yahweh seemed unwilling or unable to intervene in history. In the domain of political history, Yahweh appeared to have been so distant. It appears that the exilic community was at risk of losing a positive identification with Israel because it was overwhelmed by its self-knowledge as rejected by Yahweh. Their shaming identity as the defeated people and rejected by God was conveyed and reinforced by liturgies of lament. Allusions to these liturgical traditions can be found in passages such as Isa 40:27; 49:14; 50:1; 51:9-11.

Van der Veer uses two categories to classify the causes of the psychological and sociological issues that the deported people faced: "traumatization" and "uprooting." Traumatization refers to experiences of repression, torture and other kinds of violence that are likely to result in psychological dysfunction both in the short and long term. Uprooting refers to experiences of separation from familiar surroundings, loss, attendant hardships and exile in an unfamiliar environment for an indefinite period.[23]

Analogies exist between sociological problems faced by contemporary populations of displaced people and those exiled by the Babylonian empire after the destruction of Jerusalem.[24] It is possible, therefore, that contemporary descriptions of sociological problems faced by displaced persons could apply to the victims of the Babylonian exiles. Daniel Smith in his survey of refugee studies has noted the interest in old traditions as a matter deeply related to the identity formation.[25] Here the remembrance

---

[23] See Van der Veer, *Counseling and Therapy with Refugees and Victims of Trauma Psychological Problems of Victims of War, Torture and Repression*, 2nd ed. (Chichester, UK: John Wiley & Sons, 1998), ix.

[24] Deportation is not itself an isolated or unique event in history. The transport of Lithuanians, Estonians, and Latvians in the Soviet Union, Japanese-American in United States or Zulu tribes in modern South Africa, refugees of East Bangladesh to Dhandakarnya after the Indo-Pak war; all of these make up the long trail of history's deportees to foreign lands. For a detailed description of this kind of deportation story, see Daniel L. Smith, *The Religion of the Landless*, pp. 69-88. However, considering these cases are exactly like the Babylonian exile is an oversimplification of the issue. But it helps us to identify the patterns of behavior of the deported people.

[25] Daniel L. Smith-Christopher, *A Biblical Theology of Exile* (Minneapolis: Fortress Press, 2002), 105

of old traditions is the regenerative force in which the community's self-understanding is reinforced. So, as an antidote to their internal pessimism and to revive their self-esteem, DI reminds the exilic community about their creator and his creative purpose. That is, the creation theology in DI, in a sense, was to meet this crises faced by the exilic community during their Babylonian exile.

Even though Isaiah 40:12-31 forms a new unit, it is closely related to the preceding section in vv.40:1-11. In that section, DI had announced a decisive turning point in the life of the broken and humiliated community. The term of hard service that was entailed by Israel's sin is over. Now the time has arrived for the life-giving glory of Yahweh to be revealed, and the lost nation was again to be gathered and shepherded. But the people who heard the message could not understand or believe it. Two questions rose in their minds: Given the might of the Babylonian captors and the splendor of their gods, did the God of Israel possess the power to deliver? How could the glory of Yahweh be revealed in a world dominated by emperors and their armies?[26]

Isaiah 40:12-31 addresses and argues with the doubts that pinned down the exiled people. The main purpose of this oracle is to encourage the exiles to put aside their doubts and give their assent of faith in Yahweh as the all-powerful creator. The strategy he follows is by means of a series of rhetorical questions. Rhetorical questions, usually in series, can serve a variety of purposes. They are used by teachers as a highly interactive way of holding the attention of the students, imparting information, and eliciting appropriate responses, that is, responses deemed to be appropriate by the instructor.[27] Rhetorical questions can also be hostile in the manner of a cross-examination in a forensic context, or they can aim at reducing the opposition to silence.[28] The last seems to be the point of the long sequence in Job 38-39. However, according

---

[26] See P. D. Hanson, *Isaiah 40-66*, Interpretation (Louisville: John Knox Press, 1995), 26.

[27] J Blenkinsopp, *Isaiah 40-55:A New Translation with Introduction and Commentary*, AB 19A (New York: Doubleday, 2002), 190.

[28] J. Blenkinsopp, *Isaiah 40-55*, 190.

to Blenkinsopp, the present series is neither didactic nor forensic but to *persuade* the exiles.[29]

Thus, in order to persuade his hearers, DI opens his discourse with five rhetorical questions focusing on the creation of the world.

> Who has measured (the) waters in the hollow of his hand
> and marked off the heavens with the span of his hand,
> and enclosed the dust of the earth in a measure,
> and weighed mountain in a balance,
> and the hills in the scales?
>
> Who has directed the spirit of Yahweh
> or instructed him as his counselor?
> Whom has he consulted for his enlightenment,
> and who taught him in the path of justice
> and taught him knowledge
> and showed him
> and made him known the way of discernment? (40:12-14)

The first exegetical task lies in determining the force of the series of interrogative phrases beginning with מִי. 'Who measured the waters…and marked off (תִּכֵּן) the heavens…?; 'Who directed (תִכֵּן) the spirit of Yahweh…?'. The verb תִכֵּן in v.12 appears to have a concrete meaning such as "determine" or "gauge," but in v.13 there is a slight shift of meaning to suit the context, and best translated as "directed". Here, the prophet affirms the incomparability of Yahweh in implicit contrast with the Babylonian imperial deity Marduk who, in creating the world, needed the advice of god Ea. Whether v.13b is to be understood as parallel to v.13a is not clear. It can be understood as "Who as his counselor instructed him?" or "with whom he (Yahweh) shared his plan?" According to Childs, the latter seems preferable.[30] The point seems to be that

---

[29] J. Blenkinsopp, *Isaiah 40-55*, 190.
[30] Brevard S. Childs, *Isaiah: A Commentary* (Louisville: Westminster John Knox Press, 2001), 309.

no one can fathom the hidden mysteries of God, either in the case of creation or in his administration of the world.

Verse 14 deals God's infinite wisdom. "Who taught him the path of מִשְׁפָּט." Beuken has pointed out the crucial role of the word in Deutero-Isaiah in encapsulating the redemptive purpose of God for Israel, which then culminates in the election of the servant in 42:1 toward bringing מִשְׁפָּט to the nations.[31] However, here DI was probably thinking of God's omnipotence in creation through his supreme wisdom (cf. Ps 104:24).

Verses 15-17 reveal the political motive behind the disputation. The metaphor of scales and balances borrowed from the previous verses implies that in the scheme of the created order, these nations are nothing and emptiness in comparison to the Creator God. In order to make this point clear, DI contrasts Yahweh's absolute sovereignty with the nothingness of the nations. At the very historical moment when exiled Israel is feeling the tremendous threat from the great powers of the world, such as Babylon, and remembering the humiliating annihilation of the Jewish state, the prophet boldly pronounces the rulers of the world to be meaningless before God as "a drop from a bucket"![32] The social conditions of the exile persuade the people to think about the insignificance of the people before the world events which they have no role in controlling the event. So DI calls them to ponder on the incomparability and supremacy of Yahweh in contrast to the inferiority and weakness caused by the Babylonian exile.

Since v.16 does not perfectly harmonize with vv.15 and 17, Volz and Muilenburg think that the verse may be a later addition. But, as Westermann has pointed out, this is not necessarily so, since the extravagant metaphor very well accords with DI's style.[33] Here DI takes a specific figure to illustrate his point. That is, God

---

[31] See W. A. M. Beuken, מִשְׁפָּט. The First Servant Song and Its Context," VT 22, 1972, 8-11.

[32] B. S. Childs, *Isaiah*, 309.

[33] C. Westermann, *Isaiah*, 51.

is so great that even the vast cedar forest of Lebanon could not provide enough material for the kind of sacrifice he deserves. However, the mention of the word "Lebanon" stands out in the hymn because it seems to be the only specific reference. Duhm concludes from this that DI was living in Lebanon.

The prophet may have had another thought in his mind. Lebanon was known for its wealthy forests. Wood, especially cedar wood, was needed for the building work in Babylon. In this connection, F. H. Weissbach discusses a cuneiform inscription on Nebuchadnezzar II that reads, in part: "the lands of Hattim, from the upper sea to the lower sea, the land of Sumer and Akkad, the land between the two rivers,... the rulers of the lands of Hattim across the Euphrates where the sun sets, whose rulership, at the bidding of Marduk my lord, I overcame, and the mighty cedars of the mountain of Lebanon were brought to the city of Babylon, the whole races, people from places, whom Marduk my lord delivered to me - I forced them to work on the building of Etemenanki - I imposed on them the brick-basket."[34] Inscriptions are not to be taken as dispassionate historical documents. However, the term used in this inscription is noteworthy: "*I forced them to work*" refers clearly to the forced labor, and "*I imposed on them the brick basket*," further employs strong terms of subservience. So, for DI, the mention of Lebanon also refers to bearing burdens and construction work done in Babylon.[35]

The final refrain in v. 17 draws the appropriate conclusion from what has been just said: "All nations (are) as nothing in his (Yahweh's) presence." The declaration that they are "like a drop from a bucket" was an extreme analogy. Here also DI takes it to its extreme: "all nations!" In order to deny their any claim, DI uses three negative words; כְּאַיִן ("nothing" in his presence), מֵאֶפֶס ("at an end" or "nothing" or "non existence"), תֹהוּ ("empty, void").

---

[34] F. H. Weissbach, *Das Hauptheiligtum des Marduk in Babylon* (Leipzig: Hinrich, 1938), 46-47.

[35] Cf. I Kgs 5:13-18. Solomon's forced labor for the construction work in Jerusalem using materials from Lebanon.

The last instance is an allusion to a key word in Genesis 1.³⁶ The possibility that there is an echo of the utterance in the creation account in the Priestly writing cannot be excluded (see Gen 1:2). While explaining the term תהו ובהו, Westermann quotes Ridderbos and Delitzsch and says that 'these notions are much more ominous for the Israelite than for us,' and 'there is something fearful about this pair of words.'³⁷ During the Babylonian exile the nations were 'ominous' and 'fearful' to the exiles. Israel had to suffer terrific threat and humiliation from the great power of the world like Babylon. At this point DI boldly pronounces that the rulers of the world to be meaningless before the Creator God. Here the language is hyperbolic. But DI uses such hyperbolic statement in order to remove the disbelief of the exiles caused by the skeptical view of the situation.

The solemn seriousness of the hymn is followed in verses 18-20 by an entr'acte in which the same theme- Yahweh's incomparability- is presented on a different level.³⁸

Then, to whom will you (plural) liken God?
or (with) what likeness compare to him? (40:18)

The listeners are addressed directly. It also expects the same answer that there is nobody with whom God can be compared. The second half of the verse asks "what likeness compares to him?" Here also the expected answer is that it is impossible to make a likeness of Yahweh, for he is the creator of all that is.³⁹

Here the name "El" (אל) is used for God, a term found in almost all Semitic languages. In the Canaanite pantheon, for example, El is the head of the gods. It is striking that DI uses the term El for God, particularly in passages where the point at issue is the dispute with foreign gods (i.e. in 43:10; 44:10, 15, 17; 45:20-22; 46:6-9).

---

³⁶ Deutero Isaiah uses it seven times: 40:17, 23; 41:29; 44:9; 45:18, 19; 49:4.
³⁷ Cf. Westermann, *Genesis 1-11: A Commentary* (Minneapolis: Augsburg Publishing House, 1984), 103.
³⁸ Klaus Baltzer, *Duetero-Isaiah*, trans. Margaret Kohl, Hermeneia (Minneapolis: Fortress Press, 2001), 72.
³⁹ See C. Westermann, *Isaiah 40-66*, 54.

According to 45:14-15, the Gentiles too can acknowledge "God," even if he is "hidden God": and in spite of all the aggressiveness of the polemic against idols, this suggests that the aim here is to win a consensus from the non-Jewish exiles. It indicates the presence of Gentile listeners among DI's hearers, the presence of a mixed community.

The following two verses (19, 20) are regarded by most of the modern scholars as secondary.[40] It lacks the logical connection to the preceding as well as to the following verse. From the stylistic perspective there is some evidence to support this view. However, we cannot simply remove these verses as intrusive:

> An image that a craftsman casts,
> and a smith overlays with gold,
> and casts for it silver chain.
>
> When one sets up an image
> chooses wood that will not rot,
> seeks out a skillful craftsman
> to set up an image that cannot move. (40:19-20)

DI is making an important theological point in these verses. The utter incomparability of God lies at the base of the Old Testament's uncompromising rejection of every attempt to represent the God of Israel by means of an image (cf. Exod. 20:3ff).[41] We may well suppose that the observation of the manufacture of images made a profound impression on the Israelites exiled in Babylon.

---

[40] The majority of modern critical scholars (e.g., Westermann, Elliger, Beuken) regard verses 19-20 as a secondary expansion which interrupts the logical connection between verses 18 and 21. From the stylistic perspective there is some evidence to support this hypothesis. (See Childs, *Isaiah*, p.310). However, one cannot simply write off these verses as intrusive, because this gives the reader a sense of being a witness to the process of bringing a god into being, which was very common in Babylon during the exile and therefore, we can best imagine them on the lips of the "speaker."

[41] B. S. Childs, *Isaiah*, 310.

AN EXEGETICAL STUDY OF SELECTED PASSAGES... 193

Did the manufacture of images persuade DI to think of a creator God? The realism and vividness in description reflects an eyewitness account of Babylonian practice. He is able to reproduce the process with an almost photographic exactness, and adds not even a single word of criticism or direct mockery. Nevertheless, the way in which he stresses the idol's solidity and stability hint at a delicate indirect mockery.[42] Westermann quotes from the Babylonian New Year Festival liturgy a description of manufacturing idols:

> When it is three hours after sunrise,
> [he shall call] a metal worker and give
> him precious stones and gold [from]
> the treasury of the god Marduk to make
> two images (for the ceremonies of) the
> sixth day (of Nisannu). He shall call
> a woodworker and give him (some) cedar
> and tamarisk (pieces). He shall call a
> goldsmith and give him (some) gold...[43]

Here the prophet expresses his deepest sarcasm to depict how foolish it is to make god out of earthly materials. The verb רקע is worth mentioning. It means the beating of metal into thin sheet and this is a laborious process. But the term is again reminiscent of Genesis 1, for it is the same root that is used for the "firmament (רקיע) between the waters that God called heaven." It is, therefore, probably this persuaded DI to ponder on the contrast between the idols and the creator God. These idol-makers used materials that Yahweh created, and skills that He gave them! God, however, is unlike any idol; He is the Creator of all things. Thus the manufacture of idols persuades the DI community to reappraise the notion of Yahweh as the Creator.

Another work to be noted is the manufacture of silver chain (רתקות). What has the chain to do with the statue of god? Of course

---

[42] Westermann, *Isaiah*, 54.
[43] *AENT*, 331.

it could be a decoration. But perhaps the catchword "chain" has greater importance than that. Klaus Baltzer has pointed out the wide traditions of "chained gods."[44] There are stories about images of gods "that did not stay in their proper place but went elsewhere." Consequently the statues were tied to their place with cords and chains, and fastened to the pedestal or the floor. Famous examples are representations with chains and cords of Artemis (Cybele) as the city goddess of Ephesus, a type of representation that was widespread in Syria and Asia Minor.[45] As late as the fourth century C.E., on the founding of Constantinople, Constantine the Great had a statue of Tyche with chains set up, so that Tyche (=happiness) might remain in his new capital.[46]

It may therefore well be that the mention of "chains" is much more closely linked with the context than the notion of mere decoration would suggest. The statue of god is firmly established. But it cannot move. That is the irony, not only with the gods of Babylon but also with the people of Israel who lived in Babylon as exiles. Their situation of confinement is indicated by this image of "chain."

The exact meaning of the first two Hebrew words of v. 20 is uncertain. The word מסכן occurs five times in Ecclesiastes with the meaning "poor" and מסכנת appears in Deut. 8: 9 with the meaning "poverty." So AV translates it "he who is impoverished."[47] But most modern scholars judge that the "poor man" is not a correct translation. The supposed contrast between the metal idol of the rich in v.19 and the wooden idol of the poor in v.20 does not seem rational, because "the wood that will not rot" is not such an inexpensive material. Moreover an

---

[44] Klaus Baltzer, "The Polemic Against the Gods and Its Relevance for Second Isaiah's Conception of New Jerusalem," in *Second Temple Studies, vol. 2: Temple and Community in the Persian Period*, edited by T. C. Eskenazi and K. H. Richards, JSOT Sup. 175 (Sheffield: JSOT Press, 1994), 52-59.

[45] Cf. Klaus Baltzer, *Deutero-Isaiah...*, 74.

[46] Klaus Baltzer, *Deutero-Isaiah...*, 74.

[47] See also Westermann, *Isaiah*, 66, who translates it "who is too poor for such a work of art."

impoverished person could not hire a skilled craftsman. Most scholars now agree that the two verses are speaking of the same idol, which v. 19 refers to the idol itself and v.20 to the base on which it was fastened.[48] Another possibility is that one Ugaritic text attests a verb *skn*, meaning "to set up." Thus, Klaus Baltzer translates: "When any one set up an image does he not choose wood that does not rot…?"[49] And his translation seems more realistic. The idol which topples over is considered a bad omen (cf. 1 Sam. 5:2-5). Whatever the word may mean, here, DI said this with a heavy sarcasm, as he looked at the manufacture of the idols.

The Creator of World and the Lord of History
Do you not know?
Have you not heard?
Has it not been told you from the beginning?
Have you not understood (from) the foundation of the earth?

He who sits above the circle of the earth,
and its inhabitants are like grasshoppers;
he stretches out (the)heaven like a curtain,
spreading it out like a tent to dwell in;

who brings the princes to naught,
and makes the rulers of the earth as nothing.

Hardly are they planted,
hardly are they sown,
hardly has their stem taken root in the earth,
when he blows upon them and they wither,
and the tempest will carry them away like chaff (40:21-24).

According to Westermann, these verses are to be read as the direct continuation of the questions in v. 18. The four questions in v. 21 exemplify a leading characteristic of DI's style, intensification by

---

[48] See John N. Oswalt, *Isaiah…*, 64.
[49] Klaus Baltzer, *Deutero-Isaiah…*, 60.

means of putting sentences with the same meaning one after the other.[50] The four questions addressed to the hearers, assume that the hearers have indeed known the answers to the questions. The structure of the verse should probably be noted very precisely. The text can be translated: "Do you not know...have you not heard? Has it not been told...have you not understood?" Here grammatically two initial imperfects are set over against two following perfects. According to Klaus Baltzer, this stresses the direction towards future and past- the one is not complete, while the other already is.[51] Thus, when DI put these questions, he was thinking both the present historical circumstances of the exiles and the liturgical traditions, in which people of Israel praise Yahweh as Creator.

According to W. Schottroff, the Hebrew word ידע means "primarily the sensory awareness of object and circumstances in one's environment attained through involvement with them and through the information of others."[52] The organs of perceptions are eye and ears. The rhetorical question: "Will you not perceive and hear?" provokes the reaction: "Yes we will!" Here, DI is referring to the exilic social context, as well as their liturgical traditions of the past, which can be an occasion to perceive God as Creator from their circumstances.

We have already noted that Israel extolled Yahweh as the Creator of the world in their liturgical traditions. Jesus asked the chief priests and the elders of the people: "Have you never read in the scripture?" This is a rhetorical question which expects the answer "yes." Surely they have read it; but they did not understand its implication for their life. In the same way DI asks, "Have you not known?" Yes, they do know. But they could not understand its implication for their present history. They had already realized and experienced in the Exodus event that their God is able to change their social situation. But they again failed to interpret it

---

[50] C. Westermann, *Isaiah*, 55.
[51] Klaus Baltzer, *Deutero- Isaiah*, 78.
[52] W. Schottroff, *yd' ידע*, to perceive, know," *TLOT* 2:511.

in another social situation. Or the difficult social situation of exile weakened their power of imagination to interpret their old faith to the situation.

Moreover, some scholars think that Yahweh is likely an Israelite derivative of the Canaanite royal god El.[53] This El was known previously as a creator, even if that meant primarily in terms of procreation. We may assume, therefore, in combination with the result of the more recent research, that Israel was conscious about the creatorship of Yahweh.

The other two questions, with their perfect tenses, are directed to tradition, particularly to their liturgical traditions of the psalms in which the praises of the creator were handed on.[54] This is where it had been told them *from the beginning*. *Foundations of earth* refers to the beginning of the earth and what he is saying is that a careful thought about the origins of the world must point to the Creator (cf. Ps 19:1). "Have you not understood from the foundation of the earth?' is taken by scholars like Volz and Duhm as meaning the direct revelation through the creation.[55]

Thus, the four questions addressed to the hearers imply that they should be familiar with and have already accepted belief in Yahweh as a creator deity. Even though it seems that DI is exaggerating things to a certain extent, it asserts that the "creation theology" was known from the beginning. DI is not asking his listeners to adopt a new belief, but simply to maintain the traditional faith. But the people in exile have completely forgotten the fundamental teaching of their tradition and failed to supply clear answers to the series of questions in the disputation. Therefore, biblical scholars can no longer claim that creation came late to biblical consciousness. Rather the exilic context has provided the occasion for the resurgence of creation theology.

---

[53] For a detailed discussion of this view, see Stefan Paas, *Creation and Judgement: Creation Texts in Some Eight Century Prophets* (Leiden. Boston: Brill, 2003), 123-43.
[54] Cf. C. Westermann, *Isaiah*, 56.
[55] C. Westermann, *Isaiah*, 56.

Verse 22 may be a remarkable development in the idea of God, which stands in contrast to the idea that Yahweh dwells in Zion. What the חוּג הָאָרֶץ (circle of the earth) means in the present text is not entirely clear. It might be the earth itself with its circular horizon (Prov 8:27), or it might be the vault of heavens (Job 22:14). However, it shows that the Babylonian context made the exilic community to look to their God beyond the boundaries of Palestine. God's distance from human kind is accented here. From that distance, they appear as insignificant *grasshoppers*.

Westermann has pointed out that this verse contains some rare words: the word for 'curtain' (דֹק) and the word for 'stretches out' (מתח). This word occurs only once or twice and always in the context of creator and creation. We may take it that DI uses the words to call to his audience's minds a version of the praise of the creator, which was still well known to them.[56] We hear echoes of liturgical psalms of praise with which the audience could be expected to be familiar. Psalm 104, for example, speaks of the foundations of the earth (v.5), God's lofty abode (Ps. 104:13 cf. Isa 57:15; 66:1; Amos 9:6) and heaven stretched out like a tent (Ps 104:2).

Another remarkable feature is that the creation is to "dwell in" (45:18). Here one can see a clear echo of Gen.1:10, 12, 30 etc: "and God saw it was good." Thus, the positive purpose of creation is highlighted.

With the next verse, as in 40:15-17, the focus suddenly shifts again from creation to the "rulers of the earth." The one who sits above the circle of the earth and *stretches out* the heavens also *bring the princes to naught*. We cannot ignore the assonance: "who stretches out" (הַנּוֹטֶה) and "who gives" (הַנּוֹתֵן). Here, once again, DI is bringing creation and history together. For God, both creation and history belong to his domain. As Westermann has correctly pointed out, these passages deal with the situation in which Israel then found herself, and with the challenge to which she was

---

[56] C. Westermann, *Isaiah*, 56.

exposed. What the prophet's audience is to make out of his words is not, as Westermann points, that 'it was Yahweh who created the world,' but that Yahweh, who created the world, is the absolute lord of the nations and powers.[57] Thus, the lords of this world come and go. But the true Lord remains! The exile has given them full of bitter experiences from the powerful Babylonians. But DI is giving them an opportunity to discern the "nothingness" of their oppressors. Mary's song of praise in Luke 1:46-55 once more takes up these ideas about the relative nature of earthly power.

Acknowledging the Creator
And with whom will you compare me,
that I should be like him?
says the Holy One.
Lift up your eyes on high
and see! who created these?
he brings out their host by number
all of them he calls by name
because he is great in strength,
mighty in power,
not one is lacking. (40:25-26)

In this small unit, DI asks two questions: "With whom will you compare me?" (v.25) and "Who created these?"(v.26). The text is bound into its context in a number of different ways. The question: "With whom will you compare me?" was already asked in v. 18, in the introduction to the 'idol manufacture passage.' It is later repeated in 46:5. Moshe Weinfeld interprets this as a statement of opposition to the idea of humanity that is made in "the image" of God as asserted in Gen.1:26-27.[58] However, the context suggests that this is probably a polemic against the lifeless idols of Babylon.

---

[57] C. Westermann, *Isaiah*, 57.
[58] See Moshe Weinfeld, "God the Creator in Gen. 1 and in the Prophecy of Second Isaiah," Hebrew, *Tarbiz* 37 (1968), 122-126.

Verse 25 is not a direct divine speech; it is a quotation. The imperfect יאמר implies God's determination to reveal himself as the Creator God in the future history of Israel. And this is declared by the "Holy One." The word קדוש without the article and without a dependent noun is not simply an attribute of the Deity but has become almost a proper name.[59] It is then generally translated "*the* Holy One." "Holy One" as a name for Yahweh has a long history. קדוש was an important concept in the interpretation of the relationship between Yahweh and his people. In Isaiah 6, Yahweh's holiness is proclaimed as a prominent point in the installation of the prophet. The concept originally stresses God's tremendous "distances."[60] But surprisingly, DI takes up the term and links it up with the idea of redemption (41:14; 43:3; 45:18ff; 47:4)[61] Thus, to the exilic community in Babylon, the idea of God as the Holy One was not only the designation for God, but also it was the hope for redemption.

The question in verse 25 is followed by the earnest appeal, "Lift up your eyes on high and see! Who created these?" The very existence of creation testifies to its maker's ultimate power and the futility and absurdity of resistance to him by mortals. It is noticeable that neither here nor elsewhere DI uses the term "stars." We may compare Genesis 1 here, where creation account avoids the words for "sun" and "moon," using instead the word "lights" or "luminaries" (מְאֹרֹת - Gen 1:14-16). The names for sun and moon might have been misunderstood as meaning the names of gods. (However, the stars are mentioned in Genesis 1:16). But here DI was very sensitive in avoiding such terms, instead he deliberately uses the demonstrative pronoun "these" (אֵלֶּה) to denote the heavenly bodies. Thus he put down the heavenly bodies as only created things that come and go at the command of Lord who actually created all *these* things. The question "who created these?" categorically denies every claim of divinity of the heavenly bodies

---

[59] Cf C. R. North, *The Second Isaiah: Introduction, Translation And Commentary to Chapters XL – LV* (Oxford: Clarendon Press, 1964), 88.

[60] Klaus Baltzer, *Deutero-Isaiah*, 81.

[61] Cf. Klaus Blatzer, *Deutero-Isaiah*, 81.

that was one of the temptations of the exiles. Thus DI urges his hearers to look up at these objects in order to acknowledge Yahweh as its creator and not to worship them (cf. Deut 4:19, using the same language).

Many commentators see a polemic in these words about astral bodies.[62] The statement about Yahweh's creation and control of the celestial bodies should be seen in the context of Babylonian astral worship. It was the general conviction of the Babylonians that the stars determine the fates of human beings (Isa 47:13). Babylonians believed these astral bodies as gods. We may assume that the Jewish exiles also were tempted to choose this Babylonian faith. Therefore the community of DI asks; "Who created these?" By this DI urges his exiles to look up at these astral bodies in order to acknowledge Yahweh as its creator. Consequently, the social context of Babylonian astral theology necessitates the creation theology of DI.

Also this is not an appeal to imagine something with their inner eyes. In 51:6 the appeal to 'lift up the eyes to the heavens and look at the earth beneath' is something that is going to happen in the future. But the creation and creative power, which is working at present, can really be seen in their present exilic context. That is, the social and political condition of DI's time was practically helpful to generate new hope among the exiles.

Once again, as in vv.22 and 23, the rhetorical question is answered with a participle. Who created these? *He is the one who brings out their host by number and calls all of them by name.* Yahweh's leading the host of heaven out from their place and summoning them by name recalls the title יהוה צבאות (the Yahweh of hosts) and therefore suggests the image of a military parade. In the exilic context, especially in the wake of Persian advancement, it is not unlikely that DI was thinking a military parade under the control of the Lord of the hosts.

---

[62] See. Westermann, *Isaiah*, 58; J. Blenkinsopp, *Isaiah.*, 193.

DI uses the technical term ברא to indicate creation. The root ברא, "create" occurs 16 times in Deutero-Isaiah. It occurs more frequently in P source. It is a theological word. It does not in itself carry the meaning of creation out of nothing, but it was never used except with God as subject.[63] The motif of creation has a prominent role in DI's theology. Yahweh's creating the universe is described in 40:26, 28; 42:5; and 45:7, 18. He is the creator of light and darkness (45:7). He is the creator of human kind (45:12; 54:16). He is the creator of Israel (43:1, 7, 15).

The concept of 'creating' is supported by other creation vocabulary.[64] יסד "established" (seven times), יצר "form" (fourteen times), עשׂה "make" (twenty seven times with God as subject). All of these words portray God as actively creating, forming, shaping, and stabilizing the universe and the historical social order from the beginning on into the present. That means there is no place for chaos or lack of control, in either sphere. God is in control. And this Creator, Maker, Stabilizer is identical with Israel's Savior and Redeemer who has willed that Jerusalem be restored.[65] Thus, DI's portrayal of Yahweh as Creator functions as an ideological answer to the problem of homelessness of the exilic Israel. Therefore, DI uses creation theology to encourage and stabilize the exilic community and to help them to continue in hope.

Israel's Hope is on Creator's Sovereignty
Why do you say, O Jacob,
and speak, O Israel
My way is hidden from Yahweh,
and my right is disregarded by my God?

---

[63] Cf. C. R. North, *The Second Isaiah*, 88.

[64] For the creation vocabularies used by DI, see: Carroll Stuhlmueller, *Creative Redemption in Deutero Isaiah* (Rome: Biblical Institute Press, 1970), 209ff.

[65] John D.W. Watts, *Isaiah 34-66*, WBC vol. 25 (Nashville: Thomas Nelson Publishers, 1987), 94.

Do you not know?
Have you not heard?
An everlasting God is Yahweh,
Creator of the end of the earth
He will not grow weary,
and will not become faint;
His understanding is unsearchable.

He gives strength to the weary
and to him, who has no power,
he multiplies strength.

But youths may be faint and be weary,
and choice young men will surely fall.
But those who wait for Yahweh will renew (their) power;
they shall go up (with) wings like eagles,
they shall run and not be weary,
they shall walk and not be faint. (40:27-31)

This is the last unit in the complex 40:12-31. Westermann has rightly pointed out that the complaint of exiled Israel in v.27 forms the center of the entire passage. Here DI takes up the crucial question Israel faced during the exile. Israel had never doubted the existence of Yahweh. Also they had a faint idea about his creative power which was handed down through the liturgical psalms. So the fundamental question during the exile was whether Yahweh is concerned with their life and destiny. In order to answer this doubt DI calls their attention to Yahweh's creative power and purpose.

The text begins with the question "Why?" By quoting A. Jepsen, Baltzer writes: "The human 'why' to God is generally (46 times) introduced by לָמָּה; that is to say, it is a reproachful question with which the community or an individual comes before God. This reproach is initially always evoked, no doubt, through a contradiction between the divine promise and election on the one hand, and what God does on the other."[66] A "why" of this kind has its place especially in communal laments (Pss. 44:24; 74:1, 11; 79:10; 80:12; 115:2; Lam. 5:20; Isa.63:17; Jer.14:8; Joel 2:17). The 'why' with which he begins combats the 'why' that introduced the charge which the nation made against God.[67] We may therefore take it for granted that here, in v.27, DI cites words from a lament in actual use by the exiles at the time.[68]

The sociological crisis of the exile is reflected in these verses. Those who were deported to Babylon experienced a deep social uprooting. They had not only lost their homes but also their land and social status, which was usually influential. They were removed from the solidarity of their kinsfolk. And they had a bitter experience of seeing how quickly they were written off by their own people who were left in Judah and of being robbed of their property (Ezk 11:15; 33:24)

Therefore, verse 27 should be understood as a sociological imagination of the community about their task in the context of exile. The ability to see personal experience and tragedies as part of larger patterns of social problems is a vital element of the sociological imagination.[69] Sociologist C. Wright Mills suggests that the sociological imagination is developed when we can place such personal troubles as poverty, hardship, or loss of faith into a larger social context, when we see them as common public issues.[70] They have to do with society as a whole, its historical development, and the way it is organized.

Passages like Psalm 137 depict the mental distress Israel experienced during the Babylonian exile. The DI community was the product of this exilic society. However, they were not fully under the control of the society. They continued to be faithful to

---

[66] Klaus Baltzer, *Deutero-Isaiah*, 82.
[67] C. Westermann, *Isaiah*, 59.
[68] C. Westermann, *Isaiah*, 60.
[69] C. Wright Mills, *The Sociological Imagination* (Oxford, England: Oxford University Press, 1959), 15.
[70] C. Wright Mills, *The Sociological Imagination*, 15.

AN EXEGETICAL STUDY OF SELECTED PASSAGES... 205

their calling and to the old traditions. And all the members of this community felt that they were called by Yahweh to perform the task given to them by Yahweh for the redemption of the exiles.

The complaint is explicitly cited by DI. "My way is hidden from Yahweh; and my right is disregarded by my God." However, both of these complaints are not uncommon in times of crisis. These questions, why God has hidden his face (Pss 13:2; 44:25; 88:15) and why the way or right of the plaintiffs is being disregarded (Pss 35:23; 37:5-6; 140:13; 146:7) have been borrowed from the liturgy of communal lament. The "way" should not be understood in terms of Israel's former life-style. It is the condition in which Israel lives in Babylon, it is the fate that Yahweh does not see. And word מִשְׁפָּטִי is here probably the legitimate claim based on election and promise. In the context of exile, DI quotes the words of community lament, to express Israel's complaint, and protests against the way in which God has acted.

In the context of this socio-historical crisis, DI asks: "Do you not know? Have you not heard?" This question is already asked in v.21. But here it is in perfect tense, reflecting that the information has long been available.[71] By these words, DI once again refers to the majesty of the creator. 'Yahweh is an everlasting God, and Creator of the end of the earth.' The reality of God as creator and redeemer is not a new discovery. It was in their confessions from the beginning. One of the creator's properties is his limitless extension in time (everlasting) and in space (the end of the earth). The creator's unrestrained vastness is set over against the narrow lot of Israel and the challenges which faced her.[72] The only thing demanded from Israel is to listen, look and remember.

With verses 29-31, the prophet reaches his goal, the hope for Israel. Those who hope in Yahweh will never be disappointed. Once again, the prophet mentions the name Yahweh explicitly.

---

[71] John N. Oswalt, *Isaiah*, 73.
[72] C. Westermann, *Isaiah*, 60.

Yahweh is the one who can give new strength. Therefore, DI concludes this unit by emphasizing Yahweh's creative power and purpose of creation. This creative power is especially efficacious in "the weary" and "the powerless." The faint, the one who has no might, is the Israel of the day. Yahweh gives new life to "those who put their hope in Yahweh." DI thus, affirms that God's creative power is focused redemptively on Israel's distress, however, the promise is directed to those in Israel who "trust in the Lord"

Two assertions about the "youths" (נערים) and "young" (בחור) are contrasted with four statements about "those who hope for Yahweh." נער means the status of someone who with a few rights, a subordinate and a dependent person.[73] A man is נער as long as he is single. נער is the quintessence of youth and hence also of youthful strength. בחור is really "the chosen one" or "choice young men," specifically selected and trained for military service.[74] (See Judges. 20:15; I Sam 24:2; Jer 51:3; Ezk 23:6). It precisely means the people whose power is extolled. But, even the most vital on earth must eventually wear down. Human strength is limited. Human at their most vigorous are mortal and fallible.

"But those who wait" are contrasted with the young men and the chosen warriors. Those who wait for Yahweh will receive new strength. The idiom "wait for Yahweh" implies two things: a complete dependence on God and a willingness to allow him to decide the terms.[75] This is a life of confident expectation and imagination.

They shall go up with wings like eagles. This is a difficult clause both in translation and in interpretation. The verbal form יַעֲלוּ can both *Qal* ("they will mount up, go up") and *Hiphil* ("cause to rise up i.e. "grow")[76] The causative meaning of *Hiphil* reflects the ancient belief that eagles grow new feathers every ten years for a hundred years (see Ps 103:5). That is, those who hope for Yahweh

---

[73] Klaus Baltzer, *Deutero-Isaiah*, 84.
[74] John N. Oswalt, *Isaiah*, 71.
[75] John N. Oswalt, *Isaiah*, 74.
[76] See J. Blenkinsopp, *Isaiah 40-55*, 190.

receive new strength to move forward. However, in this context *Qal* ("they will mount up") is equally appropriate. In Jewish tradition, the root עלה is a technical term for going up to Jerusalem,[77] and the return of the exile is symbolically anticipated.

Conclusion

As we noted above, the theology of creation in DI, in its literary, social, and religious dimension, is both a reflection and a response to the crisis that Israel faced in Babylon. Several passages in DI confirm the crisis they had undergone during their exilic life in Babylon. DI's quotation from the lamentation of the exilic community in v.27 reveals serious sensitivity of social pressure and subordination. It was a crisis that centered on a self-consciously religious group.

This crisis can be described in several dimensions. First of all, it was a crisis of faith. The experience of exile evoked several profound questions of faith. It has shaken their faith in Yahweh's power and his faithfulness. It shattered their hope. Secondly, it was a crisis in understanding Yahweh's guidance. Their cherished picture of Yahweh as the Shepherd 'who leads them to the green pastures and still waters' was distorted. Many Old Testament commentators have referred to those exiles who went to Babylon in terms of "prisoners of war," "refugees," or even "slaves." Each of these terms implies the socio-political condition of Israel in exile. "Self-preservation was the major concern of the exiles - preservation of not only traditions and values, but perhaps on occasion even physical survival."[78] The preservation of identity in the context of intercultural contact is an important focus of sociological analysis.

How can they cope with the problem of identity? If a social group is facing a crisis, people make theologies or ideologies to deal with the issue of crisis. Therefore, the theology of creation

---

[77] Klaus Baltzer, *Deutero-Isaiah*, 85.
[78] Daniel L. Smith, *The Religion of the Landless...*, 49.

can be reckoned as an identity reformulation of the exilic community.

Above all, there was a crisis in deciding the true god. The power of the Babylonian empire and the splendor of their god Marduk were set against the defeated nation Israel and their God Yahweh. So in Isa 40:12-31, DI deals with the subject of Yahweh's incomparability and uniqueness among the gods and he presents Yahweh as the Creator of the world and the Lord of universal history. In the face of his sovereign power, neither the nations and their rulers nor their gods amount to anything. Before the absolute power of Yahweh, they cannot thwart the creative goal of the Creator God. Thus the theology of creation functions as a solution to the crisis with regard to the identification of the true god.

It also reflects the psychological distress. The psychological distress was added to the religious distress, which intensified as the exile went on. This was so, as the eager expectation of an imminent return home had long died and Yahweh had not intervened on behalf of Israel in more than a generation. He simply seemed to be passing over his people's right to live (v.27)

The doubt and hesitancy concerning Yahweh's power raised by the exile provided the need for the prophet to argue persuasively against these. But a prophet who drew his message from the language of the cult is limited by the fact that the cultic salvation oracle does not deal with the question whether Yahweh can save. His ability to save was taken for granted. The question was whether he *would* save. It was a new situation of exile which created a new theological problem to the community. So the challenge before DI was to establish Yahweh's *willingness* to save along with Yahweh's *ability* to save. How can one prove Yahweh's *ability*? In the Babylonian exilic context, the idea of creation is understood as the supreme example of power to do things. Creation theology, thus, becomes a theology of hope. In the frustrated social context of the exile, it encouraged the exiles to look to the future with a renewed hope.

This also shows that the notion of a creator God is not quite new to the people. The prophet declares that Israel has known Yahweh as the sole creator from the beginning. Therefore, the prophetic community is not asking their listeners to adopt a new belief, rather to appreciate its implication in their exilic context.

6.1.2. Creator is the Protector

Text: Isaiah 41:17-20

17 The poor and [the needy][a] seek water,
   but there is none[b]
   their tongue is parched with thirst;
   I, Yahweh, will answer them,
   I, the God of Israel, will not forsake them.

18 I will open rivers on the bare heights[a]
   and rivers in the midst of valleys;
   I will make the desert into a pool of water[b],
   and the dry land into springs of water.

19 I will put in the wilderness cedar,
   acacia, myrtle, and oil tree;
   I will set cypress in the desert
   elm and box-tree[a] together.

20 that they[a] may see and know
   and consider[b] and understand together
   that the hand of Yahweh has done this
   and the Holy One of Israel has created it.

Textual Notes

17 a   ואביונים as an addition, absent in Ethiopic and Arab versions, as a secondary result of haplography, overloads the line and has probably been added since עני and אביון are often paired. (E.g. Ps. 40:17; 86:1; 109:16) They occur frequently in parallelism. (See Joseph Blenkinsopp, *Isaiah 40-55*, 202). The heavy stich may be intentional; it exactly describes a

procession, weary and footsore. (See C. R. North, *The Second Isaiah*, 101)

17 b Note the assonance of the Hebrew מים and ואין lit. 'water and none.'

18 a C. R. North translates it as 'barren regions.' The usual translation 'bare heights' is agreed with the LXX ἐπι των ὀπεὶν.

18 b MT has sing. לאגם־מים, but pl. seems to be required, as in LXX. (See J. Blenkinsopp, *Isaiah 40-55*, 202).

19 a On the various tree species, see *IDB* Vol. 2, p. 284ff.

20 a Since no subject is specified for the verb, it is possible that the intended subject are the "poor and the needy" of v. 17. But most of the commentators think that the reference is to the entire human race. See John N. Oswalt, *The Book of Isaiah. Chapters 40-66*, (1998), 88.

20 b Lit. "to put," that is, put into heart; for its full form (שימו לבבכם) Hag. 1:5

Form, Structure, and Setting

Most commentators consider the section 41:17-21 as a single unit. However, some scholars keep different views regarding the delimitations of the entire chapter. For example, scholars like R.J. Richard and Muilenburg consider Isa 41:1-42:4 together as a unit.[79] Verse 17a introduces an entirely new event with the description of the condition of the people, which is followed by Yahweh's determination to answer to the situation and end with Israel's acknowledgement of Yahweh as the Creator, and therefore, this can be considered a separate unit.

---

[79] Cf. R. J. Richard, "The Function of Idol Passages in Second Isaiah," *CBQ* 42 (1980), 453; J. Muilenburg, "The Book of Isaiah: Chapter 40-66," 447.

With regard to the form, Westermann thinks, this is a "proclamation of salvation."[80] Stuhlmueller also considers it as an oracle of salvation.[81] However, this is essentially distinct from the two oracles of salvation which precede it (vv.8-13 and 14-16), in which the emphasis falls on the fact that the assurance bears upon the present. This proclamation of salvation is related to the future. Moreover, the entire oracle, in contrast with the preceding oracle, is in third person.

Since it begins with a complaint that 'when the poor and needy look for water, but there is none,' Westermann suggests the passage may be understood as the divine response to the communal lament.[82] The poor and the needy felt that Yahweh is not answering them in their distress. We can see an allusion to the lament in this verse. However, the particular setting of this passage is difficult to identify.[83]

This announcement of the future is dominated by the image of an oasis created in the desert. The purpose of Yahweh in answering the needy is that "all may see and know; all may consider and understand that the hand of Yahweh has done this, the Holy One of Israel has created it" (v.20). Most of the commentators assume that these generous acts are to facilitate the anticipated return from the Babylonian diaspora, but the passage says nothing of this. Rather the passage focuses on the ecological transformation as the result of Yahweh's creative action.

An important key to understand this unit is to recognize its relation to chapter 40. Israel has complained that its משפט has been disregarded (40:27). The Hebrew term has a wider and a narrower meaning. It can refer to a larger social order or a specific instance

---

[80] C. Westermann, *Isaiah*, 79; F. F. Melugin, *The Formation...*, 95.

[81] Stuhlmueller, *Creative Redemption...*, 17

[82] According to Westermann, this oracle of salvation is actually given as an answer to the individual lament, although it has affinities with the community lament. See Westermann, *Isaiah*, 79.

[83] See F. F. Melugin, *The Formation...*, .95.

of a legal decision that adjudicates a case.[84] The statement in v.17a: "the poor and needy seek water, but there is none, their tongue is parched with thirst," reflects the same mood and situation of v. 27 in the previous chapter. Therefore, once again, in order to counter their argument and uphold their faith, DI jogs their memory about the cultic traditions in which Israel confessed her God as Creator.

The structure of this passage is as follows:

1. An allusion to the lament (v.17a)[85]
2. Yahweh's turning towards Israel with a determination to redeem them
3. The ecological transformation as the result of Yahweh's creative act.
4. The end result: Recognition of Yahweh as Creator.

So, as Westermann has pointed out, this oracle of salvation, which was given as an answer to the lament of the community, ends with a great recognition of Yahweh's creative power and purpose. Yahweh as the God of creation is not only willing but fully able to transform their fate and execute his purpose with Israel and the world.

Socio-historical comment focusing on the creation motif

Verse 17a offers a description of the distress.[86] The syntax of the sentence can be understood in the following way. 'Verse 17aα is a nominative clause with a predicative participle, which stresses the enduring character of the action. Verse 17aα emphasizes the

---

[84] B. S. Childs, *Isaiah*, 317.
[85] See Westermann, *Isaiah*, 79.
[86] Stuhlmueller seems correct: "BH suggest changes in TM *metri causa*, but the alliteration and assonance are too exquisite to be tempered with: the four opening words ending in *îm* (the long seeking), and the quick reversal *maim wâ'ain*; then the rasping, dry sound of seven successive *â* vowels." (*Creative Redemption*... 70-71 n. 229): See also North, *The Second Isaiah*, 101.

urgency by using the perfect tense of the verb: there are tongues already parched.[87]

The people are described as "the needy and the poor" (העניים והאביונים). This pair *"poor and needy"* is frequent in OT (e.g., Deut. 15:11; 24:14; Job 24:14; Ps. 35:10; 37:14; 40:17; 70:5; 86:1; 109:16; Prov. 31:20; Jer. 22:16; Ezk.16:49; 18:12). It describes men and women who are low in the social scale, without any influence and whose rights are denied (cf. Lev. 19:10; Ezek. 22:29; Isa 58:7; Isa 10:2). However, except here, this phrase does not appear elsewhere in DI. For DI, it means not merely material poverty but also a more generalized powerlessness. The sense here is almost certainly figurative.[88] It is not water that these people need, especially in well-watered Babylon or on the return from Babylon, the likely route being by way of the Euphrates Valley to Aleppo and then southward.[89] Thirst is a powerful image of human need physically, spiritually and emotionally. So DI was using this image in order to describe the conditions of the exiles in Babylon.

Because God is the creator, he takes up the cause of the underprivileged. The ancient West Asian creation faith was concerned not only with the origin of the world, but also with the present world and its proper order. In the wisdom theology, God's special concern for the poor and the needy is one of the main themes. (see Prov. 14:31; 17:5; 22:2; 29:13). Almost all the recent scholars have recognized DI's connection with wisdom. It implicitly warns not to oppress the poor man but have mercy upon the needy (Prov. 14:31). God is on the side of the poor and needy. So when DI used these terms for the people, their social setting indicates that he was not talking about the water in the literal sense.

God declares that he will respond to their cries personally: "I, Yahweh will answer them" (v.17b). The earthly distress is not

---

[87] Klaus Baltzer, *Deutero Isaiah*, 108.
[88] John N. Oswalt, *The Book of Isaiah*, 95.
[89] See Y. Aharoni and M. Avi-Yonah, Macmillan Bible Atlas (New York: Macmillan, 1968), map 170, for a representation of the routes of the return, cited by John N. Oswalt, *The Book of Isaiah*, 95.

hidden from Yahweh. He learns directly how desperate the situation is, and, therefore, he takes the decision to help. The promise "not forsake" (עזב) is noteworthy. In Israel's covenant tradition this verb means the falling away, or defection from Yahweh and the breach of the covenant.[90] If Yahweh then "forsakes" his people, this means that they are cut off from salvation and life (Deut 31:17; Josh 24:20). This was one of the serious concerns in their lament (See Ps 22:1). The Book of Lamentations, a collections from the generation to which DI belonged, agonized over the dread possibility that God abandoned Israel to hostile powers. It concludes with this impassioned plea:

> Why have you forgotten us completely?
> Why have you forsaken us these many days?
> Restore us to yourself, O LORD, that we may be restored;
> renew our days as of old-
> unless you have utterly rejected us (מָאֹס),
> and are angry with us beyond measure (Lam. 5:20-22).

This was the lament of the exilic people too. To them DI assures: 'Yahweh has not rejected (מָאֹס) you, God of Israel will not forsake (עזב) you.' DI gives them the assurance of God's presence for his people. This means hope, and that hope is grounded upon God's creative power (see vv.18-20). It is God's creative power that will change their fortunes.

Verses 18-19 are closely related to v.17. The sovereign statement "I, Yahweh' in v.17 is followed by four pronouncements in the first person imperfect: "I will...." These sound like a government declaration.[91] All the activity is God's. The desert highway will become an oasis. Rivers flow continuously from highlands. What was once a barren desert will be transformed to productive land with bubbling spring water. However, what does

---

[90] See H. P. Stähli, "עזב 'zb to abandon," *TLOT* 2:866-68. (Cf. Deut 29:25; 31:16-17; Josh 24:16, 20; Judg. 2:12-14; I Sam 8:8; 12:10; I Kings 9:9; 11:33; Isa 65:11; Jer. 22:9).

[91] Klaus Baltzer, *Deutero-Isaiah*, 110.

DI actually mean by this? Is DI referring to the return of the exiles to the home country through the desert, which becomes an oasis as a result of Yahweh's creative act? Or, is it only a prophetic imagination of the future? According to Westermann, 'it thus ceases to be the pitiless, insurmountable barrier between the exiles and their homeland. It becomes the highway. The same power of miraculous transformation which Israel had time and again experienced in the past, when, death from drought staring her in the face, she prayed to her God – this same transforming power can turn the desert into fertile country and thus prepare the way that leads to the homeland.'[92] Most authors admit the presence of the Exodus motif in 41:17-20.[93]

However, in its socio-historical context, the community of DI wanted to show more than a new Exodus, which is described to be more glorious than the first one. Many scholars think that DI's language at this point is symbolic.[94] The "desert" poses a threat to life. The dislocation from home, dispossession of the land of promise, life under conditions of political, and social and religious estrangement were a frustrating experience for the exiles, which shaped their language and symbolism of religious despair and hope. It could be interpreted as the exilic condition by giving a moving description of the socio-economic plight and the degrading experiences of the exiles.

Verse 20 is remarkable at this point. What is the result of this transformation? That the people may "see," "know," "consider" and "understand" that Yahweh has done it and the Holy One of Israel has created it. By this, DI challenges Israel to recognize God by reflecting on his creative act, and to have a proper perception about God. It challenges Israel to review its history with the insight of Yahweh's plan and purpose in every historical event from the beginning of creation. The imperfect forms of these verbs are significant. Even in the midst of confusion and suffering of exile, they can uphold the true faith in God and hope for the future.

---

[92] C. Westermann, *Isaiah*, 80.
[93] North, Muilenburg, Rignell, Marti et al. see exodus motif in this unit.
[94] See C. Stulhmueller, *Creative Redemption...*, 72.

The Function of the Creation Theology

The description of the people as "needy and poor," as noted above, indicates their socio-economic status, without any right or influence in the society and as those who suffered under the powerful Babylonians. The social 'rootlessness' of the people put them under socio-economic pressures and made them dependable on their foreign overlords for all their needs. They could no longer support themselves for their daily needs.

Therefore, these people were in need of some special back-up and protection and it was an obligation laid on the community of DI. God's special concern for the "poor and needy" is frequently acknowledged in Israel's liturgical traditions (see Pss 9:18; 10:8-10; 18:27; 35:10; 74:19). We have already noted that the same concern is explicitly stated in the wisdom theology (chapter 3). God is on the side of the people who are without any right. God, as the creator has concern for the poor (Prov.14:31; 17:15 etc.) As Creator, he takes up the cause of the underprivileged. Therefore, the DI community as the inheritors of those traditions took the responsibility to give these people special protection and hope as the obligation of the community. Through the creation theology, the community of DI was assuring the exiles Yahweh's special protection to them, who were economically exploited by the Babylonian overlords. The creation theology, thus, functions as a protecting and an upholding factor to the suffering community and as an ideology for an egalitarian view of the society.

The connection between the social reality and the theology of creation should not be overlooked. The socio-economic-political factors had a crucial role in formulating the life and thinking of the exile. The book of DI does not conceal the economic factors behind its social life. The social 'rootlessness'[95] made the exilic Israel dependable on their foreign lord for all their daily needs, and often it led them to forced labor. As we have noted elsewhere,

---

[95] Gerd Theissen, *The Sociology of Early Palestinian Christianity*, (Philadelphia: Fortress Press, 1978), 33.

the harsh vocabulary[96] used frequently by DI in association with the Babylonian exile indicates the hardship they experienced in Babylon. So, the expression "poor and needy" must not simply be dismissed as purely metaphorical with no historical basis. The social rootlessness connected with the socio-economic pressures which Israel underwent during the exile made the DI community to revitalize the traditional concept of the Creator who has a special concern for the poor and needy. Thus the theology of creation was not only the result of the social situation of the exile but also a response to the social situation of exile. Also the relatedness of creation theology to the socio-economic-political condition of the exile means that the primary intention of the creation theology is to encourage the exilic community to take a stance against the Babylonian power.

Thus, the theology of creation is not to be seen as a development out of the contemplation of the exilic community on the reality; rather the life in exile was the determining factor behind the formation of the creation theology. But to what extent one can consider the creation theology as a product of exilic society or the product of the exilic social condition? Why do the other exilic communities do not form such a theology? It would seen then that the social condition itself cannot create such a theology. The social condition plus the already existing ideas and values together prompt the DI community to form the theology of creation. The influence of Babylonian creation myth was another factor behind the formation of DI's creation theology. Thus, these three factors together worked behind the formation of the creation theology.

Creation and Universalism

God's purpose in answering the needs of his people and delivering them from the sufferings of their social condition is stated clearly:

> that they may see and know
> and consider and understand together

---

[96] See chapter 4.

that the hand of Yahweh have done this
and the Holy One of Israel has created it

The purpose is the shared understanding of God's power in creation. The word "together" (יַחְדָּו) is significant. This gives the text its wide scope. The immediate beneficiary of Yahweh's work is only a small group of people. But its implication will spread out beyond the small group. By this Yahweh is going to be recognized as the Lord of the whole world. Israel is thus redeemed not for its own enjoyment but as a vehicle of God's revelation.[97] This emphasis is prominent in DI (see 49:6; 52:10). Israel will therefore become a living evidence of God's unique deity, through whom the world will recognize Yahweh as the sole Creator.

The word "together" implies another sociological factor. This word signifies a harmonious life with all kinds of people without given consideration to their ethnic diversity. Thus, creation theology functions as an integrating factor which gave the exiles in Babylon a sense of belonging and integration. Creation theology functions as a unifying factor in society. It brings people together to express their hope and solidarity and concern for the entire humanity.

6.1.3. *Creator's Commission*

Text: Isaiah 42:5-9.

5   Thus says the God, Yahweh[a],
    who creating[b] the heaven and stretching them out[c]
    who spread out the earth and its produce[d]
    who gives breath to the people on it
    and spirit to those who walk on it.

---

[97] See John S. Oswalt, *The Book of Isaiah*, 96.

6   I, Yahweh, have called[a] you in righteousness
    and I will take you by your hand
    and I will guard[b] you
    and make[c] you as covenant to the people[d]
    and light to the nations.

7   to open blind eyes[a]
    to bring out the prisoners from the dungeon[b]
    [and] from the prison[c]
    those who sit in darkness.

8   I am Yahweh, that is my name
    and my glory to another I will not give
    nor my praise to idols.

9   The former things, behold, have come to pass,
    and new things I am declaring,
    before they spring forth I will make you hear.

Textual Notes

5a. 1QIs[a] reads האל האלהים in place of MT האל יהוה. However, other versions such as Targum, Peshitta and Vulgate support MT. LXX has κυριος ὁ θεος (Lord God). The word האל may be to convince the audience that Yahweh is the only God, who is in absolute control over his creation.

5b. The participle form בּוֹרֵא denotes the creative act of Yahweh as a continuous process and it indicates its influence on the present as well as on the future.

5c. Here heavens are referred to as a tent.

5d. The word for that which comes out of the earth, צאצא, appears only in Job and Isaiah (Isa 22:24; 34:1; 48:19; 61:9; 64:23). As both of these texts deal with the issue of suffering of God's people, this word has an economic connotation.

6a. According to MT, the four verbs in verse 6- נתן, נצר, חזק, קרא - are given respectively perfect, imperfect, imperfect,

220 EXILE AND THEOLOGY OF CREATION

6b.   imperfect form. Syr. and Vg. translate all four with the past tense, while Tg. does so with the first and second as past. This diversity argues for retaining the MT reading. According to Oswalt, 'the holding, keeping, and giving are present and future outworking of the past calling.'(See John S. Oswalt, *The Book of Isaiah*,116).

6b.   וְאֶצָּרְךָ has been translated differently. LXX: και 'ενισχυσω σε ("I will strengthen you"). This is followed by Peshitta (ואצרך). Targum has ואתקנינך ("I will establish you"). MT's וְאֶצָּרְךָ can be either from יצר (='form') or נצר (= 'keep') DI uses יצר more frequently (8 times), so commentators like Duhm, Elliger, Mckenzie, Westermann, Baltzer et al. translate it as "I form you." However, in the present context MT וְאֶצָּרְךָ is taken to derive from verbal stem נצר, (See C. R. North, *Second Isaiah*, 110) and this counterparts with the preceding phrase.

6c.   Following Vulgate and Peshitta, commentators Mckenzie, Baltzar et al. translates it in perfect tense.

6d.   לברית עם a variety of translations are possible to this phrase. It can be translated as 'covenant people' or 'covenant with the people' or 'covenant of a people' etc.

7a.   Targum reads, "to open the eyes of the house of Israel who are as blind to the law."

7b.   Targum reads here 'to bring forth their exiles from among the nations where they are like prisoners."

7c.   Lit. "from the house of confinement."

Form, Structure and setting

Various views have been expressed by commentators with regard to the limitation of the unit. Since the publication of B. Duhm's book "*Das Buch Jesaja*" in 1892 with the hypothetical thesis that Isaiah 42:1-4; 49:1-6; 50:4-9; 52:13-53:12 form a separate literary unit which must have been composed by some one other than DI and inserted later in the book,[98] commentators struggle with the question of the limitation of the servant songs. There are however two dominant views with regard to the limitation of the unit. The most generally accepted view since Duhm is that Isaiah 42:1-4 is a unit in itself. Another trend is to view Isaiah 42:1-9 together as a literary unit. Scholars like K. Koch, K. Baltzer, J. Blenkinsopp et al. have treated Isaiah 42:1-9 as a unit.

However, there is a general agreement today that 42:5-9 form a unit.[99] The structure and form of the passage also seem to suggest that Isa 42:5-9 is a separate unit. It is most natural to take v.5, with its 'Thus says Yahweh' and its participial relative clause as the beginning of a new section.[100] (cf. Isa 43:16f.). In both cases (vv.1-4 and vv.5-9), the speaker is Yahweh himself. Nevertheless, the addressee varies. In addition, the "place" of the first one (according to the form) should be the council of the heavenly court. (cf. Job 1:6-12). But verses 5-7 form the commissioning of the servant and the commissioning is mediated through a spokesman who has been empowered to utter the formula: "Thus says Yahweh."

The sociological study also shows that verses 5-9 constitute a separate unit. The sociological analysis of the manner in which the servant accomplishes the task is different in both sections. According to the section 42:1-4, the manner in which the servant has to carry out the task of bringing justice to the nations stands emphatically in contrast to the manner of conflict or through the use of force (see 42:2-3). But in 42:6-7, the manner in which the servant functions is different. Here, one can detect the presence of the idea of conflict, the use of force to accomplish the task.

With regards to the genre, as Melugin has pointed out, it is more difficult to define precisely the genre with its setting and intention.[101] Begrich understands it as an oracle commissioning a

---

[98] B. Duhm, *Das Buch Jesaja*, 284ff.
[99] See Westermann, *Isaiah*, 98.
[100] See, C. R. North, *The Second Isaiah*, 110.
[101] Roy F. Melugin, *The Formation...*, 65.

prophet.¹⁰² Klaus Baltzer suggests that verses 5-7 indicate the actual installation, with direct address to the Servant.¹⁰³ Westermann also identifies this text as a commissioning, but it is not clear who is being commissioned.¹⁰⁴ However, without doubt these verses reflect a commissioning.

The structure of this passage: The introductory messenger formula is followed by a series of creative attribution to the האל יהוה. He is the creator of heaven and earth and humankind. This forms the introduction to the oracle proper, which comes in vv.6 and 7 and speaks of someone who is given neither a name nor a designation, but whom God intends to make the 'covenant of the people' and the 'light to the nations'(v.6), in order to open blind eyes and bring out prisoners from the dungeon (v.7).¹⁰⁵ Thus, the second part provides the purpose of commissioning. According to v.7, the purposes are "to open the blind eyes and bring out the prisoners from the dungeon." A series of catchwords points to the servant's function in the sphere of social-psychological realm of the hearers. The conclusion takes the form of self-prediction on the part of Yahweh, by which he insists that he alone is God (v.8). The last verse (v.9), which has no apparent connection with the preceding verses, is a prediction of the 'new things' which Yahweh is going to accomplish.

In sum, as Melugin has rightly pointed out, although this unit is based on the traditional forms of speech, it can be considered as a free creation which at the same time does not stray far from the genre which they imitate.¹⁰⁶

Socio-historical comment focusing on the creation motif

According to Stuhlmueller, for at least two reasons this poem is important in assessing the creation theology in DI. This text may

---

[102] Begrich, *Studien zu Deuterojesaja*, 61
[103] Klaus Baltzer, *Deutero Isaiah*, 125.
[104] See Westermann, *Isaiah*, 98.
[105] Westernann, *Isaiah*, 98.
[106] See Melugin, *The Formation*..., 69.

AN EXEGETICAL STUDY OF SELECTED PASSAGES... 223

very likely be DI's last reference to "creation" in his poems, chronologically considered.[107] Secondly, this aspect of cosmic creation may be responsible for DI's important shift from the redemption of a particular group of people (Israel) to the redemption of the whole world.

After the description of the servant and his ministry in verses 1-4, these verses are given as an address to the servant directly with more specific task. However, the identity of the servant is an enigma. Who is the servant in verses 5-9? This question has indeed been asked continually. Commentators do not have consensus in this regard. There is no sufficient evidence for assuming that the servant of 42:1-4 is the same person as is addressed in verse 6. Some scholars (S. Mowinckel, Hans Schmidt, et al.) think that verses 5-9 are addressed to Cyrus. This view is tenable only with difficulty. True, Cyrus is "called" (45:3f.; 46:11; 48:15), in "righteousness" (45:13). Yahweh has taken his right hand (45:1) and he is to free the exiles (45:13). But imagine him as ברית עם is difficult, or speak of him as "a light to the nations."[108] Another assumption is 'Israel.' However, because of the singular nature of the addressee in verse 6, the servant cannot be Israel.

A detailed discussion about the identity of the servant is beyond the scope of this study. However, DI's commissioning of the servant with the creation motif is significant.

He who called the servant is the creator of heaven and earth and the creator of humankind. Therefore the commissioning of the servant begins with the praise of God's power and wisdom shown in creation. The mention of creation indicates that the

---

[107] See C. Stuhlmueller, *Creative Redemption...*, 205-6. Westermann also thinks that the description of the salvation which Israel is to bring to the nation is similar to that of Trito-Isaiah and therefore these verses as a later expansion to the Servant Song in 42:1-4. (See Westermann, *Isaiah*, 101). However, it is impossible to prove and therefore many scholars do not accept his assumption about this text as the 'last reference to creation chronologically considered'.

[108] See C. R. North, *The Second Isaiah*, 111.

servant might be a group of people who identified and worshiped Yahweh as the creator. Here we are offered a clue to understand the servant: The servant is not an individual, rather a community who worshiped Yahweh as the creator and the Lord of history. Here the language is familiar to the Psalter. We have already noted DI's connection with the temple singers, who were in charge of the Psalter which extolled Yahweh as the creator and lord of history. (Ch. 5 a) Albertz Rainer also suggests that by 'Deutero Isaiah' we can understand a community of theologians gathered around a master who came from circles of descendants of the temple singers and cult prophets of the Jerusalem temple with their nationalistic attitude.[109] Therefore with all probability we can adduce that the servant in DI's mind was this community.

The one who calls this community to establish God's loving order on earth is in fact the Creator of the earth. Thus, DI describes the vocation of the servant community in the context of the creation of the world. The designation of the Creator as "the God Yahweh" is significant. This is the sole instance in the Old Testament where God is termed הָאֵל יְהוָה (the God Yahweh).[110] The designation is an acknowledgement of Yahweh's uniqueness. The creative attribute of Yahweh follows in three relative clauses: creating the sky and setting out the heavenly bodies in it, laying out the earth like a landscape gardener and filling it with people, and imparting to them breath (נְשָׁמָה) and the spirit of life (רוּחַ). The order of creation here resembles the order of creation in the Genesis creation account.

DI's use of "El" as name for God is especially significant in its Babylonian social context where they became a mixed group (see chapter 4). DI is touching on the relationship to the gentile people (see, e.g., 45:14-15). Behind the link between "God" and "Yahweh"

---

[109] Rainer Albertz, *A History of Israelite Religion*, 415.

[110] cf. Ps 85:9: יְהוָה הָאֵל (*BHS*). But here this phrase is unusual and metrically suspect. So Duhm suggests the inversion of יְהוָה הָאֵל. See H -J. Kraus, *Psalms 60-150: A Commentary* (Minneapolis: Fortress Press, 1993), 173.

is the hermeneutical decision to put together the names used for God in Genesis 1 and 2. It is the same God, who has created both the world and human beings. The cardinal catchwords in Genesis 1 can be recognized: "create"(ברא) v.1; "heaven (שמים) v.1; "firmament" (רקיע) v.6; "earth" (ארץ) v.1; "bring forth" (יצא) v.12. But they are newly interpreted.[111]

The most interesting change is that the heaven is "stretched out" (נטה), where as the earth is "firm" (רקע). This is a correction of Genesis 1, made because of the presuppositions of a modified worldview due to their exilic experience.[112] Here the description of God is identical to the description of God in 40:12-26. It speaks of the incomparability of Yahweh and his exclusive control over the world and as the one who maintains an exclusive care for it and for its inhabitants. The same concern for humans is expressed in vv.6-7.

The 'produce' (צאצא) of earth at this place has a special significance. Does it indicate any economic oppression that Israel underwent during its exile? According to the Marxian theory, "produce" is always related to the labor forces of the workers group. Bustenay Oded has suggested that the exiled community eventually became land-tenants of royal land.[113] Thus, it is conceivable that the exiles were employed as laborer in the agricultural production of the land. But the produce of the land were taken away from them.

"Breath" (נשמה) is the key word at the creation of the human being according to Gen.2:7. However, the older concept of the creation of one man (as in Gen. 1 & 2) no longer appears here. "Breath" is given not only to "Adam," the human being (האדם) as an individual; it is given to all "the people on it" (לעם עליה), that is, on the earth. This can hardly mean a single people. DI relates the term "people" (עם) inclusively, being applied to the whole community. The word for people, whose most frequent usage is

---

[111] Kalus Baltzer, *Deutero Isaiah*, 131.
[112] See Kalus Baltzer, *Deutero Isaiah*, 131.
[113] Bustenay Oded, "Judah and the Exile", 483.

as a designation of the people Israel, is here expanded to designate all peoples, the human race.¹¹⁴ The רוּחַ also is given to all those who walk on the earth. After Yahweh has put his spirit upon the servant in v.1, he now puts his spirit upon all human beings. Thus a universal scope of the servant's mission is implied here.

From creation to mission

It is interesting to note why the call of the servant is substantiated by the reference to God's work of creation. The creation of human beings is the reason for sending the Servant. Also creation is the reason for the universality of the Torah and its validity for all human beings. Here the whole dynamics of the statements about creation become evident.¹¹⁵

After the description of the creation, DI straight away moves to describe the purpose of the calling. "I make you a covenant of the people." It is very difficult to interpret the expression ברית עם (covenant of the people). Scholars have given a great deal of attention to ברית עם in an attempt to understand what 'people' is being referred to and what the phrase actually means.¹¹⁶ The sense implied here is almost certainly that the Servant represents the covenant. But to whom does the Servant represent the covenant? Those who take the Servant as an individual identify "the people" as Israel, while those who take the Servant as Israel must identify "the people" as humanity. What actually עם means? The same word in v.5 is shown by the context that it refers to humanity. The structure of the sentence is synonymous parallelism; therefore the meaning of עם is considered as synonymous with its parallel member גּוֹיִם (nations). However, this cannot be taken as conclusive, because recent studies of parallelism have shown that in the so-called synonymous parallelism it is normal to have a progression from the first to the second member. ¹¹⁷

---

[114] Westermann, *Isaiah*, 99.
[115] See Klaus Baltzer, *Deutero Isaiah*, 131.
[116] See D. R. Hillers, "*Brît 'âm*: Emancipation of the People," *JBL* 97 (1978)175-82.
[117] See R. Alter, *The Art of Biblical Poetry* (New York: Basic, 1985), 62-63.

A survey of DI's use of the term עם shows that in most cases they use this term to mean 'Israel.' (eg. 40:1; 42:22; 43:8, 20, 21; 47:6; 49:13; 51:7).[118] Here as well as in 49:8, עם is coupled with ברית. As we noted above, the servant is not an individual, rather a community which was trained properly in Torah to be a ברית to the people of Israel and illuminated properly to be the "light" to the nations. This means the DI community will be the link that connects the people of Israel properly with Yahweh. And 'the light to the nations' mean that the community of DI will provide the needed insight to the nation about the blessing of a life in relation with Yahweh. Here the prophet is talking about the twofold task of the community. As a 'covenant to the people' they have a task of bringing the people of Israel to the living relationship with their redeemer Yahweh, and as the 'light to the nation,' their task is to bring the whole nation into a right relationship with their creator (cf.49:6).

Therefore, limiting the significance of the term ברית to the 'people of Israel' will be inappropriate in the views of DI. The term ברית therefore needs to be understood in its universalistic background, as in the case of the covenant with Noah in Gen.9. The Servant's vocation as a covenant mediator between Yahweh and the people of Israel does not confine his task to Israel only. His commission is extended to the whole world since he is appointed as the light to the nations. The Servant is therefore called by the Creator God to perform his purpose of creation through his servant.

The *opening of blind eyes and releasing prisoners from dungeon* need not be treated only figuratively. It refers most naturally to the physical hardship of the exiles (cf. 47:6). However, in either case, the servants are called by the Creator God to perform his creative purpose through them. Thus the biblical basis of mission begins with the concept of creation. Creation is the platform of

---

[118] It is true, in some places DI uses this term to mean explicitly the humankind as whole (e.g. 40:7; 42:5).

mission, and creation gives the basic biblical worldview of reality. The thought of God's creative power that called the world into being leads into the thought of how the same creative power can bring a new world into being. Thus, the idea of mission gave the community a sense of responsibility to the rest of the community.

With these implications for the mission of the community, creation theology finally moves toward the final stage in which the whole nations recognize him as the true God (v.8). The declaration "*my glory to another I will not give,*" is significant at this point. Following this, it was presumed and taken for granted that the rise of Cyrus and his victory would bring an end to exile. And it was the fundamental reason for the contention between DI with other exiles. So, DI categorically states that it was not Cyrus but Yahweh is going to be glorified by this. The credit for Israel's deliverance does not belong to Cyrus; it wholly belongs to Yahweh. Thus the creation theology at this point reduces tension within the exilic community with regard to the use of Cyrus as God's agent of deliverance.

To sum up, Yahweh's commissioning of the servant is closely linked with the idea of creation. Yahweh as the sole creator is calling his servant to perform his creative purpose through his servants. The creation of humanity is the reason for the sending of the Servant, and also the reason for the universality of his Torah- its validity for all human beings. Here the whole dynamics of the statements about creation becomes evident.

And the functional analysis of mission begins by examining its social structure. It identifies the recurrent pattern of relationship between Israel and the nations. It provides a sense of purpose of life, meaning for life to the individual. It provides an opportunity to the believers to do something meaningful for their God. In its structural functional analysis, mission seeks a harmonious interaction among different communities.

6.1.4. Creator of Israel

Text: Isaiah 43:1

43:1 But now[a], thus says Yahweh
   who created you, Jacob
   and who formed[b] you, Israel
   Do not be afraid, for I have redeemed[c] you
   I have called[c] (you)[d] by name, you are mine.

Textual Notes

43:1a. The phrase ועתה indicates its connection to the preceding passage. The hopeless plight in which the exiles now find themselves is going to be changed by their Creator.

b. יצר (*form*), a word used particularly to indicate the work of a potter (Isa 29:16; 41:25; Jer. 18:1ff; Similarly in Phoenician and Ugaritic).

c. Scholarly views differ considerably as to the significance of the perfect tenses of "redeemed" and "called." Some believe that both are the so-called prophetic perfect in which the future action is seen as already completed.[119] Calling by name is most likely a past action, referring to the naming of a child at its birth, as God named his people Israel. Also seeing the act of redemption as having occurred at the Exodus, some scholars see both as completed actions in the past. But the phrase "do not fear" suggests that the redemption is something that is anticipated in the future.

d. *BHS*, following the versions, suggests קְרָאתִיךָ (I have called you) by supplying 2nd person masc. sing. suffix to קָרָאתִי. However, following Elliger, Watts writes: Elliger is correct that this does not necessarily presume a change in the Hebrew." (See J. D Watts, *Isaiah 34-66*, 126).

---

[119] See Muilenburg, "The Book of Isaiah," 480.

Form, Structure, and Setting

This verse is an introductory messenger formula with an expansion[120] of a participial clause about creation and Yahweh's protective assurance of a salvation oracle in vv.1-7. Although Begrich treated the oracle in verses 1-7 as a unit, scholars like A. Schoors, H. E. von Waldow et al. split up vv.1-7 into two oracles (vv.1-4 and 5-7). According to Schoors, both sections show the characteristics of a complete oracle of salvation.[121] Westermann, though treated this passage as a unit, think that this oracle is constructed in two parts, vv.1-4 and 5ff, which are parallel.[122] Melugin prefers two oracles (vv.1-3a and vv.5-7) with an intervening promise that Egypt, Ethiopia, and Seba will be given up in ransom for Israel.[123] Therefore, Melugin writes, "It is better to think in terms of three parts rather than two." V.1-3a, as we saw, displays the form of the salvation oracle. The same is true of v.5-7: "Fear not" and substantiating clause expressing Yahweh's intervention may be seen in v.5b-6. Despite the fact that v. 1-7 can be isolated into three parts on the basis of both form and content, we must not assume that the text is not a unit. Melugin continues: "It is uncertain whether Isaiah 43:1-7 is the work of a collector or an originally unified poem. The overbalanced line in v. 7 suggests that we have to do with a collector who tried to relate the end to the beginning, but the evidence is not clear enough for certainty. In the present form of the text, however, it may be read as a unified poem."[124]

Watts's citation from Mark Worthing's arch structure of vv.1-7 also suggests it as a unit.[125] According to this structure, this oracle begins and ends with the creation theme. In the beginning and in its conclusion, DI reminds the people that just as God created and

---

[120] The enlargement of the messenger formula is a usual style of DI. See 43:14, 16-17; 44:2; 48:17; 49:7; 54:8.
[121] A. Schoors, *I Am God Your Saviour*, 68.
[122] Westermann, *Isaiah*, 115.
[123] R. F. Melugin, *The Formation* ..., 105.
[124] R. F. Melugin, *The Formation* ..., 106.
[125] See John D. W. Walts, *Isaiah*..., 129.

AN EXEGETICAL STUDY OF SELECTED PASSAGES... 231

shaped the heaven and the earth, so he brought them into existence as his own people. The way in which *qara' bᵉšem, bara'*, and *yasār* are used in v.1 and v.7 shows that all the seven verses must be taken together.[126]

Its intricate structure is framed (v.1 and v.7) with a depiction of God as Creator. The first depiction of God as Creator is followed by an assurance "Do not fear," with a description of God's redemptive act in the history. Thus, as Paul D. Hanson has pointed out, 'it highlights the constancy of divine compassion as evidenced in the creation of Israel.'[127]

Socio-Historical Comment focusing on the creation motif

In chapters, 40 and 41 the theme of God as creator of the heaven and earth had been dominant and thereby DI elucidated Yahweh's supremacy over the earth and its history. Now Israel is the focus of God's creative power. God not only created Israel but also redeemed her. Moreover, DI extends the theme of God's creation to the historical relationship with his people. Verses 1 and 7 make the point that it is because of God's special relationship to Israel, she is going to experience his grace. He created and shaped Israel long ago and will not forsake it now.

According to Westermann, these words take us to the very heart of DI's proclamation. Here we can most easily feel the assurance with which the community of DI was able to proclaim to their fellow-captives that the decisive change in their lot had already taken place.[128] And the ground for that change is nothing but the fact that Yahweh is their Creator. It stands in marked contrast to the preceding unit in 42:18-25, where Israel is described as blind and deaf. DI portrays Israel's inability to recognize and respond to God by this metaphor. In the previous section, DI deals with a challenge to God's ability and desire to save. Having shown

---

[126] Melugin, *The Formation* ..., 105.
[127] Paul D. Hanson, *Isaiah 40-66*, Interpretation (Louisville, Kentucky: John Knox Press, 1995), 61.
[128] Westermann, *Isaiah*, 115.

that the problem is not on God's side, he once again returns to the creative power of Yahweh.

The introductory ועתה ("But now") link this oracle to the preceding one.[129] Israel's blindness and insensitivity may have been in the past. This is a new hour and a new situation. The hopeless plight in which the exiles now find themselves is to be followed by a glorious future in which they enjoy a special relationship with their Creator.

The theme that Yahweh created the world and the people upon it has already been elaborated in the previous passages. (cf. 40:12-26, 28 and 42:5). Now DI leads us to a more fundamental theological aspect of the doctrine of creation. The use of the term ברא is significant. This is a theological term, which is used elsewhere to denote the absolute creation of the universe. DI uses ברא very frequently (40:26, 28; 41:20; 42:5; 43:1, 7; 45:7, 8, 12, 18; 48:7; 54:16) In the OT, ברא is a technical term for God's creation, since in the *qal* its only subject is God.

יצר is a characteristic word of the second creation story (Gen. 2:7f, 19). The word is used particularly of the work of a potter (Isa 29:16; 41:25; Jer.18:1ff). At the end of this unit (in verse 7), a third word "I made" (עשה) is used. This word is common to both creation stories.

יצר also is a cosmological term, as in Gen. 2:7, since it is given as parallel to ברא. But here there is no suggestion of creation in a cosmic sense. But there can be no doubt that the doctrine of creation

---

[129] According to von Waldow, (*Jesaja 43*, BibS 29, 15) this particle belongs to the terminology of the oracle of salvation. It indicates the reversal from the lament to the corresponding oracle (cf. 44:1; 49:5). It thus comes from the original setting and has no direct bearing on the actual context in the book. (See A. Schoors, *I Am God Your Saviour*, 68). But most of the other commentators doubt this, noting the decided appropriateness of the contrast. (See Westermann, *Isaiah 40-66*, p.115). The phrase וְעַתָּה is a favorite expression in the book of Isaiah, occurring 15 times, either indicating a contrast between the former situation and a present one, or a present conclusion growing out of a description of what has been the case in the past (See J. N. Oswalt, *The Book of Isaiah*, 136).

AN EXEGETICAL STUDY OF SELECTED PASSAGES...

is in the background. Here the emphasis falls upon the coming of a people. The verbal form in v.1b גְאַלְתִּיךָ (I have redeemed you) is significant at this point. It refers strictly to Israel the nation, the words can only mean 'who created you as a nation that is, by delivering you from Egypt and leading you through the wilderness and bringing you into the Promised Land.'[130] The "creating" and "forming" would then refer to an actual historical act of God, the saving act by which he brought Israel into being.[131] The use of these terms to indicate the creation of the cosmos and the formation of Israel, underline the unity of the creating and the saving act of God.

More than once DI uses the terminology of creation in order to display Yahweh's activity in history (42:9; 48:3, 7). In Isa 44:2, 24, creation and redemption run parallel to each other. This view of creation is echoed in some of the psalms also (Ps. 100:3; 95:6 etc.). That is, as Yahweh created the world out of chaos, in the same way he created a people for himself out of the chaotic condition of slavery. The first creation was a miraculous act. The creation of Israel was also done in the same way, that is, through the miraculous act of Exodus (cf. Isa 51:9f).

At this point DI marks the appearance of something new in the relationship between God and his people.[132] For ancient Israel, just as it was with their neighbors, the question about creation was not about the origin of things. Rather it was a question of God's relationship with nature and people. DI, thus, by using the cosmological terminology elucidates Yahweh's relationship to his people. As the creation of the world shows God's purpose for the world, so the creation of the people also shows God's purpose about that people. Yahweh the Creator, who brought the world out of chaos, now as the creator of Israel will redeem them from the present chaotic condition of Babylonian exile.

---

[130] C. Westermann, *Isaiah*, 117.
[131] C. Westermann, *Isaiah*, 117.
[132] C. Westermann, *Isaiah*, 116.

Thus DI points out another dimension of his creation theology. In 42:5, as we saw, DI described the creation of the world and the creation of humanity as a whole. But here, DI focuses on Yahweh's creation of a people.

This can be seen more clearly, when we look at the social context. Already we have noted that these verses are related to the preceding passage (42:18-26). The sharp discipline of humiliation and suffering made them to ask a number of questions seeking to understand the necessity for their exile. The suffering in Babylonian exile not only brought hardship on the individual; it posed a threat to the whole people of Israel. The positive picture of Israel as Yahweh's chosen people had vanished. The prophet draws a paradoxical picture of a man who stands in the midst of a blazing fire and does not notice it (42:25). The servant is blind because he does not draw the correct implications from the experiences he has had with God (cf.42:18-20). The judgement of exile did not result repentance.

This is a chaotic condition. The connection between the social reality and DI's notion of creation is to be seen here not merely as the effect of the situation but mainly as the response to the situation. In the language of Gen. 1 and 2, DI reminds the people that just as God created and shaped the physical universe out of chaos, so he brought them into existence as his own people. Although the emphasis here is not on the doctrine of creation, there can be no doubt that the doctrine is in the background. The argument that Israel is a particular creation of God could have weight only if the hearers understood the allusion to creation: "Just as he created the heavens and shaped the earth, so he has created Israel; do you think he will forget us?"[133]

So, the oracle "do not be afraid" is prophet's answer to their basic question of that time. Because Yahweh is your "creator" and "fashioner," he will be your redeemer (גאל) also. The enlarged messenger formula strongly underlines the fact that Yahweh

---

[133] John N. Oswalt, *The Book of Isaiah*, 137.

himself restores his people. He will make the same creative power subservient to his will to sustain them and conduct them on the path of salvation. And this exhortation is substantiated by another declaration that "I have called you by name." According to ancient West Asian thinking creation is also brought about by giving the name.[134] But here the emphasis falls on the relationship between God and his people. But this relationship is based on the fact that Yahweh is the "creator' and 'fashioner' of the people.

Function of Creation Theology

The functional proposition means that creation theology is viewed as dependably related to the socio-political and religious condition of the exile in the sense that it strengthens the faith in Yahweh during the dark times of exile.

By human standards, this dispersed people without a king should have vanished in the giant Empire of Babylonians as those settled by Assyrians. Remarkably that did not happen in the Babylonian exile. The dispersed people of Judah preserved their identity at least in part. By 'identity' we mean that the positive picture of a group constructed on the basis of an adequate consensus and is balanced with the picture of other group which has been arrived at.[135] How the exilic community could create a positive picture about themselves? How could they maintain their identity?

As we noted above (in chapter four), the loss of centralized political power led to a strengthening of decentralized form of organization based on kinship. Thus, during the exile, the family became the primary social entity,[136] and the family played a decisive role in finding a new identity for Israel. In contrast to the official Yahwism, where the relationship with God was based on God's saving act in history, the family piety emphasized the

---

[134] See *NERT*, 82; see also Isa 40:26; Ps. 147:4.
[135] G. Theissen, *Sociology of Early Palestinian Christianity* (Philadelphia: Fortress Press, 1977), 31.
[136] Rainer Albertz, *Israel in Exile*, 136.

relationship with God based on God's creation of each individual.[137] To the person who feels himself forsaken needs an assurance about his identity. The DI community drew on this personal relationship with God to build confidence in their prophecy of salvation (see also 44:2, 21, 24; 54:5). Thus DI, after his analytical description of Israel's state, utters one of the most encouraging passages of the prophecy. Yahweh is Israel's creator, maker and redeemer. Now Israel's status as the direct object of Yahweh's creative and redemptive work enable them to cope with the situation in exile.

Secondly, the exiles were elevated to an honored position by the creation theology. Honor and shame was the core, the heart, the soul of social life in Mediterranean antiquity.[138] Concern for honor permeated every aspect of life. 'Honor is a positive value a person in his or her own eyes plus the positive appreciation of that person in the eyes of his or her social group.'[139] But Israel lost this positive value when they were taken as refugees to Babylon. Israel's honored position as God's chosen race blemished. To this people, honor is ascribed by creation theology.

Another notable point is Yahweh's exclusive claim on his people. Neo-Babylonian texts assert Nebuchadnezzar's claim to authority over conquered peoples. Langdon's early translation of one of these texts effectively illustrates this: "I called into me the far dwelling peoples over whom Marduk my lord had appointed me and whose care was given unto me by *Šamaš* the hero from all lands and of every inhabited place from the upper sea to the lower sea from distant lands the people far away habitations kings of distant mountains and remote regions who dwell at the upper and the nether seas with whose strength Marduk the lord has filled my hands that they should bear his yoke and also the subjects of

---

[137] Cf. Ps 22:9-10; 71:5-6; 119:73; 138:8; Job 3:8-12.
[138] Bruce J. Malina and Richard L. Rohrbaugh, *Social Science Commentary on the Gospel of John* (Minneapolis: Fortress Press, 1998), 121.
[139] Jerome H. Neyrey, ed. *The Social World of Luke and Acts: Models for interpretation*. (Massachusetts: Hendrickson Publishers, 1999), 25.

Šamaš and Marduk I summoned to build E-tem-in-anki."[140] Here DI set his creation theology against Babylonian's claim of authority over the exilic Jews. Creation theology asserts that God's children are not subjects, not under the control of any earthly authority, except Yahweh.

6.1.5. Creator leads the History

Text: Isaiah 44:24-28

44:24 Thus says Yahweh, your Redeemer,

> who formed you from the womb
> I am Yahweh, who made all things,
> I alone stretched out the heavens,
> spread out the earth,
> who is with me?[a]

25 who frustrates the omens of liars[a]
who make fools of diviners,
who turn the wise men back
and makes their knowledge in foolishness[b]

26 who confirms the words of his servants[a],
and fulfills the counsels of his messengers[b],
who says to Jerusalem, "she will be inhabited[c],"
[d]and to the cities of Judah, "they shall be rebuilt,"[d]
and I[e] will raise up her ruins.

27 who says to the deep[a], 'Be dry up!'
and I will dry up your rivers.

28 who says of Cyrus, 'My shepherd[a']
and all that I wish, he[b] will fulfill
and who says[c] to Jerusalem, 'It shall be rebuilt'
and to (the) temple[e], "Be founded".

---

[140] Langdon, *Building Inscriptions*, 149, cited by Daniel L. Smith, *A Biblical Theology of Exile* (Minneapolis: Fortress Press, 2002), 67.

Textual Note

24 a This reading, מי אתי (who was with me) follows the Kethib, 1QIs\u1d43, LXX, and Vg. The Qere supported by Syr. reads the words as one: מאתי (from with me). Though the reading of Qere seems to have a good parallel in the preceding לבדי, it lacks the necessary textual support. LXX read (τις έτεροσ) as interrogative "who was with me?" A rhetorical question meaning no one was with me.

25 a The meaning of בדים is not clear. Versions and commentators have rendered this differently. NRSV translates it as "liars," NIV as "false prophets", McKenzie translates it as "soothsayers." *Soothsayers* and *diviners* designate two types of professional interpreters of omens. Westermann translates it as "interpreters." בדים usually means "idle talk." Only here and in Jer 50:36 does it refer to a person. (See J. D. W. Watts, *Isaiah 34-66*, 151). Some scholars suggest בָּרִים in the place of בַּדִּים. (see Westernann, *Isaiah 40-66*, 52) The *baru* priests in Babylonian culture were those who were specifically assigned to read omens. In the Babylonian context, DI is denouncing the soothsayers and diviners as "liars."

25 b 1QIs\u1d43 has יסכל (make foolish) for MT's ישכל (make wise). Elliger points out that MT's *aîn* is simply an abnormal spelling. However, note that the two Hebrew words sound alike but have opposite meanings. This is a solid example of double meaning, or tongue-in-cheek sarcasm, which is difficult to translate. (See Watts, p.151)

26 a MT has עבדו (his servant) singular. But for the sake of parallelism with "messengers" in the second line, some emend it to plural "his servants." (עבדיו). See also *BHS*. The reference to the servant formed from the womb in 44:2 and 49:5 favors the singular. (See Joseph Blenkinsopp, *Isaiah 40-55*, 244). However, if we take it from the sociological perspective, here the servant means the community of DI, and hence the plural form is appropriate.

AN EXEGETICAL STUDY OF SELECTED PASSAGES... 239

26 b   One MS has only וַעֲצָתוֹ "and his counsel" instead of "the counsel of his messengers' (See John D.W.Watts, *Isaiah 34-66*, 151)

26 c   *BHS* suggests תִּוָּשֵׁב, niphil "she will be inhabited" or "be inhabited"

26 dd The unusual length of verse 26 suggests that it can be a later addition. See *BHS*. Moreover, the phrase "her ruins" in the next line refers back to Jerusalem. However, this is not a conflicting view in DI (cf. 40:9)

26 e   LXX reads in the third person: "her ruins shall spring forth."

27 a   צוּלָה is hapax i.e., this word found only once is DI. Tg add "concerning Babylon."

28 a   MT's רֹעִי ("my shepherd") is supported by Aquila, Symmachus, Theodotion, Peshitta, and Vulgate. It could also be read רֵעִי ("my friend" : see *BHS*) But the title "shepherd" as a metaphor for ruler is well known in ancient West Asia and therefore the MT reading seems authentic.

28 b   Vulgate's "you will fulfill" make the address to Cyrus explicit.

28 c   The reading of MT, לֵאמֹר, lit., "to say", is supported by 1QIsa[a] and 1QIs[b]. However, the previous three lines begin with הָאֹמֵר "the one who says." So this can be emended to make the line parallel to the first three. LXX suggests the emendation. Since DI is emphasizing Yahweh's creative power, it is better to accept LXX reading here.

28 e   *BHS* לְהֵיכָל adds the preposition where MT simply uses a dative without preposition. Another issue is the gender of הֵיכָל, which is usually masculine. Here the verb, תִּוָּסֵד is in the feminine which implies that this word is also thought to be feminine. However, v.28b is probably an addition, repeating 26b in order to include a prediction of the rebuilding of the temple; and it is not the practice of DI to

repeat himself mechanically in a single context.[141] Moreover, the restoration of the temple became the major concern only at a later stage. (cf. 63:18; 64:11). The restoration of the temple is mentioned nowhere in DI. However, according to Schoors, this is not a convincing reason to treat v.28b as an addition. This does not mean that DI could not have mentioned it once, and his interest in the restoration of Zion as the centre of the nation, is hardly conceivable without any reference to the temple.[142]

Form, Structure and Setting

There is no consensus among scholars with regard to the unity and literary genre of Isa 44:24-28. Some scholars regard Isa 44:24-45:7 together a unit. However, a majority of scholars argue in favor of a separate unity of this passage. According to Melugin, this is a self-contained disputation.[143] But Westermann views these verses not as an independent unit, but as a hymnic introduction to the following oracle. He argues that vv.24-28 are incomplete without the following portion. He thinks that 44:24-28 are designed as an introduction to 45:1-7.[144] Westermann's argument has some merit. The prophet's use of a series of participial clauses gives us the impression that the prophet has something to proclaim based on the attributes portrayed in the series of participial clauses. But the messenger formula, especially the כה (*thus*) at the beginning of 45:1-7 indicate that it is a separate unit. As Melugin has rightly pointed out, we do not possess texts which exactly parallel to the grammatical structure of 44:24-28. But Psalm 103 is sufficiently analogous to illumine the problem. Ps. 103, like Isa 44:24-28, contains a series of participial clauses, which are attached to the introduction (v.3-7). But these participial clauses are not subordinate grammatically to what follows; they stand on their

---

[141] John L. McKenzie, *Second Isaiah*, AB Vol. 20 (New York: Doubleday & Company, Inc, 1968), 74.
[142] See A. Schoors, *I Am God Your Saviour...*, 269.
[143] R. F. Melugin, *Formation...*, 39.
[144] C. Westermann, *Isaiah*, 154.

own as independent affirmations.[145] Moreover, it is obvious that the words in 44:24, following the opening "Thus says Yahweh, your Redeemer," are addressed to Israel. But what in fact follows in 45:1ff, is addressed to Cyrus and Israel is no longer addressed.

In all likelihood, this is true also of the participial clauses in Isa 44:24-28.[146] In sum, we can say that the form and content of the passage support the view that Isa 44:24-24 is a unit in itself.

Also there is much disagreement among scholars regarding the exact form represented by 44:24-28. Gressmann treats the text as a hymn dividing it into a "prophetic introduction (24a) followed by "the self-prediction" of the Deity (24b-26a) and the promise for Jerusalem (vv.26b-28).[147] This "self-prediction" or "self-introductory" formula (אני יהוה) is followed by a series of participles. According to Gressmann, the special mark of the hymn is the "participial style" that runs throughout. So the genre could be determined as a broadly elaborated self-praise (*Selbstprädikation*) of Yahweh, a genre in which the deity presents himself in terms of self-glorification.[148] The series of participles refer to Yahweh's creative activity of stretching out the heavens spreading out the earth and his continuous re-creating actions of fulfilling the words of his prophets and finally commissioning the Persian King Cyrus to perform his purpose. In all these things, Yahweh discloses his creative sovereignty.

Westermann suggests that Isa 44:24-28 is a descriptive praise of Yahweh's action in the past and the present in creation and history.[149] The participles which follow the self-introductory formula; "I am Yahweh", are praises of God or, more exactly, praises turned into the first person of self-glorification. It is obvious that vv.24-28 employ the style of the hymn. However, the fact that that vv. 24-28 begins with a messenger formula suggests that these

---

[145] R. F. Melugin, *The Formation*..., 39.
[146] R. F. Melugin, *The Formation*..., 39.
[147] Gressmann, "Die literarische Analyse Deuterojesajas," , 289-90.
[148] Gressmann, "Die literarische Analyse Deuterojesajas," , 289-90.
[149] C. Westermann, *Isaiah*, 154-55.

verses do not form a genuine hymn. Usually the prophets used the messenger formula to introduce oracles (e.g. Amos 5:3, 16; 7:17: Isa 28:16). But DI's use of the messenger formula at the beginning indicates that the hymn style is employed here for a purpose other than praise. As Begrich has correctly pointed out, here these serve as a disputation.[150] He argues that, אנכי יהוה is not a "self-glorification formula" but a "self-introductory formula" by which Yahweh tries to convince his hearers (Israel) that the God who at present says to Jerusalem "You shall be inhabited," and to Cyrus "my shepherd," is identical with the God who has created the world and guided the historical process in Israel's salvation history.[151]

However, as Fohrer has pointed out, one can discover a mixture of genres at this point.[152] There is evidence of the fusion of genres in DI, and sometime he combined and transformed traditional genres in a way hitherto unknown in order to convey his message to the exiles.[153] Thus, Melugin's assessment seems correct: Isaiah 44:24-28 stands out from its context as a disputation in hymn style.[154]

With regard to the socio-historical setting of this passage, there is no direct evidence to show as to when DI proclaimed this oracle. However, this passage and the following one in which God guarantees his support to Cyrus, makes it probable that this was proclaimed during 537 B.C.E., i.e., during the period when Cyrus was beginning his march on Babylon.

---

[150] J. Begrich, *Studien zu Deuterojesaja*, 51.
[151] J. Begrich, *Studien zu Deuterojesaja*, 50-53.
[152] Fohrer has pointed out that Isa 44:24-28 is a mixture of hymn and discussion: the hymn praises Yahweh for his creative action in the history of the world, and the discussion passes from the undisputable assertion of Yahweh's redemptive action in favor of Israel to the disputable one of appointing a foreigner as Yahweh's instrument and calling him as "Yahweh's shepherd." See G. Fohrer, *Das Buch Jesaja*, 80-82.
[153] See R. F. Melugin, *The Formation*..., 24.
[154] R. F. Melugin, *The Formation*..., 38.

Socio-historical Comments focusing on the Theology of Creation

These five verses which culminate in the naming of Cyrus as God's agent for the deliverance of Israel from the exile are considered the center of DI's message. The theme of creation once again becomes prominent. Yahweh's lordship over creation is extended to his lordship over history

The oracle begins with a self-prediction formula, "I am Yahweh." In the self-introductory formula, scholars have drawn for comparison on the ancient oriental hymns in which the deity (or king) extols himself.[155] Israel is addressed here as she is required to listen to the word from Yahweh who is her redeemer and who formed her from the womb. These self-acclamatory hymns have the function of "legitimating the ruler."[156] And this self acclamatory hymns always extol the deity as creator, and his creatorship is the legitimacy for his sovereignty.

At the outset, Yahweh is introduced himself as their redeemer (גֹּאֲלֵךְ) and creator (יֹצֶרְךָ). גאל was the next of kin who had the responsibility of recovering his kinsman from slavery (cf. Lev.25: 47-55) or buying back the property that had been alienated (Lev. 25:25) or avenging the death of the kinsman (Num. 35:12). In the monarchic period, the idea of גאל has been extended to the ideology of kingship.[157] The king was responsible to redeem the poor from affliction and oppression, and to protect their rights (Ps 72: 12-14). In DI, this image of גאל very often has been ascribed to Yahweh (cf. 44:6, 24; 47:4; 49:26; 54:8). DI's attribution of kingship on Yahweh can be ascribed to the election of Israel. But here DI means something more than mere election. He is the one who formed them in the womb (יצרך מבטן). Yahweh, as creator of the world is none other than "your redeemer."

---

[155] Westermann, "Sprache und Struktur..." 145ff.
[156] See Klaus Baltzer, *Deutero-Isaiah*, 211.
[157] See, A. R. Johnson, "The Primary Meaning of גאל," *VT* Sup. I (1953), 67-77.

Yahweh's sovereignty rests on his act of creation is emphasized in the phrase "who formed you in the womb." Creation is not something belonging to the primordial era. It takes place in the present too, and justifies both the past gift and the future claim.[158] God's creative power is still at work.

Verse 24b draws in the universal horizon of creation. He is not only the Lord who made Israel, but he has made all things, and without assistance or advice. In "Who make all things" (עשׂה כל), not even the definite article (which one would expect in Hebrew) is found. As Klaus Baltzer has rightly pointed out, it is impossible to think of any thing more comprehensive than this.[159] DI's comprehensive concept of creation is significant at this point. The commissioning of Cyrus is not outside of Yahweh's creative purpose.

The way in which the creation is brought about is described as "*stretched out the heaven and spread out the earth*." N. C. Habel has worked out the presuppositions of the formula *who stretched out the heavens* in DI.[160] He sees a specific tabernacle tradition in it. He writes: the phrase stretching out the heavens 'is designed to identify and magnify Yahweh as the unique living God of the entire earth who is in the process of revealing his magnificence.'[161] In the Psalms, these statements are bound up especially with the theophany which indicates the coming of God from the heavens in order to save his people or nations (cf. Ps 144:5-7). However, Habel's conjectures as to the origin of this imagery do not shed much light on its use here. The emphasis on "*I alone*" (לְבַדִּי), may be significant from the socio-political point of view. By this, the DI community is trying to mitigate their conflict with the other exilic community with regard to gentile king Cyrus and also justifying their support to Cyrus.

---

[158] See Klaus Baltzer, *Deutero-Isaiah*, 213.
[159] Klaus Baltzer, *Deutero-Isaiah*, 212.
[160] N. C. Habel, "He Who Stretches out the Heavens," *CBQ* 34 (1972), 417-30.
[161] N. C. Habel, "He Who Stretches out the Heavens," 417.

AN EXEGETICAL STUDY OF SELECTED PASSAGES... 245

The question, *"who is with me?"* does the same function. By this question DI asserts that God is the sole Creator of the universe, with neither consort nor adviser. Therefore, no one has any right to advise God in his dealing with his creation.

In vv. 25-26, Yahweh's lordship in creation is the basis of his lordship over events or history. Here DI introduces the false prophets and diviners. Mesopotamia was an ancient home of the art of divination, which is built on the principle that every event and phenomenon foretells the future. The diviners attempt to know the future, and think themselves as wise, but Yahweh exposes their wisdom as folly. The events of the future are not under the control of the foreign gods, but are under the control of Yahweh, the Lord of history. The course of events is governed by the sovereign will and purpose of Yahweh, and only those to whom Yahweh has revealed his counsels can interpret events. Here DI asserts the fact that the world and its affairs are completely under the control of Yahweh. It is Yahweh who decides what to do with this world, and how the history unfolds. If it is true that Israel's God is the only Creator, he alone has the absolute freedom to direct history.

It is thus further affirmed that, not only is God able to confound the predictions of the diviners, but he is also able to confirm the word of his servants.[162] Here, if we read between lines, one can sense the conflict which the DI community experiences during its prophetic ministry. DI's message of Yahweh's commissioning of a foreign king, who did not even know him (cf. 45:5), to redeem Jewish exiles sounded completely improbable to the Jewish exiles. Moreover, it seemed contrary to their traditional theological understanding. Yahweh might use a foreign king for his act of

---

[162] Is the text talking about "his servant" (sing.) or "his servants" (plur.)? The Masoretic textual tradition supports singular reading. But LXX, Targum, BHS and many scholars prefer plural reading. However, as DI uses this term with different connotations, the identification of the servant in both cases is difficult. Those who take the singular reading consider the servant as Deutero-Isaiah himself and the context also suggests that the reference is probably to prophet himself. However, the prophet should not be viewed as an individual but as a community (see chapter 5)

judgment upon Israel, as the prophet had taught (cf. Isa 10; Jer 27:6), but that he should choose a foreign king as "shepherd" and deliverer has no support in the tradition. According to the Jerusalem kingship theology, only a member of the house of David could be assigned to such a title and function. Thus, the DI community's message was theologically highly offensive. So this text should be understood as an attempt to defend the pro-Persian view of the DI community as well as to alleviate the tension among the exiles with regard to the Persian policy.

The DI community asserts that all these things take place according to the sovereign will and purpose of Yahweh. The community of DI is also attempting to persuade the Jewish exiles by disclosing Yahweh's ultimate purpose for them. "Jerusalem will be inhabited." Jerusalem is the center of all hope. The theme of rebuilding of Jerusalem and the cities of Judah and freeing the exiles was already heard right at the beginning (cf. 40:2, 9). Here the same theme is similarly addressed as a whole. The first and most important thing is that Jerusalem will be inhabited. The reason for the rehabilitation goes back to the creation of the earth: "He did not create it a chaos (תהו); he formed it to be inhabited" (cf. 45:18).

The reference to the deep[163] (צולה) in v.27, is significant at this point. Various explanations have been given to the word "deep." The Targum paraphrases it as Babylon. The older commentators like Delitzsch considered it as Euphrates. That is, it is a prediction of Cyrus's stopping at the Euphrates as a means of access into Babylon, as reported in Herodotus (1:188-91). According to McKenzie, this is an allusion to the victory of Yahweh the Creator over the monster chaos, embodied in the ocean (Isa 51:10; Ps 74:12-17).[164] Volz, too, identified it with תהום רבה of 51:10, and therefore, here the prophet is uniting the mythological victory of Yahweh with

---

[163] There is no consensus among scholars about the precise meaning of *the deep*.
[164] John L. McKenzie, *Second Isaiah*, 73.

the saving act of Exodus. The subduing of the sea as a deity or monster is common to the traditions. In Ugarit, this subjugation is the result of Baal's struggle with Yamm. Many passages in the book show DI's interest in such mythological allusions.

But does such an ancient myth have any bearing on DI's thought? The direct address to the "deep" and to Cyrus and the mention of the rebuilding of the Jerusalem temple is not an unintentional effort. In the Babylonian creation myth, Marduk's defeat of Tiamat and his beneficent ordering of creation are commemorated in the construction of the temple (Enuma Elish VI. 47-120)[165] In Ugarit mythology, Baal's victory over Yamm is similarly rewarded with the construction of a temple.[166] Also in the Babylonian creation epic, when Ea slew Apsu (the god of primordial water), he built a temple "upon Apsu." It was in the heart of Apsu in turn that Marduk was born to Ea and his wife Damkina.[167] So, as Hanson has rightly pointed out, "the deep" in this oracle in the light of mythopoeic background reveals itself to be an ancient aspect of temple ideology.[168] Therefore, in order to restore the nation and rebuild the temple, subduing such powers is essential.[169]

Function of the Creation Theology

The oracle concerning Cyrus is unique in its importance for DI's proclamation. His name is explicitly mentioned in this text. Cyrus' legitimacy and his commission to rebuild Jerusalem and the cities of Judah is theme of this unit. The so-called Cyrus cylinder[170] is similar to the present DI text.

---

[165] *AENT*, 68-69.
[166] *AENT*, 131-35
[167] Enuma Elish 1.51-82; *AENT*, 61-62.
[168] Paul D. Hanson, *Isaiah 40-66*, 100.
[169] The restoration of the Jerusalem temple became a major concern only at a later stage (cf.63:18; 64:11) and therefore 28b is considered as a later addition to the text.
[170] This political propaganda justified the Persian king Cyrus's conquering of Babylon.

It is hard to determine the socio-political background with any precision, in which the DI community raised its voice among exiles. However, it is presumed that as the religious and psychological distress continued, the expectation to return home gradually weakened. As the exile prolonged, most of the exiles came to the conclusion that the return to the homeland is not possible in the near future. Further, as they thought, Yahweh apparently lacked the will or power to intervene in their history. So they set aside their national hope and tried to find happiness in the family and in the advancement of their work. So, the majority of exiles did not notice or looked with indifference on the political shift in power under the Persian king Cyrus, which was developing from the middle of the sixth century. However, a small prophetic community in the colony of exiles, concealed behind the designation "Deutero-Isaiah" recognized that these political developments represented a new beginning.

The DI community, which was inspired to carry on the prophetic ministry to the exiles, through the study of scripture and the theological interpretation of history, were sensitized to the surprising insight that Yahweh is at work in the spectacularly victorious course of the Persian king Cyrus. They recognized that it was Yahweh who raised Cyrus (41:2, 25; 45:13); and that Yahweh called him to execute his plan (44:28; 45:4f; 46:1; 48:15); and this is for the sake of Israel (45:4). He could liberate God's people from captivity in Babylon (43:13f) and rebuild Jerusalem (45:13). With this insight and conviction, the DI community presented Cyrus as the "Messiah" of the exile and encouraged the exiles for a pro-Persian position.

However, the electrifying message of the DI community met with a barrage of criticism. The DI community's introduction of a foreign king as the "Shepherd" and "Messiah" of the exiles sounded completely improbable. The message that God makes Cyrus, the heathen king, his agent through whom he intends to perform his purpose, that is, setting Israel free and re-people Jerusalem and re-build the temple, was a shocking message. As we noted above (in chapter 5), it was not only politically incredible

AN EXEGETICAL STUDY OF SELECTED PASSAGES... 249

but also theologically highly offensive. Against this background the DI community presents its theology of creation in order to justify its political stand.

Here one can see the forceful effect of the doctrine of creation upon history; and since history is under the control of the Creator he can direct this history for the redemption of his people. As von Rad has rightly pointed out, Yahweh the Creator, who raised up the world out of chaos, does not leave Jerusalem in chaos, he who dried up the elemental waters will also raise up Jerusalem anew. Here, obviously, the doctrine of creation has been fully incorporated into the dynamic of the prophet's doctrine of redemption.[171]

Accordingly, even when DI portrays the creation of Israel in mythological imagery, his thinking is on the present reality, i.e., he is thinking of the present socio-political context of the exile. Yahweh's past act of creation cannot dissociate itself from the present reality or the present social context of the exile. The past act of creation by subduing the chaotic forces still continues. The chaotic force which was conquered once is still at work and continues to subjugate his people.

The dependable relatedness of creation theology to the socio-political condition of the time, especially to the rise of Cyrus, means that the fundamental intention of creation theology was to encourage the exilic community to take a pro-Persian policy of the DI community. The description of the pagan king in terms appropriated to a Davidic king must have been troublesome to a pious Judean. How could such a one be called *My Shepherd* (cf. 2 Sam 5:2; 1 Kings 22:17; Ezk 34:23)? Or how could it be said that some such as this, unclean and unconsecrated, could fulfill God's wish (cf. Ps. 5:4)? The creation theology is precisely DI's answer to these questions. Thus, the creation theology functions at this point as a harmonizing principle among the exilic community.

---

[171] G. von Rad, *The Problem of Hexateuch and Other Essays*, 136.

Could it have been this way, as some scholars think that because the house of David had demonstrated its craven disregard for God (7:13; 39:7), God finds a new way to keep his ancient promises, even to the house of David?[172] But this argument has its defect. It shows that Yahweh was unable to foresee the disloyalty of Davidic dynasty, so when Davidic dynasty failed, Yahweh finds a substitute to fulfill his promise. Calling Cyrus for the deliverance of his people Israel is not the result of reconsideration because he could not find a faithful servant among his chosen people. Rather it was part of his divine plan. The sociological considerations suggest that the figure Cyrus was central to DI's preaching. The declaration in verse 24b, "I am Yahweh who made all things....who was with me," not only claims Yahweh's power over his creation but also his freedom to do things as he desired. Yahweh as the creator "of all" has the absolute freedom to choose anyone who is his desire. Yahweh's sole authority as the Creator of the world and the lord of the history is proclaimed by his sovereign selection of Cyrus as his "*shepherd*" and "*Messiah*." Therefore the rising of Cyrus corresponds to the rising of Yahweh to redeem his people (cf. Judg. 7:2).

Thus the creation theology at this point functions as an integrating ideology or a harmonizing principle among different exilic groups who were divided themselves on their different political views.

6.1.6. *Good and Evil, Both from the Creator*

Text: Isaiah 45:7

45: 7 The one who forms light, and creates darkness
who makes peace[a] and creates evil.
I am Yahweh, who do all these things[b].

---

[172] See John N. Oswalt, *The Book of Isaiah...*, 197.

AN EXEGETICAL STUDY OF SELECTED PASSAGES... 251

Textual Notes

7 a. 1QIs^a has טוב instead of MT's שלום, which balance רע.

b. Am. 3:6 and Deut 32:39 show that this idea was not quite new to Israel. However, these verses provide no exegetical support to the present text.

Form, Structure and Setting

This is the last verse of the Cyrus oracle which is recorded in 45:1-7. As we have discussed in the previous passage, there are difference of opinions with regard to the unity of this passage. Although a majority of scholars consider 45:1-7 a separate unit, from the literary standpoint, it is still possible to divide this into two separate oracles: verses 1-4 and 5-7.

Verses 1-4 is a promise given to Cyrus and most critics identify this as a royal oracle.[173] But with verses 5, the focus of the oracle completely turns to Yahweh alone. It was given as a self-prediction of Yahweh. "I am Yahweh" is uttered three times. Also these three verses contain three statements in which Yahweh's all-embracing sovereignty is acknowledged. In each case they are paired antitheses that embrace the entire created world (כל־אלה). "From the rising of the sun (the east) to its setting (the west)," means the whole world. Yahweh is not the God of a single country, and cannot be identified with a single people. His lordship is therefore not nationally limited.[174] "Light and darkness" – the antithesis explicitly declares that both are created.[175] "Peace and evil" also come under his control.[176]

This verse is given as the last part of Yahweh's self-prediction, which begins in verse 5. However, it aims at the despairing

---

[173] See Westermann, *Isaiah*, 157.
[174] See, Klaus Baltzer, *Deutero-Isaiah*, 226.
[175] Note the difference with P account of creation, where only 'light' is created.
[176] "Peace" and "evil" do not form a suitable paired antithesis. But, when we look at it from the above mentioned two antitheses, it is probable that 'peace' and 'evil' too establish an "everything".

Israelites who struggle to understand the way Yahweh is dealing with his people. Melugin has rightly pointed out that it 'is not an oracle actually delivered. Rather an imitation of that genre functions here as a promise to Israel.'[177] The main intention of this oracle was to convince the people of Israel that Yahweh has determined to deliver them from the exile, but he will do it in his own way.

Socio-Historical comments focusing on the Creation Motif

The theme of creation, which had been so prominent in the previous passage, continues to control the thinking of the prophet. Yahweh's lordship in creation is the basis of his lordship over the events. The course of events is governed by the sovereign will and purpose of Yahweh. DI asserts his argument declaring Yahweh's sole authority and sovereignty: "I am Yahweh and there is no other" (v.5). This is the ground of DI's assertion. Everything that happens is a result of the plan and purpose of the one divine, transcendent being. Therefore, it does not matter whether Cyrus knew about Yahweh already or whether he acknowledges him now.

In verse 6, DI states categorically the ultimate purpose of Yahweh's action. The reason for choosing and empowering Cyrus was that the whole world might know Yahweh the only God. The work of Cyrus is a manifestation of the power and purpose of Yahweh. The focus is on Yahweh and not on Cyrus. For example, one of the dramatic differences from Cyrus Cylinder is that whereas in the Cyrus Cylinder Cyrus's virtues, strength, and leadership skills are put forward as the reason for Marduk's choosing him, here in the DI they do not even enter into the picture. The three reasons given (vv. 3, 4, 6) have solely to do with the nature and character of God. It is not human perfectibility on which the world's hope rests, but on the grace and the providence of God.[178]

---

[177] R. F. Melugin, *The Formation...*, 124.
[178] See John N. Oswalt, *The Book of Isaiah*, 200.

In the socio-political context of the exile, this statement has a profound implication. The experience of loss and displacement evoked in the exilic Israel profound questions of faith. Is Yahweh not powerful? Is Yahweh not faithful? How do we move beyond exile? Is there life after exile? These questions required a clear and imaginative thinking. It required the ability to see the signs of the time. Unfortunately, most of the exiles, perhaps except the community of Deutero-Isaiah, were led to despair and loss of faith. This is why DI describes them as being blind and deaf, people who neither want to see the signs of the time nor hear the word of God which interprets them (42:18-20; 43:8). Their failure to interpret the signs of the time prevents them to see the purpose of God in every historical event. According to DI, they were thus unable to distinguish the meaning of "light" from "darkness," "peace" from "evil."

In order to deprive their opponents of any possibility of evading their arguments, the prophetic group even moved to a final statement in describing the omnipotence of Yahweh. Yahweh is not only the one who creates light and peace (salvation), but also the one who creates darkness and disaster. Here DI goes beyond the teaching of the Priestly writer,[179] according to which Yahweh creates only light (See Gen 1:2). But here, in the end of exile, DI makes a bold proclamation that God is the creator of everything, even of evil. According to the Priestly theology, darkness is primordial and merely accommodated through creation into a new order of things. Now darkness too, no less than light, is a creation of the God of Israel.[180] And no longer God is responsible only for the good that there is. Now he is the creator

---

[179] However according to Stuhlmueller, DI's idea of creation is undeveloped and somewhat inconsistent and this fact places him *theologically inferior* to "P" and for that reason presumably *chronologically prior* to P. (See *Creative Redemption...*, 156)

[180] Moshe Weinfeld believes that a number of affirmations in DI were intended as critique of the Priestly creation story. See Moshe Weinfeld, "God the Creator in Gen.1 and in the Prophecy of Second Isaiah," Hebrew, *Tarbiz* 37(1968), 122-26.

of evil (רע) as well, and no more is the existence of evil a blemish on his claim to absolute mastery over all that is.[181]

In fact, it was not a new discovery by DI. According to J source Israel believed that Yahweh was the sole source of good or evil, or light and darkness or life and death. In the Exodus story for instance, Moses' complaint that he was slow of speech evoked the divine rebuke: "Who gives speech to mortals? Who makes them mute or deaf, seeing or blind? Is it not I the Lord?" (Ex 4:11). But Israel has failed to realize its implication in the changed context. Therefore this ancient insistence that Yahweh alone is the source of good and evil was reiterated with theological profundity in the prophecy of DI, perhaps in oblique criticism of Iranian (Zoroastrian) dualism, which regarded the world as a battlefield between Ahura-Mazda, the supreme god of light and goodness, and evil Angra Mainyu with his legions of demons.[182]

However, with this statement, Israel's theological horizon reaches well beyond itself, into a gentile world, in order to locate the continuing working of Yahweh. Yahweh's all-embracing sovereignty is acknowledged by this. Yahweh does all these (כל־אלה) things! History is a stream in which light and darkness, good and evil are constantly mingled. But everything works out of the sovereign will of Yahweh. Likewise all men and all nations are under the sovereign control of Yahweh. Yahweh is not the God of a single country and cannot be identified with a single people. His lordship is therefore not nationally limited. At this point DI's creation theology moves towards the concept of universalism.

Function of creation theology

We have already noted that the exilic community considered the Gentile world, as evil (darkness). This provides the possibility of understanding the usage of "evil" (רע) in its socio-political context. The Hebrew word רע has a wide range of meanings. רע can also

---

[181] See Jon Levenson, *Creation and Persistence* ..., 124.
[182] See Bernhard W. Anderson, *Creation verses Chaos: The Reinterpretation of Mythical Symbolism in the Bible* (Philadelphia: Fortress Press, 1987), 152.

mean evil men or women.¹⁸³ We have already noted that the exilic community to which DI addressed his oracle was a mixed community, consisting both Jews and Gentiles. Passage like Isa 55:1 ff shows that DI was addressing a mixed community. In many instances the prophecy of DI shows the mixed character of the society.¹⁸⁴ We assume that the negative attitude developed soon among the orthodox Jews towards the non-Jewish exiles and these non-Jewish folks were considered as the "children of darkness" and "unholy" or "evil" whereas orthodox Jews considered themselves as "children of light." The conflict with the Gentile world contained in these verses cannot be satisfactorily explained. However, the context suggests that a conflict developed with regard to Yahweh's selection of Cyrus as his *anointed*.

Therefore the statement about creation of both light and darkness and good and evil has special significance in the socio-political context of exile where the community lives as a mixed group. Therefore, one of the objectives of the creation theology is to encourage the audience to recognize a connection between different ethnic groups which otherwise was considered as evil and darkness. At this point, the main purpose behind forming the creation theology is not to encourage the exile to depart from Babylon, rather to find a meaningful and reciprocal coexistence among different communities in Babylon.

Secondly, according to sociology, every individual and every society must struggle to find explanation for events and experiences that go beyond personal experience. When an individual is thus struck by misfortune like Job, he wonders "why

---

¹⁸³ See *BDB*, 948.

¹⁸⁴ It was possible that many non-Jewish exiles were incorporated in to Judaism during their exile in Babylon. In the list of Ezra 2 and Nehemiah 7, for instance, it is explicitly stated that certain groups sought their genealogical titles in vain: "they could not prove their families or their descent, whether they belonged to Israel" (Ezra 2:59-63; Neh. 7:61-65). The frequent mention of the issue of mixed marriage shows that there were conservative Jews who vehemently opposed the inclusion of the Gentile as they were considered evil. See also Exodus 12:38 for the mixed character of the society.

me?" When a community is struck by misfortune like that of the author of the Book of Lamentation, they wonder "why us?" Individual and society alike therefore struggle with questions like these, searching for meaning and explanations in real life. The answers vary widely from culture to culture, but each culture furnishes answers that help individuals and society to understand their place in the universe. Creation theology helps them to interpret and cope with events that are beyond their understanding. Exile, Droughts, Tsunami etc., becomes meaningful when they are attributed to the working God.

Here the community of DI also wanted, though indirectly, to remind their audience about God's judgement and the purposefulness of divine action in divine judgement. The evil (רע), in their exilic context, also means the national catastrophe that hit Israel like a blind stroke of fate. It should be seen as a consequence of sin (42:24; 43:26-28). By justifying the exile as a logical outcome, DI reminds them that their God can teach a lesson to them through defeat as well as victory, through suffering as well as joy.

In sum, as in the previous passage, this also bears witness to the fact that Yahweh, the Creator of the world, and creator of Israel, has chosen a foreign king Cyrus, to perform his new creative action, which is basically redemptive not only for his chosen people, but also for all nations. Everything in this world is his creation and therefore at his disposal. And everything in this world works for good (cf. Rom 8:28).

6.1.7. *Creator's Plan Cannot be Questioned by Creatures*

Text: Isaiah 45:9-13

45: 9   [a]Woe to the one who strive[b] with his maker
an earthen vessel among the vessels[c] of the earth
Does the clay say[d] to him who fashions it,
"What are you making?"
or your work (say) "he has no hands?"[e]

10 Woe[a] to him who says to a father[b]
What are you begetting?
Or to a woman[c]
What are you bearing?

11 Thus says Yahweh, the Holy One of Israel
and his Maker
Will you question me[a] about my children?
or command me concerning the work of my hands?

12 I[a] made the earth and created man upon it
My hand stretched out the heavens
And I have commanded all their host.

13 I have aroused him in righteousness[a]
And all his ways I make straight
He will build my city
and set free my exiles[b]
not for price, nor for bribe
Says, Yahweh of hosts.

Textual Note

45:9a. The text of this verse is ambiguous. LXX gives a quite different translation of this verse: *"What excellent thing have I prepared as clay of the potter? Will the ploughman plough the earth all say? shall the clay say to the potter, What art thou doing that thou dost not work, nor hast hands? shall the thing formed answer him that formed it?"*. Targum also differs remarkably from MT. This suggests that neither of those translations followed a clear textual tradition, rather they were simply trying to make sense of a difficult original. See John Oswalt, *The Book of Isaiah 40-66*, 206.

9 b. MT רָב qal participle from רִיב (one who strive). *BHS* suggest הֲיָרִיב (interrogative + imperfect) "should one strive...?" Some scholars, therefore, eliminate הוֹי ("woe") form, which they consider as foreign to DI. (See Blenkinsopp, *Isaiah 40-*

55, 250-51). G. R. Driver, C. F. Whitley, and P. Volz also eliminated the first woe-formula by changing it to הָיָרֵב. (See A. Schoors, *I Am God Your Saviour*..., 261). However, MT seems more probable.

9 c. *BHS* suggests חֶרֶשׂ חׇרְשׂוּ, reading *shin* for *sin*. NRSV translates 'earthen vessel with the potter' in order to keep parallelism with 'maker' in the previous line. However, it seems best to keep MT.

9 d. 1QIs[a] has "Woe to the one who says...." By inserting this third "woe," 1QIs[a] provides evidence against the suggestion of *BHS* to eliminate the "woe" from the other two places.

9 e. *BHS* emend this to וּפׇעֳלוֹ אֵין־יָדַיִם לָךְ 'and his work, "You have no hands." LXX ὅτι οὐκ ἐργάζῃ οὐδὲ ἔχεις χεῖρας 'that you do not work nor do you have hands." NRSV 'Your work has no handles' presuppose יָדוֹת instead of יָדַיִם and is not acceptable. Stuhlmueller translates this line "Your work has no value (*yâdaim*)" in an attempt to make sense of a difficult sentence. However, none of these attempts solves the problem, and therefore what MT seems more appropriate.

10 a. *BHS* suggest הֵיאָמֵר in order to eliminate 'woe-form,' however, MT seems more appropriate.

10 b. Stuhlmueller pointed that parents are not being addressed here by their unborn child or by their child who is just coming forth from the womb. (See *Creative Redemption*..., 201).

10 c. LXX "mother."

11 a. Most scholars think that here the words are wrongly divided. As the context shows, the original must have been הַאֹתִי תִשְׁאָלוּנִי, "will you question me" (your creator). (See Westermann, *Isaiah 40-66*, 164). C. C. Torrey, A. Schoors, J. Blenkinsopp et al. prefer this emendation.

12 a. Stuhlmueller, in his translation, adds the word "indeed" at this place (also in v.12b and v.13a) in order to bring out the

AN EXEGETICAL STUDY OF SELECTED PASSAGES... 259

presence of אנכי and thus emphasizes authoritative power of the Creator. See *Creative Redemption*, p.201.

13 a. P. Volz suggests that בצדק here means "with a salvific intention, for a salvific purpose." (See Stuhlmueller, *Creative Redemption*, p.201; North, op.cit, 155).

13 a. LXX add here τοῦ λαοῦ μου "of my people." See *BHS*.

Form, Structure, and Setting

Most commentators argue in favor of the unity of Isa 45:9-13. However, some scholars have proposed to extend the scope of the unit by linking it with the preceding portion (Isa 45:1-13).[185]

Nevertheless, this unit presents a serious structural problem to the question of unity. Verse 11 begins with a new introduction, and therefore, Westermann assumes that 'it could be an independent text.' He also doubts the authenticity of verses 9-10, because only here DI makes use of the so-called "woe-oracle' in his entire book. Moreover, the opening question in verse 11, "Will you question me about my children?" is considered as a question directed toward other people.[186] In addition, Israel is addressed in the third person, and Yahweh defends his sovereign right as the creator against their recriminations. Therefore, some recent scholars think that these verses are directed not at Israel, rather at the nations against their criticism about Yahweh's treatment to the people of Israel.

However, considering verses 11-13 as a separate unit (as an answer to the nations against their charges against Yahweh's treatment of his children Israel), seems incoherent to the present context. When verses 9-10 are included, then the meaning of the poem changes to an argument with Israel. As Westermann has pointed out, if we read verses 11 ff. in the light of verses 9 f., it will become very clear that this too is addressed to Israel who questions Yahweh about his actions. However, the exact nature of the

---

[185] See John L. McKenzie, *Second Isaiah*, 75-79.
[186] See Westermann, *Isaiah*, 164-65.

objections is not given. Presumably, the prophet's audacious words about Cyrus seem to have been met with refutation. Consequently, this oracle has been constructed as a disputation between Yahweh and Israel in which Yahweh defends his use of a foreign king in order to end Israel's exile.

In this view, verses 9-13 can be regarded as a single unit constituting a disputation in which the prophet inveighs against the hearers who find his description of Cyrus as Yahweh's anointed intolerable and unacceptable. Thus, the form and content of this passage support the view that Isa 45:9-13 is a unit in itself.

What is the *Gattung* and *Sitz im Leben* of this unit? As we noted above, most scholars have assigned this unit to the 'disputation speech.' This disputation responds to the objection raised against Yahweh's plan to choose Cyrus, the Persian king, who even does not know Yahweh, as His instrument for Israel's salvation. This brief oracle is given as an argument from the part of Yahweh to validate his action.

We have seen that the disputation, including a series of aggressive rhetorical questions, have been employed as a strategy for persuading the hearers or readers of the truth of an argument. However, as Childs has pointed out, at the end of this oracle, the disputation form is transformed with a messenger speech affirming what will indeed take place: "He will build my city and set free my exiles."[187] The repetition of God's creative power in verse 12 underlines this basic theme of the entire composition.

Socio-Historical Comment focusing on the Creation Motif

As we noted above, this section has often been described as a disputation evoked by Israel's objection to God's unusual plan to use a foreign king to deliver Israel.

It is not difficult to imagine the state of mind of the exiles. When they think of return from Babylonian exile, they thought it in terms of a second exodus with the same wondrous and mighty

---

[187] B. S. Childs, *Isaiah*, 354.

act of being led by another messiah like Moses. But DI's message of deliverance from the exile by a pagan king was shocking news. The exact nature of objections is not given. Perhaps the opponents of the prophet took offence at the identification of a foreign king as the 'anointed' and the 'shepherd' of Yahweh. Would not the God of Israel see fit to select a Davidic king to carry out the task of bringing the exiles to their homeland and rebuilding the temple?

So, it is generally agreed that DI's message is directed against those who raised their objection against the idea that Yahweh will choose the Persian king as the instrument of Israel's salvation. DI was so confident that the words he delivered were from Yahweh. Therefore he addresses his opponents with a sharp refutation and with a series of aggressive rhetorical questions.

Therefore DI begins his oracle with a "woe." "Woe" cries are one of the basic forms of prophetic speech.[188] Westermann presumes that they developed out of a curse oracle. "Woe" (הוֹי) announces doom to evildoers, a doom that in the final analysis can end in death. Accordingly, the oracle here in 45:9ff ought to be included in the prophetic oracle of doom. But in DI, this is the only place in DI where the utterance of a woe is spoken against Israel, and therefore, many scholars think that this style is foreign to DI. Westermann rightly points out the significance of "woe" in DI. According to Westermann, 'there is a development in the usage of the 'woe form,' that the woe no longer signifies the terse proclaiming of doom, but theoretically and in abstract condemn [sic] an attitude or a fixed mode of action.'[189] As Muilenburg has pointed out here, there is no real judgement at all, but only condemnation of Israel's caviling.[190]

DI deals the issue in terms of the right of the Creator. Yahweh, as the Creator of the whole universe and the whole humanity, has every right to use every creature in a way he chooses. No creature

---

[188] See Westermann, *Basic Forms of Prophetic Speech* (Philadelphia: Westminster press, 1967), 190-98.
[189] See Westermann, *Isaiah*, 166.
[190] J. Muilenburg, *Isaiah*, 526.

is in a position to direct Yahweh in this regard. If they do so, it is a serious offence on the part of the creatures. The utterance of "woe" emphasizes the seriousness of thinking or acting against the supreme plan of the creator. The disagreement with God's plan is not a matter of different perspective. At the bottom, it is a refusal to let God be God, a reversal of roles, in which the creature tries to make the Creator a servant to carry out the creature's plan.[191]

V.9 evokes the well-known metaphor of the potter. This metaphor is used more than once to express God's absolute liberty in disposing of his material, which is wholly powerless in his hand (cf. Isa. 29:16; Jer 18:1-6; Rom 9:20-21). On what basis, then, humans can pass judgement on God's methods of accomplishing his will? It is nonsense for the product to attempt to fight a case (וְרִיב) against the one who produced it.[192] Human being is a "clay vessel among the earthenware vessels," or "a product of clay among clay products." Therefore, it is nonsense for human beings to quarrel with the one who has made them.

The second verdict begins as a question, thus underlining the discussion character of the text.[193] It is equally nonsensical for the clay to call the potter to account for his plans- "what are you making?" As clay, the material had no right of consultation in the potting process. The potter decides about the form or process of making the vessel. The clay too is created. In the same way, the community of DI is teaching the exilic Israel, through the creation theology, that they have no right to question the way of Yahweh's dealing. Creation theology, thus, reminds them the nonsense of questioning the Creator as well as the insignificance of the human being.

---

[191] John S. Oswalt, *The Book of Isaiah*, 208.
[192] Klaus Baltzer, *Deutero-Isaiah*, 234.
[193] Klaus Baltzer, *Deutero-Isaiah*, 234.

In verse 10, the prophet continues his argument from a different point of view. God is not merely the Maker of a material universe; he is also the father of the human world. A human father does not know whether he is going to beget a son or daughter. But this prophesy, about both the "father" and "woman," must be understood against the background of the context. God is the true father. He alone knows what kind of child is engendered and born. He also determines the birth. Everyday experience makes God's sovereignty over human beings clear. Therefore, anyone who calls it in to question, puts him/herself outside the coherent warp and woof of this life; he/she becomes subject of the "woe."[194]

Thus, both the oracles arrive at the same conclusion and intensify the assertion with another: the human being can neither question nor determine what God does. What can be said of clay can be said of human beings too. Their view of reality is totally distorted. They are like clay on the potter's wheel objecting to the design of the potter, or like an infant breaking through the birth canal with protests against the father and the mother. They need instead to call to mind that God is the Creator of the earth and its inhabitants and of the heavens and their hosts. Yahweh is the one behind the astonishing success of Cyrus. Questioning Yahweh on account of Cyrus is the product of a distorted faith. The antidote for this is an awakening to the majesty of the one who both stretched out the heavens and at the same time cared for the small exiled community. Yes, Cyrus the daunting conqueror is in the service of the one true God. "He shall build my city and set my exiles free." From the perspective of worldly wisdom this all seems absurd. That is, those who do not have the broad perspective of the reality and faith cannot understand this. Creation theology provides this broad perspective about reality.

After a graphic description of their rebellion against the Creator, the prophet gives the reply to the implied objections in

---

[194] Klaus Baltzer, *Deutero-Isaiah*, 235.

the form of an oracle in which Yahweh speaks in his own name (vv.11-13). Yahweh's absolute sovereignty is asserted here and this sovereignty is based on his creatorship. The two solemn titles "the Holy One of Israel" and "his Maker" stress Yahweh's special relationship with his people. The word "Holy One of Israel," carries a connotation of the covenant relationship. But the emphasis falls on the second title; "his Maker" (יֹצְרוֹ). The word יצר stresses the idea of a careful workmanship, like a potter at work.[195] Out of fourteen occurrences of יצר in DI, Israel is almost always the object, and thus DI underscores the creation of the people through Yahweh's redemptive act. The allusion to the covenant here is significant. Using the imagery of the potter fashioning clay and of a parent giving birth to a child, DI speaks of the creation of Israel through the action of Yahweh. So they need to heed that God is not only the Creator of Israel but also the sole Creator of the universe. As the Creator of the world, he has every right to do what he thinks right.

As the creator of the universe, Yahweh can make use of the universe and any part of it as he wishes. As the creator of whole humanity, he can make use of any person he wishes. Therefore his decision to choose Cyrus as his instrument ("anointed") to release his people and to rebuild the holy city is a matter of his absolute sovereignty. No one has any right to question his sovereignty.

The interpretation of v.11b is difficult. "Will you question me about my children?" To whom does the prophet ask this question? Who is questioning Yahweh about his children? And finally who are the "children"? Some scholars believe that this is not addressed to Israel, rather this disputation is addressed to the nations and Yahweh defends his sovereign right as creator against their accusation with regard to his treatment of Israel. But, North has rightly pointed out that it is directed against DI's fellow exiles

---

[195] C. Stuhlmueller, *Creative Redemption..*, 214.

who were scandalized by his making Yahweh assert that he would carry out his purposes through a non Davidic king.[196]

And who are the "children"? As Blenkinsopp has pointed out "my children" here does not refer to Israelites.[197] One can observe a conflict among the exiles with regard to Yahweh's decision to make a foreigner as his "anointed." So the group which predicts Yahweh's plan becomes the object of their contention. Thus, the "children" can be identified with the DI community who prophesy Yahweh's plan to employ Cyrus, the Persian king, as his instrument for the redemption of Israel. It was however very difficult for the DI community to convince the exilic Israel about this.

Here, "my children" (בני) parallels with "the work of my hand" (פעל ידי). The structure of this sentence is synonymous parallelism. Therefore the meaning of *children* and *the work of my hand* can be meaning the same person. But as we noted above, in the synonymous parallelism it is normal to have a progression from the first to the second member.[198] Therefore these two attributes- *my children* and *the work of my hands* need not be parallel and therefore do not mean the same thing. One can observe a development here. Thus, in the first place, *my children* mean the "DI community"; while in the second line *the work of my hands* refer to Cyrus. Thus as a creature, Israel cannot question "his children" for predicting Yahweh's plan or cannot command Yahweh with regard to his use of Cyrus as his instrument.

The proper reply to the implied objection comes in verses 12-13. Yahweh's supreme authority and his right to do things as he likes, lie in the fact that he is the creator. As the creator, Yahweh has absolute authority to use any of his creation for his purpose, and Cyrus, as his creation, is completely under his control and at his disposal. Cyrus did not arise by his own choice. *I have aroused*

---

[196] See C. R. North, *The Second Isaiah*, 154.
[197] See J. Blenkinsopp, *Isaiah 40-55*, 252.
[198] See R. Alter, *The Art of Biblical Poetry*, 62-63.

him. This emphasis continues throughout the verse. The idea of creation and history are entwined at this point in DI's message. History is solely in the hands of the Creator. Thus, Yahweh's large claim moves from cosmic scope to the reality of Israel and the rhetoric moves quickly to Cyrus and the freedom of the exiles.

Function of creation theology

Scholars of DI are in general agreement that a conflict of some sort between DI and the Jewish exiles were the major issue with which DI is dealing. The DI community's interpretation of history and its approach to Cyrus becomes the main reason for the conflict. Thus, in this passage, we encounter a community, whose faith gave them the courage to struggle with the opposition of those who refuse to accept their message. Thus, the functional position of creation theology is viewed as dependably related to the socio-political context of the exile. The dependable relatedness of creation theology to socio-political condition of exile means that the fundamental intention of creation theology is to encourage the exilic community to take a pro-Persian stance against the Babylonian authority. The DI community's opposition to the Babylonian structure of government can be seen in their radical claim that Yahweh is the sole Creator. All that the opposition movement wanted was to realize the rule of God constantly.

Moreover, in this passage the theology of creation contributes in a variety of ways towards fulfilling the basic aims of society, namely achieving the integration of its members by overcoming conflicts. Thus the theology of creation functions at this point as an integrating ideology of the exilic society and thus eliminates or minimizes the conflict that comes out as a result of different views with regard to their political stand.

6.1.8. *Creation: a Purposeful Act of Yahweh*

Text: Isaiah 45:18-19

45:18   For thus says Yahweh,
           who created the heavens (he is God)

AN EXEGETICAL STUDY OF SELECTED PASSAGES... 267

    who formed the earth and made it[a]
    (he established it)
    he did not create it as a chaos[b]
    but formed it for habitation
    "I am the Lord, and there is no other.

19   I do not speak in secret
    in a land of darkness;
    I did not say to the offspring of Jacob,
    'Seek me in[a] chaos'
    I the Lord speak the truth,
    I declare what is right[b]

Textual Note

18 a J. Blenkinsopp translates it "who gave the earth form and substance." (*Isaiah 40-55*, p. 256)

18 b Both LXX and Tg. translate "in vain." 1QIs[a] adds the preposition ל and reads לתהו ("for a waste"), intent to the meaning parallel to לשבת (for habitation)

19 a MT have no preposition. But *BHS* suggests inserting ב "in." Some scholars think that this is a designation for a place (See John D. W. Watts, *Isaiah 34-66*, WBC, p.162). LXX: "seek vanity" omitting the pronoun. 1QIs[a] supports MT. Tg: "Seek the fear of me in vain."

19 b Lit. "uprightness"

Form, Structure, and Setting

There is no consensus among scholars with regard to its limit as well as to its genre. The participle conjunction כִּי ("for, because") at the beginning shows that what follows is the substantiation of what has gone before. Therefore, Muilenburg connects these two verses to the preceding section.[199] Blenkinsopp also thinks that

---

[199] See Muilenburg, "The Book of Isaiah," 531.

this section is related to the foregoing section.²⁰⁰ But some scholars attach vv.18-19 to what follows rather than to what precedes. For example, Melugin considers verses 18-21 as a unit,²⁰¹ while Begrich considers verses 18-25 as a unit,²⁰² and verses 18-19 as a subsection within it.

As Westermann has pointed out, after the Cyrus oracle, the book of Deutero-Isaiah is mainly composed of units of considerable length, which cannot be clearly assigned to any precise form. For the most part, they are composite pieces which either unite motifs taken from several forms or have small, relatively complete units placed alongside one another.²⁰³ This is also true of the passage beginning with 45:18f. Therefore Westermann argues that verse 18-19 is 'relatively complete in itself, yet it cannot be called an independent unit. It is however, meant to be connected with 45:20-25, so that it may be taken as an introduction to them.²⁰⁴

The theme of Yahweh's uniqueness can be seen throughout the chapter. "I am Yahweh and there is no other," is recurring even after v.19. To that extent, there is a connection to the following section. However, these two verses particularly highlight Yahweh's uniqueness manifested in creation, and therefore it gives good reason for considering this as a separate unit which underscores Yahweh's uniqueness as Creator. The content also suggests that this is a separate unit, which begins a new section with v.18.

With regard to the *Gattung* also there is no agreement among scholars. One can find a variety of familiar forms and formulae such as the messenger formulae, hymn, polemics, and self-prediction oaths. The discussion of the *Gattung* of the song is very much related to the discussion of its unit. According to Gressmann it is a trial speech, which passes into a missionary motif in verses

---

²⁰⁰ J. Blenkinsopp, *Isaiah 40-55*, 259.
²⁰¹ R. F. Melugin, *The Formation...*, 128.
²⁰² J. Begrich, *Studien*, 13. See also A. Schoors, *I Am God Your Saviour*, 234.
²⁰³ C. Westermann, *Isaiah*, 172.
²⁰⁴ C. Westermann, *Isaiah*, 172.

22-24.²⁰⁵ According to Schoors, these two verses belong to the trial speech which is given in 45:18-25, and therefore, verses 18-19 is not a separate unit. Begrich argues that this is a disputation speech.²⁰⁶ According to Melugin, this is a lengthy introduction of a trial speech.²⁰⁷ In its present context, it is very difficult to determine its genre unambiguously. This speech shows distinctive structural features. The declarations about Yahweh in verse 18 points to the hymnic tradition. But verse 19 shows some traits of the disputation speech. However, as Westermann has rightly pointed out, it is not easy to discover what is the position disputed.²⁰⁸

Socio-historical comment focusing on the creation motif

These verses cannot be understood apart from its exilic setting in which the Jewish exiles experienced shame and humiliation (v.17). Yahweh's announcement of deliverance through a pagan king was not a satisfactory answer to the humiliated exilic community. It sounds like rejecting them from the privileged position. Therefore DI leads them to the climax of his argument: they will not be humiliated forever, as Yahweh has some definite purpose behind the creation of the world as well as the creation of the people.

DI's beginning of this section with the participle conjunction כִּי is noteworthy. It provides the setting for DI's theology of creation. Although the exile is a shameful experience for Israel, finally it is not Israel, who is going to be ashamed or humiliated, but the idol-makers of Babylon. Israel will be vindicated before the world as the one nation in which God is truly known. In order to validate this truth, DI ties the power of God manifested in creation to the purpose of creation.

---

²⁰⁵ H. Gressmann, ZAW. XXXIV 1914, 278-79, cited by A. Schoors, *I Am God Your Saviour*, 234.
²⁰⁶ J. Begrich, *Studien...*, 49.
²⁰⁷ R. F. Melugin, *The Formation...*, 127.
²⁰⁸ C. Westermann, *Isaiah*, 172.

The combination of "creation" and "purpose" is the unique contribution of DI's theology. The influence of exilic context behind the combination is clear. According to Babylonian understanding, each stage in creation happened as a result of an afterthought. According to their creation myth, the beginning of all things was matter in chaos. Out of this chaos everything, including the gods, emerged. God who stands outside the cosmos was unknown to them. To them, gods are part of the universe. The ordering of chaos was something of an afterthought on the part of the gods to protect themselves from the ever-present danger of its reemergence. Humans are even more of an afterthought, created primarily to take care of the gods.[209] Thus, according to the Babylonian myth, their gods have no commitment or responsibility for human beings. They have no interest in human future. Therefore, those who put their trust upon such idols will be ashamed and humiliated.

All of this has profound implication for the doctrine of creation in DI. If the gods are simply an emergent form of primordial chaos, if human existence has no purpose, and if we have no reliable means for discovering what the gods are about, then there is no point or possibility in relying on them.[210] They do not have a plan. They do not have a purpose for the universe or for the inhabitants in them.

In contrast, according to DI, the creation of the universe as well as the creation of the human being is not a meaningless endeavor. God created the universe for a purpose, i.e., for human habitation. Here, DI modifies the theme of creation with some new ideas. He did not create it a chaos (תהו). Here DI uses the word תהו as a direct opposition to creation. The word תהו is remarkable and DI uses it very frequently (cf. 40:17, 23; 44:9; 45:19). DI states emphatically that chaos has no place in Yahweh's creative action. Yahweh created a world of order.[211] God established it with a good plan in mind.

---

[209] Enuma Elish, VI.1ff.
[210] John N. Oswalt, *The Book of Isaiah*, 218.
[211] At this point DI has not been completely thought out and integrated with rest of his message, cf. 45:7. Jeremiah sees the land as a תהו after the wrath of Yahweh has scorched it (cf. Jer 4:23-26).

In Gen.1, תהו is described as the chaotic state of the world before God began his work of creation (cf. Gen.1:1-2; 2:4b-5).

At this point, the Priestly writer and DI share the same outlook about creation. The Priestly tradition ends with the phrase: 'God saw that it was good.' And at the end, God looks at everything which he had created, 'and saw, it was very good.' As Westermann has pointed out, 'the good in this context does not mean some sort of objective judgment...it is good or suited for the purpose for which it is being prepared; it corresponds to its goal.'[212] Thus, DI makes use of the creation theology to remind the exilic community both the meaning and purpose of their life. During the exile, Israel forgot the goal behind the creation of the world as well as the goal behind their creation as the people of God.

Another creation term יצר is particularly important at this point. DI uses this verb twice. The verb connotes the attentive action of a potter in shaping and fashioning a clay vessel.[213]

Thus DI asserts that Yahweh makes the earth very carefully. Yahweh's determination not to create the earth in meaningless chaotic state underscores Yahweh's purpose behind the creation. Every part of the universe was created in an orderly way for habitation and that no part of it ever made תהו.

The next clause, 'he formed it to be inhabited', makes its meaning clear. For him, creation is not a *leela*[214] as in some Indian cosmogony describes. Also it is not for destruction. He formed it to be inhabited (οικουμενε). Thus the goal of creation is salvation. This view about creation is significant, especially during the period of exile. Already we have noted that DI's message seemed unbelievable to his hearers. They could see nothing but chaos.[215]

---

[212] C. Westermann, *Creation*, 61.
[213] See C. Stuhlmueller, *Creative Redemption...*, 154.
[214] *leela* literally means play or an activity which intends nothing but pleasure for the creator god. In Hinduism, creation is sometimes described as a *leela* of god.
[215] Some scholars see a polemic at this point against the Babylonian concept of creation in which *man* lived in a world that constantly moved

However, the community of DI could see the bright future awaiting his people (cf. 40:1-11). What was the basis of this hope? The Creator of the world has spoken a word in Israel in which he has revealed his intention for his creation.[216] As the community of DI was aware of Yahweh's purpose behind the creation, the exiled community needed to be reminded about that.

The second declaration in v.19 is difficult to understand. Here, Yahweh declares that he did not speak in secret. It may mean that Yahweh has not spoken by occult art of divination, as pagan religions did. The saying affirms that Yahweh has always communicated in an open, straightforward and truthful way to his people. According to Stuhlmueller, here DI appeals to the past prophecy and their fulfillment. Yahweh's words to his people were never confusing or had double-meaning, but always peace and joy.[217] He did not leave his people to grope in darkness but spoke clearly of life's purpose. Throughout their history God continued to reveal his will.

Therefore he reminds his people: "I did not say the offspring of Jacob, 'seek me in chaos.' The term תהו is noteworthy. It is the same word that occurs in Gen. 1 and elsewhere in creation context, to which the light and order of God's reign of truth and righteousness stand opposed. In this context these words are significant. According to West Asian creation concept, creation did not deal only with the origin of the world. Rather it was concerned above all with the present world with its entire environment. Thus, by applying creation theology, DI urges the exiles to find meaning and purpose in Yahweh's dealing with his people. God has not left his chosen people in lurch. Even in his

---

in a cycle from creation to chaos. Unless the primeval act of creation is repeated every year that earth may sink back to chaos. The idea of repetition of creation is connected with the New Year Festival of Babylon (cf. NERT, 81ff)

[216] James D. Smart, *History and Theology in Second Isaiah: A Commentary on Isaiah 35, 40-66* (London: Epworth Press, 1967), 132.

[217] C. Stuhlmueller, *Creative Redemption...*, 155.

AN EXEGETICAL STUDY OF SELECTED PASSAGES... 273

selection of Cyrus as his agent of deliverance demonstrates Yahweh's creative purpose. Therefore, Yahweh, the Creator of the world, has created it for order and not in vain, and this is the basis for their hope. He created it for human dwelling and therefore will not blot out the race, for all his creative work would then be futile.

The expression in v.18a, הוא האלהים emphatically proclaims that Yahweh is the only God and the sole Creator. Here the predication of God as creator is reminiscent of 44:24ff. Here the prophet puts a great stress on the divine pronoun "he." The forceful noun clause at the end of the first line (see *BHS*), הוא האלהים can hardly be translated. Literally it means "he the God." But at the end of v.18 with its solemn proclamation, that "Yahweh is the only God" we get the actual intention of the prophet. Therefore we may translate it as "he is the only God". Thus, the prophet's understanding of God as the sole creator leads him to monotheism, because monotheism asserts that there is but one creator and ruler of the universe.[218]

6.2. Summary of the Exegetical Study

From the foregoing exegetical study of the passages pertaining to the creation motif in Isaiah 40-55, we have seen how the community of DI applied and reinterpreted its traditional creation faith in various ways, to the context of the exile.

The primary observation of the creation passages in DI shows that the creation faith in DI is not a subsidiary motif used to support the message of redemption. The massive use of creation vocabulary - ברא (16 times), יצר (14 times), עשה (27 times), פעל (5 times), שמים (6 times), רקע (2 times) כון and יסך (one each) - and the frequent use of creation language shows that the idea of creation is an integral part of DI's message to the exiles. This stresses the importance and the independent status of the creation faith in the proclamation of DI's message.

---

[218] Cf. Y. Kaufmann, *The Religion of Israel*, trans. M. Greenberg (Chicago: University of Chicago Press, 1960), 127.

However, it does not deny DI's primary concern of the good news about the restoration of Israel to her homeland. But without the creation faith, DI couldn't think of the redemption of Israel from the exile. Even the Exodus event was described in terms of creation. DI epitomized the announcement of the new Exodus in clear creation words יצר, ברא, עשה. In a number of passages, creation faith serves as the context and the important basis for the proclamation of deliverance from the exile.

Another important point we have observed from this study is DI's close affinity to the ancient West Asian creation tradition. DI makes use of the traditional West Asian creation traditions substantially to pursue the hearers (44:27; 45:18; 51:9-10). But DI uses such traditions with considerable freedom and reshapes it to suit his message. For example, the West Asian tradition of the struggle with chaotic forces and the ordering of the cosmos provide DI with a theological basis for the proclamation in the continuing struggle taking place in the exile. As the chaotic figures threaten the life of the primordial community, the present Babylonians threaten the life of the exilic community. The way in which they conquered at the beginning of the world becomes a dire need of the present time. The present Babylonian chaotic power also needs to be subjugated by the Creator God (see 51:9-10).

The presentation of Yahweh as the cosmic Creator is one of the important themes of DI (see 40:12, 26, 28; 42:5; 43:1, 15; 44:24; 45:7-8, 12, 18; 48:12-13). One can see several dimensions of this theme. In Isaiah 44:18, the creation faith is closely related to the idea of the uniqueness of Yahweh. In other places, the creation faith serves as a basis for the assertion of Yahweh's sovereignty over history (e.g. 40:12-17, 21-24). In many places, DI uses the theme of creation to show Yahweh's incomparability (40:18, 25). Yahweh's incomparability is set against the nothingness of the nations and their gods. Consequently the presentation of Yahweh as the sole creator functions as an exhortation against the temptation to worship idols or the heavenly bodies which Israel faced during their exile in Babylon.

AN EXEGETICAL STUDY OF SELECTED PASSAGES... 275

Yahweh's absolute sovereignty as the Creator makes him the lord of history. Here, the one who *stretches out the heavens* is the same who *brings the princes to naught* (40:22-23). Yahweh is portrayed as the mighty Creator and the lord of history. Thus for DI, history is the continuation of Yahweh's creative activity and creation is the realm in which humanity can discern the divine plan for the world.

Another important function of creation theology in DI was to persuade the exiles to acknowledge Cyrus as Yahweh's agent of redemption. DI's presentation of Cyrus as Yahweh's "anointed" and "shepherd" met with a barrage of criticism. Therefore DI informs the dissenting group about Yahweh's authority and freedom as the sole Creator to choose any one he desires. Therefore DI terms questioning Yahweh on account of Cyrus as a rebellion against the Creator. Here, the creation theology helps the Deutero-Isaianic community to defend their pro-Persian policy.

The doubt concerning Yahweh's willingness and power to redeem His people from the exile was one of the serious issues of the exilic period. Therefore, establishing Yahweh's ability to save was an immediate concern of the Deutero-Isaianic community. In Babylon, the idea of creation is understood as the supreme example of power to do things. Thus DI presents Yahweh as the sole Creator who is powerful enough to redeem His people from the exile.

Creation in DI also means creation of a people. In several passages, Yahweh is extolled as the Creator of Israel (43:1; 43:15), the one who formed them from the womb (44:2), 'the Holy One and Maker of Israel' (45:11). Here the creation signifies Yahweh's historical relationship with the people of Israel. As Yahweh created the world out of chaos, Yahweh created people for himself from the chaotic state of Egyptian bondage. It indicates Yahweh's personal concern for his chosen people (see 43:2ff). However, according to DI, Yahweh's concern is not limited to the people of Israel, as the whole universe is Yahweh's creation; his concern is meant for the whole humanity (cf. Isaiah 41:20; 49:6). Thus the theology of creation finally leads the prophetic community to the idea of mission.

Establishing of the earth as Yahweh's orderly creation is another important concern of DI and by which they wanted to emphasize the establishing of the earth over against a chaotic condition, as an orderly cosmos in which God's people can live unharmed (see 45:18-19). It indicates God's particular concern for the earth and its inhabitants. At this point, DI shares the OT tradition of the notion of creation as a structured space.

According to DI, creation is not an event that took place once for all in the distant past. Rather DI emphasizes Yahweh's continuous sustaining of the world order, especially guarding the boundaries of the sea and the natural order through his ongoing active interventions.

Another important concern of DI's creation theology is the building of the temple or temple city (cf. 44:24- 45:7). For DI, the building of Jerusalem and the temple and the appointment of a king are part of Yahweh's creation. Here DI shares the common view of the West Asian creation tradition, which connects creation to the royal ideology.

In several passages, DI categorically states that the redemption of Israel is not the final goal of Yahweh's plan. Yahweh's goal is the redemption of the entire world, because the entire world is his creation. Yahweh's concern for his creation is the motivating factor for the redemption of Israel (cf. 49:6). Therefore, it is not creation that is subordinated to redemption; rather redemption is subordinated to the theology of creation. Therefore election and redemption could be understood properly only on the basis of creation. Creation provides the meaning and significance for the election and redemption.

God's special concern for the poor and the needy is one of the main themes in Wisdom teaching. DI as a community, influenced as such by 'Wisdom' takes up the cause of the underprivileged especially who were exploited by the Babylonians (41:17-20).

Through creation theology, DI assures the exiles, Yahweh's special concern for the people and assures them Yahweh's protection.

According to DI, Yahweh is not only the Creator of light or good but also the Creator of darkness and disaster. At this point DI goes beyond the teaching of the Priestly writer, according to which Yahweh creates only light. In order to make an enormous claim of Yahweh over creation, DI asserts that Yahweh as the Creator is ultimately responsible for everything in nature and history. No power is beyond the sphere of Yahweh's sovereignty.

Creation theology offered thus the exile unimaginable opportunities to rise in the world. In fact, 'creation' gave them a defense of faith against the temptations of foreign religion, and the totalitarian claims of foreign rulers. Creation thus helped them to realize that God is supreme in the whole arena of their history and their history. The exile community is called to be the witnesses of God's act of liberation which he performs in his absolute freedom.

CHAPTER SEVEN
Concluding Remarks

7.1. Conclusions

From the preceding study a number of conclusions can be drawn with respect to the presence of the creation motif in DI. In the first place, it has been investigated how the faith in Yahweh as Creator developed during the exile and the decisive reality of exile which facilitated the development of the creation theology in DI. In the second place, we have considered how the creation theology was functionally related to the socio-political setting of the exile; thirdly, its implication to other motifs in DI such as monotheism, universalism, and mission; and finally, the significance of DI's creation theology to the present faith community.

The primary observation of the socio-historical study of Isaiah 40-55 is the existence of a community behind the designation Deutero-Isaiah. The prophet DI was not an individual who dealt with the issue of exile, rather "Deutero-Isaiah" was a small community with a distinctive worldview and who struggled with their master in their task of communicating a distinctive message to the exile. Even though we are not told anything explicitly about the community, using the evidence of the texts themselves, the prophetic community of Deutero-Isaiah can be constructed with reasonable clarity. And we cannot properly understand the message of the book unless we understand the community which inspired the prophet to bring out the message.

CONCLUDING REMARKS

One of the important points exposed through the exegetical study was that the main concern of the DI community was not formulating a new theology of creation; instead they were revitalizing the creation motif of their old liturgical traditions with new interpretation, in order to cope with the issues which they faced in their socio-political context of the exile.

It is generally agreed that the emergence of creation faith in Israel had its setting in Jerusalem and its context in the royal consciousness.[1] Whether the creation of the world was already part of Israel's perspective prior to the establishment of the state is difficult to say.[2] There is no textual evidence to suggest that it was, but there are scarcely any Old Testament texts that date to this period. Yet, it remains quite possible.

Moreover, as we have seen above (Chapter II), there was no culture in ancient West Asia that did not speak rather extensively of creation in literary forms. Ancient West Asians generally considered their principal god as creator. We noted that some scholars think that Yahweh is likely an Israelite derivative of the Canaanite royal god El. This El was known previously as a creator, even if that was primarily in terms of procreation. We may assume, therefore, in combination with the result of the more recent research, that Israel was conscious about the creatorship of Yahweh even before the formation of the state. The strong influence of Egyptian universal creator-god Amun-Re during Iron Age I could also have been influential in this respect.

The creation of the world is first explicitly described in a few Psalms that possibly date for the early monarchic period (e.g. Ps 24). The belief in Yahweh as Creator is found in eighth century prophets (see Amos 4:13; 5:8-9; 9:5-6; Hos 8:14; Isa 17:8; 29:16). Both Amos and Isaiah of Jerusalem confess Yahweh as the Creator who like a king rules his creation.

---

[1] See B. W. Anderson, *Creation verses Chaos: The Reinterpretation of Mythical Symbolism in the Bible* (Philadelphia: Fortress Press, 1987), 63ff.

[2] Even though in Genesis 14, the title El Elyon, 'Maker of heaven and earth' is applied to Yahweh, its date is uncertain.

Therefore it must be admitted that the belief in creation existed in Israel from an early period as an integral part of their concept of God. It was a cherished idea of the cult. This is evident in DI's question in 40:28. "Have you not known?" was a rhetorical question which expects the answer "yes." Surely they did know it. In the Exodus event they realized that only the Creator-God, the One who made the sea, animals, the heavenly bodies and all nature, could employ these elements in his redemptive work. But in the changed social situation of the exile, they failed to understand its implications for their life. The adverse social situation of the exile weakened the power of imagination to interpret their old creation faith. However, through the community of DI we find a resurgence of their creation faith.

Therefore, it is difficult for us to agree with von Rad, whose view on this issue has been followed by many scholars, when they argue that creation as a concept was comparatively a later development and even then was principally an ancillary and secondary belief supportive of, but subordinate to, Yahweh's primary redemptive act.[3] According to von Rad, DI introduced the creation concept 'in order to arouse confidence in the unlimited might of his God he adverts to the fact of creation of the world.'[4] But even at this point there lies a logical presupposition that creation faith was an older tradition. If the creation faith was used to rekindle the faith of the people, when other traditions such as Exodus, Davidic, Zion become irrelevant and meaningless, it shows logically that creation tradition was an important one which existed right from the beginning.

At this point it is legitimate to ask why, then, the Bible is relatively silent about creation? If Israel already knew her God as Creator, why did she not confess it in her early writing? The main reason lies in the nature of Israelite faith. In contrast to other religions which viewed man's existence only as bound to the

---

[3] Cf. G. von Rad, "TheTheological Problem of the OT Doctrine of Creation," 131-143.
[4] G. von Rad, "The Theological Problem...," 134.

nature, Israel's faith insisted upon the radically historical character of human existence. The meaning of life was not found in the rhythms and cycles of nature, as in the Babylonian or Canaanite mythology, but in the decisive historical events in which the faith community receive the revelation of God. Thus, as scholars have already pointed out, Israel's faith was first confessed in the form of *Heilsgeschichte*. We should not forget that the whole OT scripture was written with this perspective. Therefore, the Old Testament's silence about the creation does not necessarily argue that it did not exist.

The second reason may be adduced from the sociological perspective. Sociologically speaking, all belief and ideology is conditioned by, and reflection of, a certain set of social circumstances. DI's creation theology as a theological and sociological response was affirmed at a particular time in history. It was the first occasion when the faith community has challenged in such a way to defend Yahweh's supremacy as Creator. As long as they were a people of the land, Yahweh's image as the warrior was sufficient for a successful maintenance of social and religious identity. A comprehensive picture about Yahweh as the sole Creator of the world and sole controller of history became a requirement for the faith, only when they were thrown into the Diaspora situation.

7.2. The Decisive Reality of Exile behind DI's Creation Theology

It is generally agreed that the Old Testament creation faith received its fullest articulation in the period of exile. But seldom have we paid attention to the social circumstance that caused the articulation or the decisive reality of the social context behind the theology of creation.

With the destruction of Jerusalem in 586 BCE, Israel became a people without a land. The hope for a return from the exile diminished with the passing of years. The sociological issue of 'uprooting' and the psychological issue of 'traumatization' faced by the exiles reduced their self-esteem. On one side, the symbols and images of the Babylonian gods paraded through the streets in magnificent processions disturbed the exiles (46:1-2). Babylonians through these images obviously seemed to rule over human society and world history. But on the other side, Yahweh appeared to be unwilling or unable to intervene in history. In the domain of political history, Yahweh seemed to have been so distant. The perception of divine abandonment is strongly conveyed in the citations from the complaints of the community (40:27; 49:14). It appears that the exilic community was at a risk of losing a positive identification with Israel because it was overwhelmed by its self-knowledge as rejected by Yahweh. The shaming identity as the defeated Israel and rejected by God was conveyed and reinforced by the liturgies of lament.

This situation forced them to set aside their national hope and find consolation in family life and work. Consequently, a majority of the exiles could not notice or looked with indifference at the political shift under the Persian king Cyrus. However, the prophetic community of DI recognized these political developments as they represented a new beginning, and perceived in them the hand of Yahweh in the advancement and the use of the Persian king Cyrus for their redemption. Therefore the challenge before the DI community was mainly threefold: (1) to establish that Yahweh is still concerned about his people and he is willing to redeem people from the suffering of exile; (2) Yahweh is powerful enough to redeem them from the mighty Babylonians; and (3) the Persian king Cyrus is Yahweh's agent in His redemptive plan.

How could the community of DI perform the task? One possibility was in making use of the social location to bear on the traditional conceptions of faith – creator, creation etc. However, the prophetic community who drew their message from the language of the cult found it to be limited by the fact that the cult itself became irrelevant or non-existent in the exile. In the Babylonian context however, the idea of creation was understood as the supreme power to do things. Therefore DI begins with an appeal to the power of Yahweh exhibited in creation. DI sought to lead those addressed to put aside their doubts and give their assent to faith in Yahweh as the all-powerful Creator. Perhaps the most important purpose of creation theology was to mitigate the conflict among the exiles with regard to their different political views. Thus DI's theology of creation was developed as a response to the crisis that the people underwent during the exile.

7.3. Structure of the Exilic Society and Creation Theology

Creation theology is structurally embedded in and functionally correlated to the social context of the Babylonian exile. The following is a brief discussion of the same.

a. Family structure and creation theology

In the exile, the prolongation of Israel's separation from their land and sanctuary caused a new sociological development in the structure of the society. The loss of centralized political power led to a strengthening of decentralized forms of organization based on family relationship. Thus, during the exile, family became the primary social entity. The separation from the sanctuary and the absence of official religion paved the way for family piety. And the family piety persuaded them to redefine their relationship with God, not on God's saving act or election but on God's creation of each individual (43:1). And this helped them to find access to God even in a foreign land, as the creator of the individual. Thus, creation theology developed from the family structure of the society. At the same time, creation theology functioned as the upholder of the family structure. Also creation theology helped the exilic community to find a firm ground for faith in their stateless condition of the exile.

b. Mixed Nature of the Society

In Babylon, the Jewish exiles were forced to live with the people of different regions, different religions and different cultures and share the same fate, and they underwent the same social situation and suffering. The mixed nature of the society, of course, often caused conflict. But on the other hand, the same fate of the different groups of people widened their outlook and worldview. The mixed nature of the society however, had not directly influenced them for the formation of a creation theology. But the new outlook and widened worldview persuaded them to reflect on their traditional liturgical conception about God in the pluralistic context, which finally led them to the articulation of a creation theology. Thus, from a structural functional analytical point of view, creation theology functioned as an integrating ideology among the different group of people. Creation theology thus mitigated the tension among different groups of people. It promoted a meaningful cooperative community life among the exiles with the native Babylonians. Thus, creation theology was a survival strategy for a harmonious life in the pluralistic context of the exile.

c. Oppressive Structure of Babylonian Exile

As we noted above, the harsh vocabularies employed frequently by DI in the exilic context indicates the hardship they experienced in Babylon. The expression "poor and needy" in 41:17 must not simply be dismissed as purely metaphorical with no historical basis. It clearly indicates the economic exploitation of the Jewish exiles by the Babylonian overlords. There are evidences that the Babylonian cult justified the exploitation of the weaker section of the society by emphasizing the centralized power and its hegemony.[5] DI's theology of creation was developed as a response to this social situation. Creation theology functioned thus as a protecting and upholding factor of the suffering community and as an ideology for an egalitarian view of the society. One can even detect an anti-imperialistic and anti-feudalistic element in DI's creation theology, and as a protest movement against the misuse of land and earthly resources only for the benefits of the Babylonian elite.

d. Diaspora Status and Creation Theology

One of the most significant social dynamics, by which the DI community was motivated to shape the theology of creation, was their homelessness and the subsequent result of condition such as alienation and helplessness of the Jews in Babylon. From the

---

[5] See Norman K. Gottwald, *Tribes of Yahweh*, 615.

moment of deportation, Israel no longer appeared as a group tied to a fixed geographical location. They became a people without a place. Israel as a displaced and dislocated community was in need to compensate the displacement with a theological interpretation of "place." So the "place" where they now lived does not belong to any particular people, but to Yahweh as it is created by Yahweh. Since the Lord is the Creator he is the owner too. Israel's stateless condition made them to think about their God beyond the boundaries of the state. Thus, DI's portrayal of Yahweh as Creator functions as an ideological answer to the problem of homelessness of the exiles. Thus, creation theology could be understood as an effort of the stateless community to find meaning and purpose in the stateless condition of the exile.

7.4. The Function of Creation Theology in DI

Creation theology as a functional proposition was viewed as dependably related to the socio-political and religious conditions of exile in the sense that it strengthened the faith in Yahweh during the dark period of exile.

Creation Theology as a Crisis Theology

As we noted above in the exegetical study, creation in DI, in its social and religious dimension, is both a reflection and a response to the crisis that Israel faced in the Babylonian exile.

Babylonian exile was certainly a crisis. Several passages in DI confirm the crisis they had undergone during their exile in Babylon. DI's quotation from the lamentation of the exilic community in 40:27 reveals the serious sensitivity of the social pressure and subordination. It was a crisis that centered on a self-consciously religious group. Self preservation was their major concern, preservation not only of traditions or values, but perhaps on occasion even physical survival.

This crisis can be described in several dimensions. First of all, it was a crisis of faith. Their experience of the exile evoked several profound questions of faith. It shook their faith in Yahweh's power and his faithfulness. It shattered their hope in Yahweh. Secondly, it was a crisis in understanding Yahweh's guidance. Their cherished picture of Yahweh as the Shepherd 'who leads them to the green pastures and still waters' were distorted. Above all, there was a crisis in deciding who is the true god. The power of the Babylonian empire and the splendor of their god Marduk were set against the defeated nation Israel and their God Yahweh.

Against this context, DI presents Yahweh as the Creator and the incomparable God of the whole world. DI clearly delineates Yahweh's incomparability and uniqueness as the sole Creator of the world and the Lord of history (40:12-31). DI asserts that, in the face of his sovereign power neither Babylon nor their god Marduk amount to nothing. Before the absolute power of Yahweh, they cannot thwart the creative purpose of the Creator God of Israel. Thus, creation theology can be understood as a crisis theology. Creation theology here functions as a solution to the crisis as Israel confronted in Babylonian exile.

Creation Theology as a Pro-Persian Propaganda

DI also uses the creation theology to persuade the exiles to acknowledge Cyrus as Yahweh's agent of redemption. DI's presentation of the Persian king Cyrus as the 'Messiah' met with a barrage of criticism. Therefore DI informs the dissenting group about Yahweh's authority as the sole Creator to choose any one he desires. However, DI makes it very clear, it is not Cyrus, but Yahweh is going to be glorified by this (42:8). Therefore, questioning Yahweh on account of Cyrus is revolt against the Creator. Thus, the community of DI makes use of the creation theology to defend their pro-Persian policy.

Creation Theology as a Liberation Theology

W. Brueggemann has proposed that the belief in Yahweh as Creator served in the first place as a support for the status quo, in particular that of the Judean monarchy. He writes: "the creation theology, like every theological effort, is politically interested and serves to legitimate the regime, which in turn sponsors and vouches for this theological perspective."[6] He sees it more inclined to social stability than towards social transformation and liberation. In its structural-functional analysis, Brueggemann's observation is justifiable to a certain extent, because structural functional analysis is more concerned with static structure than with the change of process. However, this view is completely in disagreement with DI's view of creation. Generally scholars connected the theology of creation in DI with the coming of Cyrus and the political liberation from exile. It is true, DI does not deny the stabilizing role of creation theology as long as it fulfills Yahweh's creative purpose (see comment on 45:7). But the main thrust of his creation theology is the liberation, not only from political subjugation but also from all forms of oppressive structures including economical, social and cultural. The ancient connection between Israel's liberation from Egypt and the creation terminology is significant at this point.

7.5. Creation Theology and Other Motifs in DI

a. Creation and Monotheism

Scholars generally agree that during the Babylonian exile a clear and theoretical monotheism developed among the group of those who were capable of such conviction.[7] We have noted that the community of DI was the rethinking group among the exile. And this monotheism set forth in the community of DI, who based their message on creation of the world. Some scholars think that DI's monotheism is grounded on Yahweh's lordship over history.[8] But the rhetorical question in Isaiah 40:25: "And with whom will you compare me" is followed by an earnest appeal to look to the Creator (v.26) clearly indicates that DI was basing his argument on creation. Here DI takes up the comparison to draw support to his

---

[6] W. Brueggemann, "Trajectories in Old Testament Literature and the Sociology of Ancient Israel," in *The Bible and Liberation: Political and Social Hermeneutics*, edited by Norman K. Gottwald (Maryknoll, New York: Orbis Book, 1983), 314.

[7] See Horst Deitrich Preuss, *The Old Testament Theology*, vol. I (Edinburgh: T&T Clark, 1995), 116.

[8] See Reiner Albertz, *A History of Israelite Religion*..., 418.

monotheistic argument. Thus, according to DI, Yahweh's incomparability, which finally led them to the monotheistic view, is grounded on Yahweh's creation of the world. However, we need not reject their argument out rightly, because according to DI, Yahweh's lordship over history is grounded on his creation of the world. However, basically it was on the theology of creation, in which DI based his teaching on monotheism.

b. Creation and Universalism

Another conclusion which the DI community draws out from the creation theology is the concept of universalism. Universalism is the extension of Yahweh's power and concern over the entire creation. The theme of universalism pervades the biblical text from the Pentateuch itself. The initial appearance of the theme can be traced in the story of Baalam, a non-Israelite prophet who performs some tasks that shows Yahweh's power (Num 22-24). However, it was with DI, the theme of universalism became an important perception.[9] If Yahweh could make use of a foreign king to rescue his people from exile, its implication could no longer be exclusively limited to Israel. Its implication will spread out beyond the small group of Israel, to the wider circle of nations (45:22f; 55:5). By this, Yahweh is going to be recognized as the Lord and Creator of the whole world (41:20). Thus, for DI, creation was the basis for their universalistic outlook.[10]

c. Creation and Mission

For most of the scholars who write on the subject, DI is not only a universalistic prophet, he is also a missionary one.[11] Yahweh's

---

[9] Perhaps the most powerful of the later universalistic stories is found in Jonah, probably written after exile. This story demonstrates Yahweh's concern for his entire creation.

[10] However, J. Blenkinsopp points out that the positive reading of universalism need to be balanced with the fact that there are certainly negative portrayals of foreign nations. See J. Blenkinsopp, "Second Isaiah – Prophet of Universalism," *JSOT* 41 (1988), 83-103.

[11] Robert Martin-Achard, *A Light to the Nations: A Study of the Old Testament Conception of Israel's Mission to the World* (Edinburgh and London: Oliver and Boyd, 1962), 8.

redemption of Israel from the exile is not for its own enjoyment, but to become a living evidence of God's unique deity. This emphasis is prominent in DI. The servant is given a mission. They must now become "a light to the nations." (See also 49:6, where the servant is made 'a light to the nations that Yahweh's salvation may reach to the end of the earth.') But what is the basis of this mission? The servant is called by the One who created the heaven and stretched them out. Thus the call of the servant is substantiated by the reference to God's work in creation. The creation of humanity is the reason for sending the servant with a mission. And the servant is called by the Creator God to perform his creative purpose (see 42:5-9). Thus, according to DI, creation is the platform of mission, and the creation theology enlightens the goal of creation.

7.6. Relevance of the Study

Metaphorically speaking, Babylon refers to a concentration of power and values which are dominant and which are fully hostile to the Christian community. Christians today are living in a situation fundamentally alien to their belief and values. Philosophies such as globalization, privatization, commercialism etc., in a variety of ways are trying to reshape our faith and values which is fundamentally hostile to the values of the gospel. Christian community is often forced to accept these values and realities. Thus, the Babylonian exile can be described as a paradigm of the conditions of the present Christian community. However, the historical event of the exile teaches us that it is not entirely impossible for a people, who think of themselves as a minority, to maintain its distinctive faith and values without controlling the land or without holding political power.

The creation theology that emerged from the socio-political context of the Babylonian exile presents us with the most challenging ideas that the present Christian community can derive from the Babylonian Diaspora. Creation gives us the basic biblical worldview of reality. Creation teaches us that God has made the world with his plan and in that plan he continues to direct and take care of the world. Creation theology underscores the basic human obligations towards God, the earth and fellow human beings.

The importance of creation is seen in God's answer to the complaint of Israel in exile. Israel complained that "My way is hidden from the LORD; my cause is disregarded by my God?" (40:27). God answered them reminding Israel that God is the Creator. "Do you know? Have you not heard? The LORD is the everlasting God, the Creator of the end of the earth. He will not grow tired or weary, and his understanding no one can fathom" (v.28). It is affirmed thereby that, God will never desert his creation or set it to run itself out in its time. Rather he guards the continuing existence of his creation. Creation is not just a thing in the past. Rather it is a guarantee of Yahweh's present power and a blueprint for the future. Creation theology offers us the most fundamental criterion to evaluate human plan and activity in history.

Bibliography

Ackroyd, Peter R. *Exile and Restoration: A Study of Hebrew Thought of the Sixth Century B.C.* OTL. London: SCM Press, 1968.

Albertz, Rainer. *A History of Israelite Religion in the Old Testament Period, Vol. I: From the Biginnings to the End of the Monarchy.* OTL. Louisville, Kentucky: Westminster / John Knox Press, 1994.

Albertz, Rainer. *A History of Israelite Religion in the Old Testament Period, Vol. II: From Exile to the Maccabees.* OTL. Louisville, Kentucky: Westminster / John Knox Press, 1994.

Albertz, Rainer. *Israel in Exile: The History and Literature of the Sixth Century B. C. E.* Translated by David Green. Atlanta: SBL, 2003.

Albertz, Rainer. *Weltschöpfung und Menschenschöpfung: Untersucht bei Deutero-jesaja, Hiob und in den Psalmen.* Calwer Theologische Monographien 3. Stuttgart: Calwer, 1974.

Albright, W. F. *Yahweh and the God of Canaan.* Garden City, NY: Doubleday, 1968.

Anderson, Arnold A. *The Book of Psalms.* 2 vols. New Century Bible Commentary. Grand Rapids: Wm. B. Eerdmans, 1972.

Anderson, Bernhard W. "Creation." *IDB* I (1962), 725-32.

Anderson, Bernhard W. *Creation in the Old Testament.* Issues in Religion and Theology 6. Philadelphia: Fortress Press, 1984.

Anderson, Bernhard W. *Creation verses Chaos: The Reinterpretation of Mythical Symbolism in the Bible.* New York: Association Press, 1967.

Anderson, Bernhard W. *From Creation to New Creation.* Minneapolis: Fortress Press, 1994.

Baltzer, Klaus. *Deutero Isaiah: A Commentary on Isaiah 40-55.* Translated by Margaret Kohl. Hermeneia. Minneapolis: Fortress Press, 2001.

Baltzer, Klaus. "The Polemic Against the Gods and its Relevance for Second Isaiah's Conception of New Jerusalem." In Second Temple Studies: 2. Temple and Community in the Persian Period. JSOT Sup.175. Sheffield: Sheffield Academic Press, 1994.

Barstad, Hans M. "On the So-Called Babylonian Literary Influence in Second Isaiah." *Scandinavian Journal of Old Testament* 2 (1987), 90-110.

Barstad, Hans M. *The Babylonian Captivity of the Book of Isaiah: "Exilic" Judah and the Provenance of Isaiah 40-55*. Oslo: Novus forlag, 1997.

Barstad, Hans M. *The Myth of the Empty Land: A Study in the History and Archeology of Judah During the "Exilic" Period*. Symbolae Osloenses Fasc. Sup. 28. Oslo: Novus forlag, 1996.

Barth, Karl. "The Doctrine of Creation" in *Church Dogmatics* III: 1-4, Edinburgh: T & T Clark, 1958.

Begrich, J. *Studien zu Deuterojesaja*. BWANT 77, 4th ed., Muchen: Chr. Kaiser. 1963.

Beyerlin, Walter, ed. *Near Eastern Religious Text Relation To the Old Testament*. London: SCM Press, 1978.

Beuken, W. A. M. "Miðpât. The First Servant Song and Its Context," *VT* 22, 1972, 1-30.

Blenkinsopp, Joseph. "Second Isaiah- Prophet of Universalism" *JSOT* 41 (1988) 83-103.

Blenkinsopp, Joseph. *Isaiah 40-55: A New Translation with Introduction and Commentary*. AB 19 A. New York: Doubleday, 2002.

Boman, Thorlief. "The Biblical Doctrine of Creation." *CQR* 165 (1964), 140-51.

Brandon, S.G. F. *Creation Legends of Ancient Near East*. London: Hodder & Stoughton, 1963.

Bright, John. *A History of Israel*, 3rd ed. Philadelphia: Westminster, 1981.

Brinkerhoff, David B. and Lynn K. White. *Sociology*, 3rd ed. St. Paul. New York: West Publishing Company, 1991.

Brueggemann, Walter. *Genesis*. Interpretation. Atlanta: John Knox Press, 1982.

Brueggemann, Walter. *Hopeful Imagination: Prophetic Voice in Exile*. Philadelphia: Fortress Press, 1986.

Brueggemann, Walter "Second Isaiah: An Evangelical Reading of Communal Experience". In *Reading and Preaching the Book of Isaiah*. Edited by Christopher R. Seitz. Philadelphia: Fortress Press, 1988.

Brueggemann, Walter. "The Loss and Recovery of Creation in the Old Testament Theology." *Theology Today* 53 (1996) 177-190.

Brueggemann, Walter. *Theology of the Old Testament: Testimony, Dispute, Advocacy.* Minneapolis: Fortress Press, 1997.

Brueggemann, Walter. "Trajectories in Old Testament Literature and the Sociology of Ancient Israel." *JBL* 98 (1979), 161-85.

Brueggemann, Walter. *The Message of the Psalms: A Theological Commentary.* Minneapolis: Augsburg Publishing House, 1984'

Carroll, Robert P. "The Myth of the Empty Land". In *Ideological Criticism of Biblical Text.* Ed. by D. Jobling and T. Pippin. Semeia 59. Atlanta: SBL, 1992.

Carter, Charles E. "Social Scientific Approaches". In *The Blackwell Companion to the Hebrew Bible.* Edited by Leo G. Perdue. Oxford: Blackwell Publishers, 2001.

Causse, Antonin. "From an Ethnic Group to a Religious Community: The Sociological Problem of Judaism". In *Community, Identity, and Ideology: Social Science Approaches to the Hebrew Bible.* Sources for Biblical and Theological Study, Vol. 6. Edited by Charles E. Carter and Carol L. Meyers, Winona Lake, Indiana: Eisenbrauns, 1996.

Childs, Brevard S. *Biblical Theology of the Old and New Testament.* Minneapolis: Fortress Press, 1992.

Childs, Brevard S. *Isaiah*, OTL. Louisville: Westminster John Knox Press, 2001.

Childs, Brevard S. *Myth and Reality in the Old Testament*, SBT 27, London: SCM, 1968.

Childs, Brevard S. *Old Testament Theology in a Canonical Context.* Philadelphia: Fortress Press, 1985.

Clements, Ronald E. "The Unity of the Book of Isaiah." *Interpretation* 36 (1982) 117-29

Clements, Ronald E. ed. *The World of Ancient Israel: Sociological, Anthropological, and Political Perspective.* Cambridge, England: Cambridge University Press, 1989. (Reprintedn1991).

Clifford, Richard J. *Creation Accounts in the Ancient Near East and in the Bible.* The Catholic Quarterly Monograph series 26. Washington DC: The Catholic Biblical Association of America, 1994.

Clifford, Richard J. "The Hebrew Scripture and the Theology of Creation." *Theological Studies* 46 (1985) 507-23.

Clifford, Richard J and John J. Collins. eds. *Creation in the Biblical Traditions.* (The Catholic Quarterly Monograph series 24).

Washington DC: The Catholic Biblical Association of America, 1992.

Coggins, Richard D. "The Origins of Jewish Diaspora" in *The World of Ancient Israel: Sociological, Anthropological, and Political Perspective*. Edited by R. E. Clements. Cambridge: Cambridge University Press, 1989. (Reprintedn1991).

Craigie, P. C. *Ugarit and the Old Testament*. Grand Rapids: Wm. B. Eerdmans,1983.

Cross, Frank M. *Canaanite Myth and Hebrew Epic: Essays in the History of Religion of Israel*. Cambridge: Harvard University Press, 1973.

Dalley, S. *Myths from Mesopotamia: Creation, the Flood, Gilgamesh and Others*. New York: Oxford University, 1989.

Davidson, R. *Genesis 1-11*, CBC. Cambridge: Cambridge University Press, 1973.

Davis, Philip R. "The Society of Biblical Israel." In *Second Temple Studies 2: Temple and Community in the Persian Period*. Edited by Tamara C. Eskenazi and Kent H. Richards. Sheffield: Sheffield Academic Press, 1994.

Eichrodt, Walter. *Theology of the Old Testament, Vol. 2*. London: SCM Press, 1967.

Eichrodt, Walter. "In the Beginning: A Contribution to the Interpretation of the First Word in he Bible". In *Israel's Prophetic Heritage: Essays in Honor of James Muilenburg*. Edited by Bernhard Anderson and Walter Harrelson. New York: Harper & Row, 1962.

Eissfeldt, Otto. *The Old Testament: An Introduction*. Translated by Peter R. Ackroyd. New York: Harper & Row, 1965.

Elliott, John H. *A Home for the Homeless: A Sociological Exegesis of I Peter, Its Situation and Strategy*. Philadelphia: Fortress Press. 1981.

Elliott, John H. *What is Social- Scientific Criticism?* Minneapolis: Fortress Press. 1993.

Emerton, J. A. "Wisdom." In *Tradition and Interpretation*. Edited by G. W. Anderson. Oxford: Clarendon, 1979.

Fisher, L. "Creation at Ugarit and in the Old Testament," *VT* 15 (1965).

Flanagan, J. *David's Social Drama: A Hologram of Israel's Early Iron Age*. The Social World of Biblical Antiquities Series 7. Sheffield: Almond Press, 1988.

Fohrer, George. *Das Buch Jesaja: 3 Band, Kap. 40-66*. Zurich: Zwingli Verlag, 1964.

Fohrer, George. *Introduction to the Old Testament*. Translated by David Green. London: SPCK, 1970.

Fretheim, Terence E. "The Plague as Ecological Signs of Historical Disaster: *JBL*, 110 (1991) 385-396.

Fretheim, Terence E. "The Reclamation of Creation." *Interpretation*. 95 (1991) 354-365.

Gersternberger, Erhard S. *Theologies in the Old Testament*. London: T&T Clark, 2002.

Gottwald, Norman K. *The Hebrew Bible: A Socio- Literary Introduction*. Philadelphia: Fortress Press, 1985.

Gottwald, Norman K. *A Light to the Nations: An Introduction to the Old Testament*. New York: Harper & Row, 1959.

Gottwald, Norman K. "Sociological Method in the Study of Ancient Israel" In *Encounter with the Text: Form and History in the Hebrew Bible*. Edited by M. J. Buss. Philadelphia: Fortress Press, 1979.

Gottwald, Norman K. ed. Social Scientific Criticism of The Hebrew Bible and Its Social World: The Israelite Monarchy, Semeia 37, Society of Biblical Literature, 1986.

Gottwald, Norman K. *Studies in the Book of Lamentation*. SBT 14. London: SCM, 1954.

Gottwald, Norman K. *The Tribes of Yahweh: A Sociology of the Religion of Liberated Israel, 1250-1050 B.C.E.*, Maryknoll: Orbis, 1978.

Grabbe, Lester L, ed. *Leading Captivity Captive: The Exile as History and Ideology*. JSOT Sup Series 278. Sheffield: Sheffield Academic Press, 1998.

Gressmann, Hugo. "Die literarische Analyse Deuterojesajas", *ZAW* 34 (1914), 254-97.

Gunkel, Hermann. "The Influence of Babylonian Mythology upon the Biblical Creation Story." In *Creation in the Old Testament*. Edited by B. W. Anderson, Philadelphia: Fortress Press, 1984.

Hanson, Paul D. *Isaiah 40-66*. Interpretation. Louisville: KY: John Knox Press, 1995.

Habel, Norman C. "He Who Stretches out the Heavens," *CBQ* 34 (1972), 417-30.

Habel, Norman C. *The Book of Job: A Commentary*. OTL. Philadelphia: The Westminster Press, 1985.

Habel, Norman C. "Yahweh, Maker of Heaven and Earth: A Study in Tradition Criticism." *JBL* 91 (1972): 321-337.

Haralambos, M and R. M. Heald. *Sociology: Theme and Perspective*. Slough: University Tutorial Press, 1980.

Harner, P. B. "Creation Faith in Deutero Isaiah." VT 17 (1967), 298-306.

Heidel, Alexander. *The Babylonian Genesis*. Chicago: Univ. of Chicago Press, 1963.

Herbert, A. S. *The Book of the Prophet Isaiah, Chapter 40-66*, New York: Cambridge University Press, 1975.

Hermission, H. J. "Observation on the Creation Theology in Wisdom." In *Creation in the Old Testament*. Edited by B. W. Anderson. Philadelphia: Fortress, 1984.

Herrmann, Siegfried. *A History of Israel in Old Testament Times*. Philadelphia: Fortress Press, 1975.

Hyatt, J. Philip. "Was Yahweh Originally A Creator Deity?" *JBL* 86 (1967), 369-77.

Kaufmann, Yehezkel. *The Religion of Israel*. Translated by. M. Greenberg. Chicago: University of Chicago Press, 1960.

Klein, Ralph W. *Israel in Exile*. Philadelphia: Fortress Press, 1979.

Knierim, Rolf P. *The Task of Old Testament Theology: Substance, Method, and Cases*. Grand Rapids: William B. Eerdmans Publishing Co., 1995.

Köhler, Ludwig. *Deuterojesaja(Jes 40-55) Stilkritishch Untersucht*, BSWA 37, Giessen: Alfred Töpelmann, 1923.

Koole, Jan L. *Isaiah, Part 3 Volume 1: Isaiah 40-48*. Historical Commentary on the Old Testament. Kampen- The Netherlands: Kok Pharos Publishing House, 1997.

Kramer, S. N. "Sumer," *IDB* VI (1962),454-63.

Kramer S. N. *The Sumerians: Their History, Culture, and Character*, Chicago: Univ. of Chicago Press, 1963.

Kraus, Hans-Joachim. *Psalms 1-59: A Continental Commentary* and *Psalms 60-150: A Continental Commentary*. Minneapolis: Fortress Press, 1993.

Kraus, Hans-Joachim. *Theology of the Psalms*. Translated by Keith Crim. Minneapolis: Fortress Press, 1992.

Laato, Antti. "The Composition of Isaiah 40-55." *JBL* 109 (1990), 207-28.

Landes, George M. "Creation and Liberation." In *Creation in the Old Testament*, Edited by B. W. Anderson, Philadelphia: Fortress Press, 1984.

Levenson, Jon D. *Creation and the Persistence of Evil: The Jewish Drama of Divine Omnipotence*. Princeton: Princeton University Press, 1988.

Malamat, Abraham. "The Last Wars of the Kingdom of Judah," *JNES*, 9 (1950).

Malamat, Abraham. "The Last Years of the Kingdom of Judah" in *Archaeology and Biblical Interpretation: Essays in Memory of Glenn Rose*. Edited by Leo G. Perdue, Lawrence E. Toombs, Gary L. Johnson. Atlanta: John Knox Press, 1987.

Malina, Bruce J. "The Social Science and Biblical Interpretation." In The Bible and Liberation. Edited by Norman K. Gottwald. Maryknoll, New York: Orbis, 1983.

Malina, Bruce J. and Richard L. Rohrbaugh. *Social Science Commentary on the Gospel of John*. Minneapolis: Fortress Press, 1998.

Martin, Dale B. "Social-Scientific Criticism." In *To Each Its Own Meaning: An Introduction to Biblical Criticism and Their Application*. Edited by Steven L. McKenzie and Stephen R. Haynes. Louisville, Kentucky: Westminster John Knox Press, 1999.

Matthews, Victor H, James C. Moyer. *The Old Testament: Text and Context*. Peabody, Massachusetts: Hendrickson Publishers, 1997.

Mayes, Andrew D. H. *The Old Testament in Sociological Perspective*. London: Pickering. 1989.

Mayes, Andrew D. H. " Sociology and the Old Testament" in *The World of Ancient Israel: Sociological, Anthropological, and Political Perspective*. Edited by R. E. Clements. Cambridge: Cambridge University Press, 1989.

McCarthy, Dennis J. "Creation Motif in Ancient Hebrew Poetry." In *Creation in the Old Testament*. Edited by B. W. Anderson. Philadelphia: Fortress Press, 1984.

Mckay, John. *Religion in Judah under the Assyrians*. SBT 26. London: SCM, 1973.

McKenzie, John L. *Second Isaiah*, Anchor Bible, New York: Doubleday, 1968.

McKenzie, Steven L. and Stephen R. Haynes, eds. *To Each Its Own Meaning*. Louisville, Kentucky: Westminster John Knox Press, 1999.

Melugin, Roy F. "Deutero- Isaiah and Form Criticism." *VT* 21 (1971) 326-37.

Melugin, Roy F. *The Formation of Isaiah 40-55*. Berlin: Walter de Gruyter, 1976.

Mendenhall, George E. "The Hebrew Conquest of Palestine," *BA* 25 (1962).

Mills, C. Wright. *The Sociological Imagination*. Oxfrod, England: Oxford University Press, 1959.

Mowinckel, Sigmund "Die Komposition des deuterojesajanichen Buches," *ZAW* 49 (1931), 87-112.

Muilenburg, James. "The Book of Isaiah: Chapters 40-66." *IB*, Vol. 5. New York: Abingdon, 1956.

Mulholland, M. Robert Jr. 'Sociological Criticism.' In *New Testament Criticism and Interpretation: Essays on Methods and Issues*. Edited by David Alan Black and David S. Dockery. Grand Rapids, Michigan: Zondervan Publishing House, 1991.

Newsome, James D. *By The Waters of Babylon: An Introduction to the History and Theology of Exile*. Edinburgh: T & T Clark, 1979.

Neyrey, Jerome H., ed. The *Social World of Luke-Acts: Models for Interpretation*. Massachusetts: Hendrickson Publishers, 1999.

Niditch, Susan. *Chaos and Cosmos: Studies in Biblical Patterns of Creation*. California: Scholars Press, 1985.

North, Christopher R. *The Second Isaiah*. Oxford: The Chlarendon Press, 1964.

Noth, Martin. *The History of Israel*. 2nd ed. New York: Harper & Row, 1960.

Oded, Bustenay. "Judah and the Exile." In *Israelite and Judean History*. Edited by John H. Hayes and J. Maxwell Miller. London: SCM, 1977.

Oded, Bustenay. *Mass Deportations and Deportees in the Neo-Assyrian Empire*. Wiesbaden: Reichert, 1979.

Oswalt, John N. *The Book of Isaiah: Chapters 40-66*. NICOT. Grand Rapid, Michigan: Wm. Eerdmans Publishing Co., 1998.

Otzen, Benedikt, Hans Gottlieb, and Kund Jeppesen. *Myths in the Old Testament*. London: SCM, 1980.

Paas, Stefan. *Creation and Judgement: Creation Texts in Some Eight Century Prophets*. Old Testament Studies 47. Leiden. Boston: Brill, 2003.

Parsons, Talcott "Functional Theory of Change." In *Social Change: Source, Patterns and Consequence*. Edited by Eva Etzioni- Halevy and Amitai Etzioni. New York: Basic Books, 1968.

Perdue, Leo G. *The Collapse of History: Reconstructing Old Testament Theology*. Minneapolis: Fortress Press, 1994.

Perdue, Leo G. "Job's Assault on Creation." *HAR* 10 (1987) 295-315.

Perdue, Leo G. *Wisdom and Creation: The Theology of Wisdom Literature.* Nashville: Abingdon Press, 1994.

Perdue, Leo G. *Wisdom in Revolt: Creation Theology in the Book of Job*, JSOT Sup. 112; Sheffield: JSOT, 1991.

Pleins, J. David. *The Social Visions of the Hebrew Bible.* Louisville: Westminster John Knox Press, 2001.

Preuss, Horst Dietrich. *Old Testament Theology*, Vol.1. Edinburgh: T&T Clark, 1995.

Pritchard, J. B. *Ancient Near Eastern Text Relating to the Old Testament.* Princeton: University Press, 1969.

Rad, Gerhard von. *Genesis.* OTL. Revised edition. London: SCM Press, 1972.

Rad, Gerhard von. *Old Testament Theology*, 2 vols. London: SCM Press, 1975.

Rad, Gerhard von. "The Theological Problem of Old Testament Doctrine of Creation." In *The Problem of Hexateuch and Other Essays.* Translated by E. W. T. Dicken. Edinburgh: Oliver & Boyd, 1966.

Rad, Gerhard von. *Wisdom in Israel.* London: SCM Press, 1970.

Rendtorff, Rolf. *The Old Testament: An Introduction.* Philadelphia: Fortress Press, 1986.

Rendtorff, Rolf. "The Book of Isaiah: A Complex Unity. Synchronic and Diachronic Reading. Society of Biblical Literature 1991 Seminar Papers. Edited by J. Eugene H. Lovering. Atlanta: Scholars Press, 1991.

Reventolw, Henning Graf. *The Problem of Old Testament Theology in the Twentieth Century.* Philadelphia: Fortress Press, 1985.

Reventolw, Henning Graf and Yair Hoffman. *Creation in Jewish and Christian Tradition.* (JSOT Suppl. Series 319). London: Sheffield Academic Press, 2002.

Richard, R. J. "The Function of Idol Passages in Second Isaiah," *CBQ* 42 (1980).

Rogerson, John. *Anthropology and the Old Testament.* Atlanta: John Knox Press, 1978.

Raitt, T. M. *A Theology of Exile: Judgment/Deliverance in Jeremiah and Ezekiel.* Philadelphia: Fortress Press, 1977.

Reventlow, Henning Graf. *Problem of Old Testament Theology in the Twentieth Century.* Philadelphia: Fortress Press, 1985.

Rogerson, J. W. *Anthropology and the Old Testament*. Atlanta: John Knox Press, 1978.

Rylaarsdam, J. C. "Hebrew Wisdom," in *PCB*. Edited by Matthew Black and H. H. Rowley. London & Edinburgh: Nelson, 1962.

Schmid H. H. "Creation Righteousness and Salvation." In *Creation in the Old Testament*, Edited by B. W. Anderson, Philadelphia: Fortress Press, 1984.

Schmidt, J.H. *The Faith of the Old Testament: A History*. Philadelphia: The Westminster Press, 1983.

Schoors, Antoon. *I am God Your Saviour: A Form Critical Study of the Main Genres in Is. XL-LV*. VT Sup. 24. Leiden: Brill, 1973.

Scott, James M. ed. *Exile: Old Testament, Jewish & Christian Conceptions* (SJSJ 56). Leiden: Brill, 1997.

Seitz, Christopher R. *Zion's Final Destiny: The Development of the Book of Isaiah: Reassessment of Isaiah 36-39*. Minneapolis: Fortress Press, 1991.

Shanks, Hershel, ed. *Ancient Israel: A Short History From Abraham to the Roman Destruction of the Temple*. Biblical Archeology Society, Washington D.C.: SPCK, 1988.

Simkins, Ronald A. & Stephen L. Cook eds., *The Social World of Hebrew Bible: Twenty- Five Years of The Social Science in the Academy*. Semeia 87. Atlanta: SBL, 1999.

Smart, James D. *History and Theology in Second Isaiah: A Commentary on Isaiah35, 40-66*. London: Epworth Press, 1967.

Smith-Christopher, Daniel L. *A Biblical Theology of Exile*. Minneapolis: Fortress Press, 2002.

Smith-Christopher, Daniel L. "Reassessing the Historical and Sociological Impact of the Babylonian Exile." In *Exile: Old Testament, Jewish, and Christian Concept*. Edited by James Scott. Leiden, New York, Köln: Brill, 1997.

Smith-Christopher, Daniel L. *The Religion of the Landless: The Social Context of the Babylonian Exile*. Bloomington, Ind.: Meyer Stone Books, 1989.

Stuhlmuller, Carroll. *Creative Redemption in Deutero Isaiah*. Rome: Pontifical Biblical Institute, 1970.

Stuhlmueller, Carroll "Deutero-Isaiah (Chaps.40-55): Major Transitions in the Prophet's Theology and in Contemporary Scholarship," *CBQ* 42, (1980), 1-29.

Sweeney, Marvin A. "On the Road to Duhm: Isaiah in Nineteenth-Century Critical Scholarship" In *SBL 2002 Seminar Papers*, Atlanta: Society of Biblical Literature, 2002. Pp.191-211.

Sweeney, Marvin A. "The Reconceptualization of the Davidic Covenant in Isaiah." In *Studies in the Book of Isaiah: Festschrift Willem A. M. Beuken*. Edited by J. Van Ruiten and M. Vervenne. Louvain: Leuven University Press, 1997.

Theissen, Gerd. *The First Followers of Jesus: A Sociological Analysis of the Earliest Christianity*. London: SCM Press. 1978.

Torrey, C. C. "The Exile and the Restoration." In *Ezra Studies* (1910) Reprint. New York: Ktav, 1970).

Torrey, C. C. *The Second Isaiah: A New Interpretation*. Edinburgh: T&T Clark, 1928.

Trible, Phyllis. *Rhetorical Criticism: Context, Method, and the Book of Jonah*. Minneapolis: Fortress Press, 1994.

Vriezen, Th. C. *The Religion of Ancient Israel*. London: Lutterworth Press, 1967.

Watts, John D.W. *Isaiah 34-66*, WBC 25. Nashville: Thomas Nelson Publishers, 1987.

Weinfeld, Moshe "God the Creator in Gen. 1 and in the Prophecy of Second Isaiah," *Tarbiz* 37/2 (1968), 105-32.

Weiser, Artur. *The Psalms: A Commentray*, OTL. Philadephia: Westminster, 1962.

Westermann, Claus. *Basic Forms of Prophetic Speech*. Philadelphia: The Westminster Press, 1966.

Westermann, Claus. *Creation*. Translated by J. J Scullion. London: SPCK, 1974.

Westermann, Claus. *Genesis1-11*. Translated by J. J Scullion. London: SPCK, 1984.

Westermann, Claus. *Isaiah 40-66*. OTL. Translated by D. M. G. Stalker. Philadelphia: The Westminster Press, 1969.

Westermann, Claus. *The Praise of God in the Psalms*. Richmond: John Knox, 1965.

Westermann, Claus. *The Praise and Lament in the Psalms*. Atlanta: John Knox Press, 1981.

Westermann, Claus. "Sprache und Struktur der Prophetie Deuterojesajas", in *Forschung am Alten Testament: Gesammelte Studien* . TBü 24. Munich: Kaiser, 1964.

Whybray, R. N. *Second Isaiah 40-66*, New Century Bible. Grand Rapids: Wm. B. Eerdmans Publishing Co., 1975.

Whybray, R. N. *The Second Isaiah*. Sheffield: Sheffield Academic Press, 1983.

Williamson, H. G. M. *The Book Called Isaiah: Deutero- Isaiah's Role in Composition and Redaction*. Oxford: Clarendon Press, 1994.

Wilson, Robert R. *Prophecy and Society in Ancient Israel*. Philadelphia: Fortress Press.1980.

Wilson, Robert R. *Sociological Approach to the Old Testament*. Philadelphia: Fortress Press, 1984.

Wilson, Robert R. "The Community of Second Isaiah." In *Reading and Preaching the Book of Isaiah*. Ed. by Christopher R. Seitz. Philadelphia: Fortress Press, 1988.

Zimmerli, Walther. Old *Testament Theology in Outline*. Atlanta: John Knox, 1978.

Zimmerli, Walther. "The Place and Limit of the Wisdom in the Framework of the Old Testament Theology." *SJT* 17 (1964) 146-58.

www.ingramcontent.com/pod-product-compliance
Lightning Source LLC
Chambersburg PA
CBHW021913180426
43198CB00034B/184